WARSPITE

WARSPITE

From Jutland Hero to Cold War Warrior

Iain Ballantyne

Pen & Sword
MARITIME

Dedicated to the immortal *Warspite*,
her crews and the casualties of all her wars

First published in Great Britain in 2001,
reprinted in 2010, 2013 and 2014 by
PEN & SWORD MARITIME
An imprint of
Pen & Sword Books Ltd
47 Church Street
Barnsley
South Yorkshire
S70 2AS

ISBN 978 1 84884 350 9

A CIP catalogue record for this book is
available from the British Library.

Printed and bound in England
By CPI Group (UK) Ltd, Croydon, CR0 4YY

Pen & Sword Books Ltd incorporates the Imprints of Pen & Sword Aviation,
Pen & Sword Family History, Pen & Sword Maritime, Pen & Sword Military,
Pen & Sword Discovery, Pen & Sword Politics, Pen & Sword Archaeology,
Pen & Sword Atlas, Wharncliffe Local History, Wharncliffe True Crime,
Wharncliffe Transport, Pen & Sword Select, Pen & Sword Military Classics,
Leo Cooper, The Praetorian Press, Claymore Press, Remember When,
Seaforth Publishing and Frontline Publishing.

For a complete list of Pen & Sword titles please contact
PEN & SWORD BOOKS LIMITED
47 Church Street, Barnsley, South Yorkshire, S70 2AS, England
E-mail: enquiries@pen-and-sword.co.uk
Website: www.pen-and-sword.co.uk

Contents

HMS *WARSPITE* Battle Honours 1596-1944

Cadiz 1596, Orfordness 1666, Sole Bay 1672, Schooneveld 1673, Texel 1673, Barfleur 1692, Velez Malaga 1704, Marbella 1705, Lagos 1759, Quiberon Bay 1759, Jutland 1916, Atlantic 1939, Narvik 1940, Norway 1940, Calabria 1940, Mediterranean 1940-43, Matapan 1941, Crete 1941, Malta Convoys 1941, Sicily 1943, Salerno 1943, Normandy 1944, English Channel 1944, Biscay 1944, Walcheren 1944.

ACKNOWLEDGEMENTS

This book would not have been possible without the generous assistance of members of the HMS *Warspite* Association.

I first got to know them at their fourteenth annual reunion dinner, at the Hotel Prince Regent, Weymouth, in May 1999. In common with many other former Royal Navy sailors and Royal Marines, and indeed ex-soldiers and airmen who also fought in the Second World War, the members of the *Warspite* Association preferred to forget their experiences for four decades. Hence their association was, like many other veterans' groups, only formed in the mid-1980s. Only after they had retired could they finally afford the time to contemplate their supporting roles in the great drama of history.

While their stories may have been shared with former shipmates during reunions since the 1980s, until I started gathering material for this book many of the *Warspite* veterans had never really spoken in any depth about their time aboard the most famous battleship in Royal Navy history. Their experiences as ordinary sailors and marines aboard a mighty ship of war proved to be the definition of true British grit. We would be well advised not to forget how freedom was saved from extinction by ordinary men like them.

Sincere thanks are therefore due to the following members of the *Warspite* Association who allowed me to interview them for this book: Reg Foster; Charles Pearson; Frederick 'Ben' Rice, Ken Smith and Jack Worth. I would also like to thank *Warspite* veteran Peter Finnigan for allowing me to use material contained in his own account of his time on the battleship.

This book is a tribute to them and also to all the association members I did not have time to interview, not least those who have 'crossed the bar', taking their experiences with them untold. I was, however, given permission to use material published in the *Warspite* Association's newsletter – *Anchors Aweigh* – which has enabled me to relate the experiences of many I was unable to interview.

Several members of the *Warspite* Association generously loaned me images from their private collections to illustrate this book and to them I also extend thanks.

Of course this book could not ignore the stories of either the six *Warspites* which preceded the battleship or the eighth vessel to bear the name, a nuclear-powered attack submarine. The *Warspite* Association embraces sailors who crewed this Cold War fighting vessel and, of their number, I must especially thank Jonathan Cooke and Tim Hale for talking to me about their experiences. They gave to me as much detail as they reasonably could without breaking the restrictions of the Official Secrets Act.

When it came to locating former members of *Warspite*'s crew, and others who witnessed her exploits, beyond the association's active membership list, the Royal British Legion's official magazine, *Legion*, played a crucial role. Its readers responded from around the world with a flood of material after reading an article about the *Warspite* Association's fourteenth reunion dinner in which I mentioned that I was writing this book. I am therefore very grateful to *Legion* magazine's Editor, Chris Boiling, and Assistant Editor, Dominic Needham, for their assistance.

I am grateful to the following for responding to the *Legion* article and providing their own eyewitness accounts: Albert Cock; Philip Gourd; Andy Hamnett; W.E. Heard; Charles Hunter; Arthur Jones; William Nichol; Frank Page; Ray Pattenden and Dougie Weyhaup. The family of one former *Warspite* sailor, H. Banks, who has sadly passed away, kindly sent me a copy of his unpublished account of service in the battleship during the Second World War, called *An Outline of My Life Aboard The Grey Lady*.

After reading the *Legion* article, John Corbett, who is also an active member of the *Warspite* Association, came forward with a very significant contribution. Many thanks are due to him for allowing me to use previously unpublished material from *The Journal of J.G. Corbett Midshipman, Royal Navy*. Mr T. Sutherland of Berlin, whose late father served on *Warspite* during the Second World War, responded to the *Legion* article by loaning me his father's superb photo album. A number of others who responded in writing to the same article also provided images. Among them, special thanks are due to John Hockley for allowing me to use pictures in the private collection of his late father, Jack Hockley, another who served on *Warspite* during the Second World War. Steve Wyles, only grandson of George Wyles, who was one of *Warspite*'s divers in the late 1930s and during the Second World War, has kindly allowed me to use images from his family's private collection.

The staffs of the Imperial War Museum's Sound Archive and Department of Documents, together with the staff of Plymouth City Library's Naval Archive were very helpful during the course of my research. The US Naval Historical Center was very efficient in providing some of the key images for this book. I would also like to acknowledge the help of the National Maritime Museum and Topham Picturepoint picture archives, even if, in the end, many of the images they provided were not used.

I am particularly indebted to Dr Robert Franklin for giving access to his father's superb collection of photographs of *Warspite* and her crew during the First World War.

Judith Ellis has given permission to use extracts from the war diary of her father-in-law, Gordon, who was a Surgeon Lieutenant in *Warspite* at the Battle of Jutland. She has also graciously allowed me to use portrait photographs of her father-in-law and pictures of *Warspite* on the rocks at Prussia Cove taken by him in 1947.

Thanks are due to the copyright holders of the various Collections held by the Imperial War Museum, extracts of which form an important element of this book. Every effort was made via the Imperial War Museum to contact all the relevant copyright holders.

I must thank Andrew M. Ramsay for enabling me to enlarge the scope of the account of the Battle of Matapan by allowing me to draw on material in his book, HMS *Formidable*.

Reg Shield and John Constantine at Devonport Management Limited – management company of Devonport Royal Dockyard – were able to help me with images of submarine *Warspite* arriving at Plymouth for, and during, her final refit in the early 1990s. My thanks to them and DML, or Babcock Marine as it is known today.

Thanks are also due to my photographic colleagues Nigel Andrews, Tony Carney, Neil Hall and Mike Welsford for helping assemble a superb range of images for this book. Tribute is due to John Pearce and to Stu Reed for helping me with research matters. Anthony Abbott and Bob Drayton are acknowledged for helping to put the word around that I was looking for *Warspite* veterans.

Thanks to Peter Hore for his blunt perspective on the book, which I am sure helped to shape it in its final stages.

I am grateful to all at Leo Cooper/Pen & Sword Books for giving me the opportunity to write this book and being so patient, especially Henry Wilson and Roni Wilkinson. Susan Ottaway should be mentioned and thanked for her judicious editing which helped sharpen the text tremendously.

And last, but by no means least, I owe a debt of gratitude to Dennis C. Andrews, maritime artist extraordinary, for his fantastic pictures and drawings, and Syd Goodman who provided not only superb images from the Goodman Collection but also no-nonsense guidance and salty encouragement. Syd, who sadly passed away in 2006, also allowed me to draw on his considerable archive of printed matter, including his excellent, and unpublished, potted history of the seventh *Warspite*'s career.

If there is anyone I have forgotten to mention please accept my sincere apologies.

Since the hardback edition of this book was published in 2001, time has thinned out the surviving *Warspite* veterans, some of them acknowledged as key contributors to this story. Hopefully, this paperback edition stands as a lasting memorial to them all.

Iain Ballantyne
May 2010

Chapter One

CREATORS AND FOREBEARS

Anxious Moments on the Tamar

On 26 November 1913, a young politician witnessed the launching of a gigantic vessel of war upon which he had gambled his political career and the safety of the British Empire. The vessel's name was *Warspite*; the politician was Winston Churchill.

Gathered around the First Lord of the Admiralty at Devonport Dockyard in the English naval city of Plymouth, was a tumultuous crowd of 30,000. Under a grey overcast sky, the assembled thousands held their breath as one, for the *Warspite* stubbornly refused to be launched. Mrs Austen Chamberlain, wife of the Government minister, had broken a bottle of wine against the bow and then, using a hammer to hit a chisel held by a dockyard official, severed a cord releasing with a massive crash, wooden supports either side of the gigantic hull. However, despite the best efforts of burly dockyard workers and hydraulic rams to send her down the slipway, the battleship had stayed put.

But then the creaking of timber blocks giving way under the hull shattered the tense silence and someone cried out: 'She's off!' With the masses cheering their lungs out, and craft on the river blasting their sirens, the *Warspite* finally went on her way, sliding stern first into the wide Tamar. She settled gracefully in the water, the cheers of sailors aboard her answered from all sides by the crowd.

With 30,000 people cheering her down the slipway, HMS *Warspite* is launched at Devonport in November 1913. *US Naval Historical Center.*

Overjoyed, Mr Churchill blew off steam by lustily joining in the singing of 'Rule Britannia', giving extra emphasis to the song - and his relief - with the enthusiastic waving of his hat.

The launch of *Warspite* at Devonport Dockyard had been delayed a month to await the arrival of heavy castings and time was of the essence. Never before had a hull of some 12,000 tons been put in the water on the Tamar and there would not be another adequate high tide for a long time. Britain was engaged in a rapidly escalating naval construction race with Germany and just under nine months later the two nations would be at war.

Churchill had fought tooth and nail to build *Warspite* and her four sister ships, in a bold bid to achieve final supremacy over the Kaiser's fleet with a class of new super dreadnoughts.

A controversial concept, they mounted 15-inch guns on a heavily armoured hull. Not only was it by no means certain such large calibre guns could be mounted and fired safely, the new super dreadnoughts also rejected plentiful British coal in favour of oil from the Middle East to fire their boilers.

But, if the First Lord of the Admiralty had needed a boost to his confidence, he had only to study the history of the six previous *Warspites*, each of which carved an illustrious career.

From Raleigh & Essex to Pax Victoriana

The first *Warspite* set the fighting tradition commanded by swashbuckling Elizabethan high seas privateer Sir Walter Raleigh.

The origins of the name *Warspite* are not clear but the most popular theory is that it was a compound creation – 'War's spite' embodies contempt for one's enemies (an obvious reflection of English feelings towards Spain at the time). The word 'spight' was also a colloquial name for the green woodpecker. A 'warspight' would obviously be ready to 'peck' at the wooden hulls of opponents.

From the first moment he went aboard *Warspite* at Plymouth in 1596, Raleigh was certainly eager to hurl spite, and peck at the Spaniards with a cannonade or two. The forty-two-year-old adventurer's new ship had been launched earlier

Standing outside Sherborne Abbey is this statue of the first *Warspite*'s first Captain, Sir Walter Raleigh. *Nigel Andrews.*

that year at Deptford, on the Thames, displacing approximately 650 tons and carrying thirty-six guns. Now Sir Walter was getting her ready to sail at the head of a squadron in an ambitious raid on Cadiz.

The year 1596 was not a good one for England.

The sheen of victory over the Spanish Armada of 1588 had well and truly dulled and everywhere the threats grew. The Spaniards had taken Calais that April and were said to be assembling a new armada at Cadiz.

England's security could therefore be assured by the destruction of enemy naval vessels in the port, so removing the means to transport troops across the Channel.

But the stars of the 'old firm', which had vanquished the previous armada, were dead – Hawkins and Drake during the Panama expedition that had set off in August 1595 and ended in disaster. Most painful for Raleigh was the loss of his cousin and mentor, Richard Grenville, killed in the Azores some five years before, after his ship, the *Revenge*, was trapped by fifty Spanish men-of-war. Two vessels that had played a leading role in destroying Grenville - the *Saint Philip*, on whose deck he gasped his last breath before his corpse was thrown overboard, and the *Saint Andrew* - were said to be at Cadiz.

Raleigh once enjoyed an intimate and unrivalled position in the Queen's favours which had brought him a knighthood, rich lands and power. But his place in the Queen's affections had been taken by the Earl of Essex who was also his rival in martial affairs. When Raleigh heard Essex was to be joint leader of the expedition with Howard of Effingham – the man who led English naval forces against the 1588 armada – he was outraged. His hatred for Essex, and jealousy of his joint command, poured more oil on his burning determination to make Cadiz a personal triumph. But when Raleigh went to Plymouth to join *Warspite* he managed to keep his temper under control and showed only courtesy to Essex.

A large force had been assembled – eighteen Royal Navy ships, ten armed merchant vessels and twenty-four Dutch warships plus 100 other assorted craft. Nearly 10,000 English and Dutch soldiers were to be carried by the fleet. *Warspite* was to lead one of four naval squadrons while Essex had charge of another, with the *Repulse* as his flagship. Despite the Queen blowing hot and cold over the whole venture this 'bristling and ferocious fleet'[1] finally set sail from Plymouth on 1 June and three weeks later was approaching Cadiz.

Things did not get off to a good start. In heavy seas an ill-fated attempt was made to disembark troops for a direct attack on the city of Cadiz.

Raleigh's squadron had been sent off to clear the approaches of any Spanish warships which might interfere, so Sir Walter had been unavailable to point out the folly of such an opening move. Its cardinal sin was ignoring destruction of the armada and capture of treasure ships. A direct assault on the city could bog down the English, allowing the Spanish vessels to slip away. Witnessing the chaos and confusion from *Warspite* on his return, Raleigh immediately intervened. Putting *Warspite* near the *Repulse*, he rowed across to have an urgent conference with Essex during which his bitter rival surprisingly bowed to his wisdom. Next he rowed to Effingham's ship and managed to persuade the overall commander to cancel the assault on the city. It was decided that on high tide in the morning the English warships – spearheaded by Raleigh's squadron with *Warspite* at the very tip – would sail straight into Cadiz Harbour.

With the *Lion*, *Rainbow*, *Dreadnought*, *Nonpareil*, *Mary Rose*, *Swiftsure* and a dozen armed merchantmen close behind, Raleigh's *Warspite* brazenly braved fierce gunfire from cannons on the port's fortifications. Ever the showman, Raleigh declined to

The first *Warspite* leads the English and Dutch naval assault on Cadiz. *Specially commissioned painting by Dennis C. Andrews.*

waste ammunition on the battlements, instead ordering trumpeters to blow blasts as his defiant response.

Raleigh later wrote that 'the volleys of cannon and culvern came as thick as if it had been a skirmish of musketeres.'

Warspite was badly damaged but still brushed off these annoyances, forcing the Spanish vessels to run before her.

Meanwhile Essex, frightened Raleigh would steal all the glory, pushed *Repulse* through the mêlée until she was also at the forefront of the action.

The *Warspite* was at this point pummelling the *Saint Philip*, her gun crews urged on by an exultant Raleigh, his blood lust for revenge knowing no bounds against this hated vessel. But he could see the *Warspite* would herself come to grief before the Spaniard was finished off unless he could send across boarders. But he had no small boats for his men to use in this endeavour. Clambering down into a skiff, he dodged through the hellfire to the nearest English man-of-war which was the *Repulse*.

Hatred of the Spanish overwhelmed any qualms Raleigh might have felt about begging his bitter rival for help. Calling up he asked for the loan of some small boats and, to his surprise, Essex eagerly agreed to his request. However, Raleigh need not have bothered for, realizing they were doomed anyway, the crew of the *Saint Philip* ran her aground and set fire to her.

Raleigh's triumph was sealed when he captured the *Saint Andrew* but he was wounded in the leg and would be lame for the rest of his life.

After several hours of fighting, and despite his wound, Raleigh was ready to push on deeper into the massive harbour, for he knew the treasure ships were trapped within. But his energetic pleas for the English force to waste no time in capturing them were ignored in favour of looting Cadiz. The merchants who owned the heavily laden treasure ships offered to pay the English a large sum to let the vessels leave. This was turned down by Effingham and Essex yet Raleigh and the *Warspite* were still not unleashed. The Spaniards then set light to the galleons, rather than let them fall into the hands of the English, with more than three million pounds worth of treasure going up in smoke.

The English troops occupied Cadiz for a fortnight and treated the town's occupants with humanity despite looting and destroying its buildings, causing twenty million ducats worth of mayhem. Two dozen major Spanish vessels were destroyed and over 1,000 cannon and other weapons captured. Raleigh advised sailing for Plymouth, as the English vessels were by then in no fit state for lengthy adventures in which they might encounter strong Spanish naval forces. Effingham agreed.

Ultimately the Queen's coffers would receive less than £10,000 in prize money from the Cadiz raid. This was a grave disappointment, particularly in light of the millions lost in the destroyed treasure ships. However some are happy to view the Cadiz raid in less dismal light.

The *Oxford Illustrated History of the Royal Navy* describes the raid as: 'One of the most efficient acts of war carried out by any Tudor government.'

Hugh Ross Williamson went even further in his book *Sir Walter Raleigh*, hailing the raid led by the first *Warspite* as an 'Elizabethan Trafalgar' which secured English naval supremacy and the decline of Spain.

The year after Cadiz, Raleigh was once more at the helm of *Warspite*, embarking on another expedition with Essex. This time the aim was to destroy Spanish warships at Ferrol, for fear they would form another Armada. The English also intended capturing treasure ships off the Azores to deny the Spaniards war-fighting funds. Known as 'The Islands Voyage', it failed miserably.

Setting sail from Plymouth in July 1597, under the command of Essex, bad weather caused disarray in the English force. The storm was 'so shattering that the bulkheads of the *Warspite* were broken and her cookroom smashed.'[2]

Raleigh returned to Plymouth and Essex sought shelter in Falmouth. He made his way to Plymouth and boarded the *Warspite* to discuss an alternative course of action with his deputy. The attack on Ferrol was abandoned and the fleet headed for the Azores. Their intention was to capture one of the islands – Fayal – to use as a base while they waited for a treasure fleet from the West Indies to appear. But, while Raleigh was delayed at another island in the Azores by some essential maintenance work on *Warspite*, which had suffered a damaged mainyard, and repairs to other members of his squadron, Essex went haring off after prize ships. Arriving at Fayal expecting to discover Essex waiting for him to mount an invasion, Raleigh found himself alone. Unable to resist the challenge, he went ashore with 500 of his sailors and took the island.

Essex eventually reappeared and was infuriated by Raleigh's fait accompli. All the

13

old enmities erupted and Essex initially threatened to have Raleigh court-martialled and beheaded for gross insubordination.

While all this was going on, the Spanish treasure fleet slipped by and reached a port in the Azores too strongly defended for the English to risk attacking.

Realizing that this disaster was ultimately his fault, Essex thought better of prosecuting Raleigh.

Demoralized, the English headed for home, only to discover, on returning to Plymouth, that the Armada they had failed to destroy at Ferrol was off the Lizard.

In port aboard *Warspite*, Raleigh despaired of mounting any kind of realistic defence of the West Country. Their crews exhausted and dispirited, the English warships were also desperately in need of refitting.

Luckily the weather intervened and scattered the Spanish Armada of 1597, saving England once more. In the fallout from this farce, Raleigh was relieved of his naval command. Essex revived his attempt to have him court-martialled and executed, arousing disapproval at Court for such an unjustified course of action.

Failure in missions to pacify Ireland soon alienated Essex from the Queen's favours. Meanwhile Raleigh revived his place at Court and was again one of the Queen's closest advisors. Embittered, Essex let his hatred of Raleigh get the better of him and in 1601 attempted to stage a rebellion against the Queen which would also rid him, finally, of his rival. He paid for it with his head. But Essex would have his revenge, for when his old friend James I succeeded Elizabeth, he had Raleigh executed for treason.

Following the Islands Voyage, *Warspite* was delegated to Channel Guard duties, but in 1601 took part in the destruction of a Spanish fleet off Kinsale in Ireland.

Under James I the English navy as a whole underwent a period of severe recession and inactivity and it wasn't until 1627 that *Warspite* saw action again, taking part in an assault on La Rochelle. This venture was launched in support of the Huguenot cause during renewed conflict with Spain and France. The expedition was a disaster.

By the mid-1630s, the first *Warspite* had been reduced to a hulk and was being used for harbour duties. She was disposed of in 1649.

Launched on the Thames at Blackwall in 1666, the year of both the Great Plague and the Great Fire of London, the next HMS *Warspite* displaced 899 tons and carried sixty-four guns. She was part of a revival in the English navy brought about by the Restoration which saw Charles II ascending the throne.

The second HMS *Warspite* (also spelt *Warspight*) could carry six months' supplies, a great step forward in English warship design, enabling extended deployment to the expanding colonies.

Initially the second *Warspite*'s enemies would be the Dutch in wars between England and Holland of the 1660s and 1670s. By the 1690s, the *Warspite* was sailing alongside Netherlands vessels and at war with the French and Spanish. In the year of her launch she took part in the victory over De Ruyter's Dutch fleet at Orfordness (the Battle of St James Day).

Warspite was present at Southwold Bay (also known as Sole Bay) when a combined British and French fleet suffered heavy casualties and the loss of their flagships. The

Dutch withdrew to the Scheldt and attempts to lure them out resulted in the battle off Schooneveld in 1673, during which *Warspite* lost her captain. In August of the same year she took part in the Battle of Texel where there was no decisive result despite heavy fighting.

In 1692 *Warspite* was to the fore in the Battle of Barfleur and the subsequent Battle of La Hogue. By this time the English were allied with the Dutch. The Anglo-Dutch aim was to prevent an invasion of England by an army under the command of the exiled King James II who had been been replaced by Holland's William of Orange in 1688.

In the period 1694-95 *Warspite* served in the Mediterranean and in 1697 entered a five year refit and rebuild at Rotherhithe which increased her displacement to 952 tons and her guns to seventy.

During 1702-03, with the start of the War of the Spanish Succession, *Warspite* was engaged in small actions off the Spanish coast, capturing the French vessel *Hasard*. The following year, the second *Warspite* achieved fame by taking part in the capture of Gibraltar under the command of Admiral Rooke. She was retained in those waters and played a distinguished part in the Battle of Velez Malaga when an Anglo-Dutch fleet clashed with a Franco-Spanish force intending to re-take Gibraltar. *Warspite* sustained severe damage and, while no ships were sunk on either side, the British suffered nearly 700 dead and almost 2,000 wounded.

In 1705 the French again tried to capture Gibraltar and were once more repulsed, with *Warspite* weighing into action during the resulting Battle of Marbella. She returned home from the Mediterranean in 1709 and, after subsequent service on the Newfoundland Station, the second *Warspite* was placed in reserve.

Renamed *Edinburgh* in 1715, she was finally broken up in 1771.

A seventy-four gunner of 1,850 tons displacement, the third HMS *Warspite* was launched in 1758 at Deptford and in 1759 fought in the Battle of Lagos (off Portugal)

The third *Warspite* in the thick of the action at Quiberon Bay. *Specially commissioned painting by Dennis C. Andrews.*

in defence of Gibraltar. Later in the same year she participated in the Battle of Quiberon Bay, under Hawke's flag, helping to destroy a French invasion force bound for Ireland by annihilating the fleet carrying the troops.

In 1783 *Warspite* was paid off into reserve at Plymouth, but the American War of Independence led to her being reactivated and pressed into service as a hospital ship. However, by 1784 she had been downgraded to a floating naval barracks and in 1800 was renamed *Arundel*.

Built at Chatham and launched in 1807, the fourth *Warspite* had a displacement of 1,890 tons and carried seventy-four guns. Her first commanding officer was the renowned Captain Henry Blackwood, who had sailed in support of Admiral Nelson at the Battle of Trafalgar and was chief mourner at his funeral. Under Blackwood she saw service in the Baltic, the English Channel and Mediterranean. Blackwood was a forceful captain and enriched himself with frequent pursuit of prize ships, displaying tenacity which frightened many in his own navy. In *The Prizes of War*, Richard Hill relates that in 1810 the mistress of the Prince Regent was heard to describe Blackwood as 'the most severe not to say tyrannical officer in the Service' who, apparently, flogged his midshipmen. As Hill points out, this was of particular concern to the lady as her son was a young officer aboard *Warspite* at the time she made these remarks. No matter to the Royal Navy – Blackwood was an outstanding captain.

He had come to *Warspite* after his previous command – HMS *Ajax* – was destroyed by fire, allegedly set ablaze by a drunken steward. Blackwood very nearly didn't survive this calamity, coming close to going down with the ship. He was subjected to a court martial but acquitted with honour. A proud and determined individual, he then set his eye on a governorship in the West Indies but was instead offered, and refused, the job of Pay Commissioner on the Navy Board. The result of all this was another sea command and six years as captain of HMS *Warspite*.

Between 1807 and 1810 the fourth *Warspite* played a supporting role to Wellington's army in the Peninsular War, taking up station off the coast of Spain and Portugal. Thereafter she was involved in the blockade of the French fleet at Toulon. In 1812 she helped to capture American vessels carrying tobacco, silks and brandy to France.

Two years later, without Blackwood, she was in North American waters and took troops up the St Lawrence to Quebec during the war with America, becoming the largest vessel to sail that far up the Canadian river. In the year of Waterloo, 1815, she was paid off, but recommissioned two years later, rebuilt and enlarged to carry seventy-six guns.

Until 1832 *Warspite* served mainly in the East Indies, South America and Mediterranean. However, she did take time out to circumnavigate the world – the first line of battle ship to do so.

In 1833 she was paid off at Portsmouth and seven years later reduced to a fifty gun frigate and dispatched to the Mediterranean to conduct anti-piracy patrols. Again paid off in 1846, she was loaned to the Marine Society as a training ship for boy sailors, but was destroyed by fire in 1876 while at Woolwich.

Following the destruction of the fourth HMS *Warspite* it was decided to rename

HMS *Conqueror* in her honour. This fifth *Warspite* was subsequently given as a replacement to the Marine Society. She survived until 1918 as a training ship when, like her immediate predecessor, she was also destroyed by fire.

A new frontline warship called HMS *Warspite* had in the meantime joined the fleet. Launched at Chatham in 1884, this sixth vessel to carry the name was considered an armoured cruiser and had a displacement of 8,400 tons, with 800 hp steam engines enabling her to reach seventeen knots. The first warship to be lit by electricity, she carried four 9.2-inch guns as her main weapons and ten 6-inch guns as secondary armament.

In 1888-89 she was involved in sea trials and exercises in home waters. In 1890 she became flagship of the Pacific Station before transferring to Queenstown where, again, she fulfilled flagship duties. Returning to the Pacific Station in 1899, she ended her career in 1902 and three years later was sold for scrapping.

And so ended the life of the immediate predecessor to the super dreadnought which is the main subject of this book.

While all the *Warspites* were kin, the relationship between the first and the seventh was particularly special.

Aside from being built at the first *Warspite*'s home port of Plymouth, the battleship of 1913 was to embody the Elizabethan fighting spirit better than any other *Warspite* since Raleigh's flagship. She served in an era when England was again in peril from powerful armadas, this time sailing forth from Germany.

The seventh *Warspite* was created by two men who aroused love or hate but never indifference. They were, like Raleigh and Essex, comrades-in-arms who ultimately fell out, in their case amid bitter recriminations over the conduct of the Dardanelles campaign of 1915.

Admiral John Fisher. *Taylor Library.*

We have already encountered one of *Warspite*'s fathers – Winston Churchill. The other was the visionary Admiral John Fisher whose brutal reformation of the Royal Navy at the beginning of the twentieth century created the conditions which gave birth to *Warspite* and her sisters. Rising to First Sea Lord in 1904, aged sixty-three, he 'did more than any single officer to drag the Royal Navy out of its nineteenth-century sloth, inefficiency, and drowsiness...' [3]

A great fan of all things revolutionary when it came to naval architecture, Fisher scrapped vast numbers of obsolete Royal Navy ships and pushed forward the development of submarines, the concept of the 'all-big-gun' battleship (the turbine driven HMS *Dreadnought* of 1906), construction of battlecruisers, the use of oil fuel and initiated construction of super dreadnoughts.

Fisher also reorientated the British fleet towards

Winston Churchill, First Lord of the Admiralty at the age of thirty-seven. *Taylor Library.*

HMS *Dreadnought*, the revolutionary battleship which paved the way for the construction of super dreadnoughts of the Queen Elizabeth Class. *Goodman Collection.*

combating the growing German threat, in the process devastating the Mediterranean Fleet, which he had commanded from 1899 to 1902, in order to bring vessels back to Britain.

When thirty-seven-year-old Winston Churchill was appointed First Lord of the Admiralty in late 1911, he was not to serve alongside Fisher as First Sea Lord, for the Admiral had resigned the previous year and soon departed for a sunny retirement in the Mediterranean.

However, the two men had been friends for some time. Before, and during, Churchill's early years as First Lord, Fisher pushed all manner of revolutionary ideas in correspondence, including his proposals for even bigger, faster battleships.

Notes

1 Henrietta Buckmaster, *Sir Walter Raleigh*
2 Ibid
3 Richard Hough, *The Great War at Sea.*

Chapter Two

BIRTH OF A SUPER DREADNOUGHT

Taking the Gamble

Suggesting a ruling monarch should authorize the naming of a warship in his very own Royal Navy after a man who had arranged the beheading of a previous king, was not perhaps the most subtle move. But here it was in black and white from the First Lord of the Admiralty... again!

King George V had already asked his Private Secretary to write to Winston Churchill and make it abundantly clear, when the Iron Duke Class was being built, that under no circumstances would a battleship be christened His Majesty's Ship *Oliver Cromwell*.

Now, in October 1912, Churchill had come back with the same suggestion, pointing out that Oliver Cromwell had done much to establish the Navy and ensure its rise to supremacy.

A new super dreadnought class was being laid down and, aside from Cromwell, Churchill was putting forward the names Queen Elizabeth, King Henry V and King Richard I.

He claimed to have prime ministerial support for putting forth Cromwell again. But, with senior naval officers warning Churchill they would take a dim view of a name so unpopular with the King being foisted upon them, Churchill eventually realized he had to concede defeat. In the end the only one of the four new warships to bear a name put forward by Churchill was the lead ship in the class, HMS *Queen Elizabeth*. The rest of the names were provided by the King – King Richard I became *Warspite*, Henry V was *Barham*, Oliver Cromwell became *Valiant*. The fifth Queen Elizabeth Class vessel, HMS *Malaya*, was so named because she was built with funds provided by the Malay Federated States.

Despite this early dispute over suitable names, the Queen Elizabeth Class vessels were to be the crowning glory of a British naval supremacy established at the Battle of Trafalgar in 1805.

The four Orion Class battleships – ordered under the 1909-10 naval construction

HMS *Iron Duke*, lead ship of the super dreadnought class which immediately preceded construction of *Warspite* and her sisters. *Iron Duke* was flagship of the Grand Fleet at Jutland. By the Second World War she was a depot ship at Scapa Flow. *Goodman Collection.*

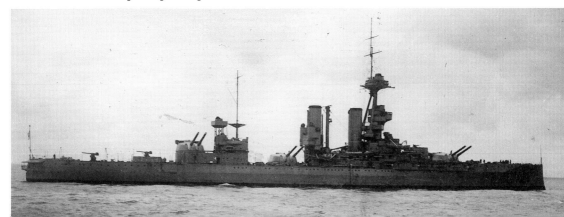

Until *Warspite*, the biggest guns mounted on British battleships were 13.5-inch guns like these belonging to the battlecruiser HMS *Queen Mary*. *Queen Mary* was to be blown apart by German shells at Jutland in 1916. *Taylor Library.*

programme – were the first of the super dreadnoughts, armed with ten 13.5-inch main guns and sixteen 4-inch secondary. They had belt armour up to twelve inches thick. These were followed by four King George V Class, ordered in the 1910-11 programme, and four Iron Duke Class, ordered in the 1911-12 programme, both classes with ten 13.5-inch guns. The former had sixteen 4-inch guns and the latter twelve 6-inch secondary armament. The King George V Class had two 3-inch high-angle anti-aircraft guns, the first time a British battleship had been fitted with AA weapons. Belt armour for the King George Vs and Iron Dukes was up to twelve inches thick.

But for every advance Britain made, the Germans were close behind. In 1911 they laid down four König Class battleships, armed with ten 12-inch main guns, fourteen 5.9-inch secondary armament and with belt armour of up to fourteen inches. In 1912, two tough Derfflinger Class battlecruisers were laid down. They carried eight 12-inch and twelve 5.9-inch guns, with belt armour up to twelve inches thick, compared with a nine inch maximum for most British battlecruisers.

To retain its lead the British fleet had to pull something big out of the hat, but had the parameters of battleship design gone as far as they safely could?

At a time of maximum danger words never failed Winston Churchill. And so it was in May 1912 when he went to the House of Commons to justify his gamble on a new class of super dreadnoughts mounting untried guns and using a foreign fuel.

The First Lord carefully explained the new vessels would carry 15-inch guns as main armament, 6-inchers as secondary and would be heavily protected, with armour up to thirteen inches thick. They would be fast thanks to oil-burning boilers. In order to inspire the House of Commons to give its broad support for these new leviathans Churchill employed vivid language to illustrate their killing power. To grasp the concept of a dreadnought duel he advised MPs to imagine,

> *a battle between two egg shells striking each other with hammers. The importance of*
> *hitting first, hitting hardest and keeping on hitting...really needs no clearer proof.*

The 1912 programme of naval construction was changed to accommodate the new super dreadnoughts. Plans for a further three 13.5-inch gun battleships and a battlecruiser were amended in their favour. Intelligence suggested the Germans were working on a new class of bigger gunned ships. There were also reports that the Americans and the Japanese were building vessels mounting 14-inch guns.

Warspite was laid down on the last day of October at Devonport, ten days after *Queen Elizabeth* at Portsmouth. *Valiant* was laid down at the end of January 1913, *Barham* towards the end of February and *Malaya* at the end of October that year. A sixth member of the class, called *Agincourt*, was ordered and destined to be built by Portsmouth Dockyard, but was ultimately cancelled at the end of August 1914. It was thought the war would be over before she could be finished. The name *Agincourt* was immediately given to a battleship originally built for Brazil in the UK, sold to Turkey at the beginning of 1914 but seized for service in the Royal Navy while fitting out at Devonport. The crew of the seventh *Warspite* would later have good cause to salute *Agincourt*'s astounding armament of fourteen 12-inch guns for they helped save the super dreadnought from destruction.

Churchill himself gives a vivid account of how he embarked on the gamble of *Warspite* and her sisters in *The World Crisis*. Originally the idea was to have a battleship that would carry ten 15-inch guns and do twenty-one knots. However, it was realized that, even with the number of main guns reduced to eight, a broadside heavier than ten 13.5-inch guns could still be achieved. With fewer guns to carry, the new super dreadnoughts could probably achieve battlecruiser speeds. But, as Churchill explains in *The World Crisis*, achieving a bigger, faster battleship was all very well as an exercise in naval architecture, but once it hit the water would it be of any use to the Admirals?

He reveals he asked of himself: 'Was it wanted? Was it the right thing to make? Was its tactical value sufficient to justify the increase in costs and all the changes in design?' The answer was yes. A division of fast battleships would be able to outpace an enemy battle fleet and, as Churchill himself explained, 'curl around the head of the enemy's line' and concentrate awesome firepower, shattering those vessels and throwing all the ships behind them into absolute disarray. The War College was asked to divine how fast the new super dreadnoughts would have to be to enable them to achieve this. The answer was at least twenty-five knots. But to nail that high speed down would require the First Lord to take a decision sure to arouse great passions in Britain.

Today oil fuels the world economy but, in 1912, coal turned the wheels of industry and commerce. It had also, since the advent of steam propulsion, pushed warships through the water.

Coaling a ship was time consuming, manpower intensive and the saving in weight achieved through burning oil would enable bigger guns to be carried, more room for boilers (to increase speed) and better accommodation for the crew. Studies carried out by the Navy had also proved coal could not possibly provide the intensity of heat needed to push a battleship of 27,500 tons (the designed displacement of *Warspite*) through the water at twenty-five knots.

Oil was very responsive to the demands of a warship. Speed could be piled on simply by increasing the number of sprayers ignited in the boiler, instead of depending on the exertions of stokers shovelling coal as fast as they could. Conversely speed could be cut easily by reducing the sprayers. A ship could also be made more stable, as it is easier to pump oil from tank to tank to achieve better ballasting than shift coal around.

Aside from the sheer convenience of enabling swift refuelling at sea, instead of having to call in at coaling stations, oil also meant the manpower aboard a capital ship could be used where it was most needed – in ensuring the killing power was fully inflicted on an enemy.

In *The World Crisis* Churchill refers to the sheer effort of feeding coal burning boilers as a poor use of manpower. He observes:

> As a coal ship used up her coal, increasingly large numbers of men had to be taken, if necessary from the guns, to shovel the coal from remote and inconvenient bunkers to bunkers nearer the furnaces or to the furnaces themselves, thus weakening the fighting efficiency of the ship perhaps at the most critical moment in the battle.

Oil made undeniable sense.

Many oil-fired torpedo-boat destroyers had been built for the Royal Navy and proved such a success that, by 1905, the Admiralty decided to invest in a flotilla of several tankers to transport oil back to the UK from the Middle East and to supply it to the Royal Navy's bases around the empire. In 1903 the Majestic Class battleships *Mars* and *Hannibal* had oil-fired boilers installed alongside their coal-fired ones to make comparative tests. It was becoming evident oil offered many benefits.

This was all very well, but for Britain to go the whole hog and start building whole classes of capital ships that depended on oil, there needed to be concrete assurances plentiful supplies could be found and secured. Naturally there was considerable

Coaling a battleship was time consuming and a sheer waste of manpower. One of the benefits of *Warspite*'s oil fuel was the eradication of this chore. *Taylor Library.*

A rare shot of HMS *Warspite* near to completion at Devonport early in the First World War, with dockyard workers swarming over her. *Goodman Collection.*

opposition to the idea of abandoning coal not only in the government but in the country as a whole. Thousands of jobs depended on coal mining. There were those who could not understand why the Navy would reject a natural resource abundantly available beneath the homeland's soil, in favour of a fuel with its source several thousand vulnerable miles away. It seemed distinctly unpatriotic and a vicious betrayal of the British coal miner.

A Royal Commission on Oil Fuel was to be formed to weigh up the pros and cons of new battleships, and indeed the whole Royal Navy, using oil. In the meantime the *Warspite* and *Queen Elizabeth* were rapidly taking shape on the slipways of Portsmouth and Plymouth around oil-fired boilers.

Churchill's decision to proceed with their construction several months before the Royal Commission gave its verdict, was a considerable gamble. He decided to mark the cards by dragging out of retirement the man who had inspired the whole concept of oil-burning battleships in the first place. Sailing to Naples aboard the Admiralty yacht *Enchantress* to meet Lord Fisher, Churchill wanted to know for certain if the Admiral would agree to chair the Royal Commission on Oil Fuel. For Churchill it was the first face-to-face meeting with the former First Sea Lord since Fisher had sent him a virulent letter condemning him for appointing to high posts in the Navy people he regarded as unsuitable.

After an initially frosty atmosphere, Fisher and Churchill set their differences aside and entered into energetic discussion. They agreed, not for the first time, that at stake was the Royal Navy's mastery of the seas and the security of Britain and her empire.

Churchill noted in *The World Crisis*: 'A decision like this involved our national safety as much as a battle at sea. It was as anxious and as harassing as any hazard in war.'

As Geoffrey Penn notes, opposition to the Royal Navy's use of oil fuel at the time was bitter:

> *Not only did foreign governments and commercial interests try to thwart the scheme, but at home, coal owners and mining unions joined in an unlikely alliance to prove it a retrograde step, arguing that it was suicidal to depend on fuel supplies unavailable from home, and attempting to prove that vast dangers from explosion existed.*[1]

The matter was finally settled in favour of oil by the Commission in 1913. It recommended all new warships should be oil-burners and fuel reserves large enough to last four years should be created. Ten million pounds for building the appropriate storage tanks was voted by the House of Commons. Churchill went back to the House in July 1914, just days before the outbreak of war with Germany, and got approval for Britain to buy a controlling interest in the newly founded Anglo-Persian Oil Company. The company had access to vast supplies of oil in what is today Iran and the Gulf States. The fifty-one per cent interest acquired cost Britain £2 million which was less than the cost of building HMS *Warspite*. Even then fears that oil would not be accessible during a war led to battleships constructed after those of the Queen Elizabeth Class initially being coal burning.

However, while these Royal Sovereign Class battlewagons may have started coal-fired, during construction they were converted to oil-burners. The majority of other Royal Navy warships also had oil nozzles installed in their boilers.

The issue of main guns for the Queen Elizabeth Class was equally complex and caused Churchill more than a few anxious nights. He had most energetically pushed the idea of the new vessels mounting 15-inch guns – the largest calibre ever proposed for a battleship – but it was by no means certain they would be a success. The dreadnought design envelope had already been stretched to its limits by earlier classes of battleship. These new beasts threatened to rip it asunder. A vessel packing a 15-inch punch would have to be much bigger than anything which had previously gone down the slipway. It was simple; the bigger the guns, the bigger the ship, and these weapons would each weigh 100 tons. Basically made of two gigantic tubes – an inner and an outer, with 170 miles of steel wire sandwiched between – the turrets they would be mounted in each weighed 550 tons. If all that wasn't enough, Churchill was informed that a full load of 900 15-inch shells to feed the new battleship's eight guns would reach 1,000 tons. To give the reader some idea of the sheer enormity of it all, it is interesting to note the total weight of guns, turrets and ammunition in *Warspite* (4,000 tons) was more than the entire tonnage of a Type 42 destroyer (or six Hunt Class minesweepers) in today's frontline British fleet. Despite the frightening dimensions, and egged on by Fisher in the background, Churchill authorized the design and production of the new calibre of gun.

Of course the easy way out would have been to stick with a smaller gun – a 14-incher perhaps, which would at least be equal to the calibres mounted in the new Japanese and American vessels and would certainly better the Germans. But being merely equal could cause uproar in the nation – since Trafalgar the British fleet had

The punch – a 15-inch shell. *Iain Ballantyne.*

The breech of a mighty 15-inch gun. *Iain Ballantyne.*

been undisputed controller of the oceans and the man who destroyed that unchallenged superiority may as well go hang himself.

To the British people of the early twenty-first century it may seem bizarre that the building of warships and the creation of their big guns, could raise such passion. But, in 1912, it did, for the dreadnoughts were the ultimate expression of imperial virility and prosperity.

More than thirty dreadnoughts, super dreadnoughts and battlecruisers were built between 1906 and 1921, providing good honest heavy engineering work for thousands of people from the Clyde to the Tamar, from the Tyne to the Solent. These great metal beasts were crewed by sailors belonging to a fleet whose White Ensign was universally feared and respected. With other countries, chiefly Germany, challenging for the seapower crown at the turn of the century, the fiercely competitive British had risen to the challenge. And if the only way to secure a clear unassailable lead over the Kaiser's fleet was to go into the unknown, and take a leap of faith with untried and untested 15-inch guns, then so be it.

To make sure Churchill understood exactly what was at stake, Lord Fisher had described any other course of action as 'treason to the empire'. But still the First Lord of the Admiralty fretted. He was to write in *The World Crisis*:

> No such thing as a modern 15-inch gun existed. None had ever been made. The advance to the 13.5-inch had in itself been a great stride. Its power was greater; its accuracy was greater; its life was much longer. Could the British designers repeat this triumph on a still larger scale and in a still more intense form?

Churchill relates that the Ordnance Board had been tasked with investigating the feasibility of the proposed calibre and had duly produced a design. Indeed Churchill reported the Director of Naval Ordnance was 'ready to stake his professional existence upon it.'

This was no time to be timid, and Churchill reflected that losing his nerve at that moment would have been a disaster. Some were counselling Churchill that it would be madness not to carry out full trials before mounting the guns. He noted: 'I hardly remember ever to have had more anxiety about any administrative decision than this.'

When *Warspite* and her sisters went to sea their 15-inch guns were still an unknown quantity. First Lord of the Admiralty Winston Churchill took a gamble on the success of the 15-inch guns, such as this one belonging to a Queen Elizabeth Class battleship. *Taylor Library.*

Starting to lose his nerve, Churchill went back to Fisher for advice which he duly received, in typical blistering tones. Churchill recalled in *World Crisis*: 'He was steadfast and even violent. So I hardened my heart and took the plunge.' Churchill gulped at the sheer enormity of it all, having only been in place as First Lord for a matter of weeks. 'Fancy if they failed. What a disaster. What an exposure. No excuse would be accepted.'

He imagined his career in ruins, with critics enjoying his downfall with relish, labelling his decision a 'ghastly fiasco' which caused the 'mutilation' of the new warships so badly needed to retain Britain's lead over the Germans.

But the Elswick Ordnance Company was supremely confident it could do the job, assuring Churchill the guns were perfectly feasible and would work without needing proving trials before being mounted in the battleships. The best they could offer was delivery of one of the weapons four months early to allow test firing and the compilation of calibration tables.

Churchill's relief at the safe launch of *Queen Elizabeth* and then *Warspite* was short lived. Yes, they were in the water, to be swiftly followed by the rest of the class, but the gunnery trials would not start for some time.

If the guns of *Warspite* and her sisters proved useless, Britain would have squandered precious ship-building resources almost on the eve of war with her greatest naval rival.

Notes

1 Geoffrey Penn, *Fisher, Churchill and the Dardanelles.*

Chapter Three

JUTLAND

Casualties of High Expectations

The railwaymen lining the Forth Bridge hurled coal to express their disgust at the battleship limping in below them apparently battered, bruised and defeated.

The super dreadnought's superstructure was pocked with shell holes, her upper decks a shambles, littered with charred lifebelts and shattered cutters. Benches and tables had been pulled up from the mess decks ready to be thrown overboard for the crew to cling onto if she went down.

The railwaymen shouted abuse at HMS *Warspite*'s crew. 'You ran away you bloody cowards,' shouted one, according to Midshipman Bill Fell.[1]

With the sorely damaged battleship coming alongside at Rosyth Dockyard other workers got their chance to show their anger too. Midshipman Fell recalled:

We were received at Rosyth with very, very great disapproval by the local people. They were all in mourning black hats and black arm-bands. They all felt the Grand Fleet had suffered complete defeat and that some ships, like the Warspite, *had run away.'*[2]

Warspite's crew were stunned by this reception, for, far from having fled from the enemy, they had fought with great bravery despite being hit time after time by heavy shells. Ordered home to Rosyth, because there was every danger she might sink, the *Warspite* had shown her defiance by almost ramming a U-boat on the way back. Behind her in the North Sea, the Royal Navy had chased the German fleet back to its bases where it would largely skulk for the rest of the war. But, in those vital first hours after the battle, the British public's perception of the titanic clash which had just taken place was of an overwhelming victory for the enemy.

In Whitehall, faced with a German tactical score sheet which included three British

The Forth Bridge was the gateway to the Rosyth Naval Base, from where *Warspite* sailed for action at Jutland. This photograph was taken from *Warspite*'s upper deck as she arrived at Rosyth in May 1916. On her return from Jutland railway workers working on the bridge would pelt the battleship with lumps of coal. *Franklin Collection.*

battlecruisers blown apart, obscuring the true strategic state of play, the Government of the day was frozen with fear, unable to decide what to do. It did nothing. While the British politicians remained mute, Germany's propagandists seized the initiative immediately, releasing triumphant accounts of their High Sea Fleet's success to the newspapers of neutral nations. And so across America, Greece, Holland and South America, via a carefully orchestrated campaign of media hype, the Battle of Jutland was initially perceived as a humiliating defeat for the Royal Navy. Britannia ruled the waves no more and the message had swiftly been picked up in Britain.

By 1 June 1916, when the *Warspite* sailed back under the Forth Bridge, the British public were convinced their Navy had well and truly flunked what should have been its finest hour. The huge investment of treasure and blood, sweat and tears in building a magnificent fleet appeared to have been in vain. National pride had apparently received a shameful blow and thousands of British sailors had died. People asked themselves how it could possibly have come to this. They had been led to believe the British Grand Fleet was more than a match for the German High Sea Fleet. An inability to catch up with the British dreadnought building capacity had seemed to leave the Germans incapable of defeating the Royal Navy in a fleet action. Everyone else lay even further behind. Battleship construction competition between France, Turkey, Austria and Italy in the Mediterranean and between Russia and Japan in the Far East, seemed irrelevant, such was the Royal Navy's apparent superiority. Meanwhile the Americans stood back from it all and quietly built the foundations of a powerful navy that was, by the middle of the twentieth century, to eclipse all others.

At the outbreak of war in August 1914, the Royal Navy's operational dreadnought fleet consisted of twenty vessels. The King George V Class battleship *Audacious* was sunk on Loch Swilly in October 1914 by a mine laid by a U-boat and many of her rescued crew ended up drafted to the *Warspite*.

HMS *Benbow* and HMS *Emperor of India*, the remaining ships of the Iron Duke Class, were completed in November 1914. By the beginning of 1915 the Royal Navy had twenty-four dreadnoughts in service to the Germans' seventeen. The British also had nine battlecruisers while their opponents had just five. The most powerful additions to the British fleet at this point were HMS *Queen Elizabeth* and HMS *Warspite*. In reply to the Queen Elizabeth ships, the Germans had laid down just two Bayern Class battleships carrying 15-inch guns, in 1913 and 1914. But *Bayern* would not be completed until 1916 followed by *Baden* in 1917 - too late to contribute to the clash of battle fleets.

The presence of the 15-inch guns of *Warspite* and her sisters at Jutland was to prove an important factor in preventing the Germans from achieving in reality the crushing victory claimed by the Kaiser's propaganda machine.

Commissioned in early March 1915, *Warspite*'s first full crew went aboard a few weeks later. She immediately felt right to her sailors, as one of her 15-inch gunners recalled:

> I immediately felt that I would be at home and happy. This happened to be so throughout the time I served in her. She was commanded by Captain Phillpotts and we were in good hands being commanded by such a gallant gentleman.

Members of *Warspite*'s crew watch another Queen Elizabeth Class battleship prove Churchill's gamble on 15-inch guns was a success, during gunnery exercises off Scapa in 1915. *Franklin Collection.*

> *The ship's 15-inch guns were a much bigger armament than any other battleship had carried before. It was something new and at the same time something strange. The ship herself soon proved everything that was expected of her, having been built in Plymouth and starting from Plymouth with a West Country Captain.[3]*

During acceptance trials that August in the Irish Sea, while on the way to Scapa Flow to join the Grand Fleet, *Warspite* proved herself fast. In a ninety minute sprint the *Spite* maintained 24.5 knots, showing she would be able to catch up with, or out-distance, German battleships only able to do twenty-two knots maximum. In initial trials her guns demonstrated superb hitting power, well capable of inflicting fatal blows on enemy vessels while still beyond the range of their smaller calibre guns. The gunnery trials were successfully completed off Scapa over three days in August 1915, with accuracy superior to the 13.5-inch guns of other British dreadnoughts emphatically demonstrated.

Weighing 1,950 lbs, the velocity of the 15-inch shell was 2,655 feet per second, compared with 2,700 feet per second for the (1,250lbs) 13.5-inch shell. Despite the slightly lower velocity the heavier weight of the 15-inch shell gave it a bigger punch. It was also able to retain its accuracy at ranges over 15,000 yards whereas smaller calibre shells could not. Geoffrey Penn[4] explains that the combined weight of a Queen Elizabeth Class broadside was 15,600 lbs whereas the German *Kronprinz*, completed in February 1915, had ten 12-inch guns which could manage barely more than half that impact. It could be said Winston Churchill's super dreadnought gamble showed every sign of paying off. Churchill wrote that the first time he witnessed the new 15-inch fired he felt 'delivered from a great peril.'[5]

Despite her design concept appearing to be a proven success, inspiring foreboding in the German high command, *Warspite*'s early career was marred by mishap after mishap. During the period May to September 1915 she deployed on routine gunnery and manoeuvre exercises with the Grand Fleet without incident. In mid-September HMS *Warspite* visited Rosyth and was grounded off Dunbar. Darkened and making fifteen knots in foggy weather at 5.30a.m., she was concentrating on avoiding enemy submarines.

She was mistakenly led down the small ships channel by escorting destroyers from the Rosyth-based Battle Cruiser Fleet.[6] Fortunately the *Spite* managed to extricate herself by going astern. An Admiralty board of inquiry held aboard *Warspite* was critical of the battleship's speed, suggesting she should have slowed by the time she reached Dunbar. However, bearing in mind wartime conditions forcing commanding officers to take risks, no members of the crew were found guilty of negligence but *Warspite*'s Captain Phillpotts and his navigator were reprimanded.

The battleship's outer hull bottom was damaged seriously enough to warrant spending two months in a floating dock on the Tyne for repairs.

Grand Fleet commander Admiral Sir John Jellicoe was deprived of one of his most effective units at a time when pressure for action against the Germans was mounting. The Kaiser's ships had staged a series of hit and run raids against ports on the north-east coast of England which had outraged public opinion, mainly because the British fleet seemed unable to stop them. The Germans managed to nip across and unleash their bombardments and then escape back home before the Grand Fleet's major vessels could get anywhere near an interception. The Royal Navy's Battle Cruiser Fleet had pursued and savaged a German force in January 1915, at the Battle of Dogger Bank, but still the raiders came. Scapa Flow was thought by many to be too far north and it was being suggested to Jellicoe that Rosyth and the Humber would be better bases for the Grand Fleet. Sir John was not, however, keen on these two bases as he considered them very vulnerable to attack. Splitting his ships would also hamper his ability to concentrate overwhelming force against the enemy when the decisive fleet v fleet action came.

This is believed to be Captain Phillpotts, seventh *Warspite*'s first commanding officer; a photograph taken aboard the battleship in 1915.
Franklin Collection.

Warspite left the Tyne and headed north to rejoin the Grand Fleet on 22 November but within a fortnight hit more bad luck. Back at Scapa she became part of a new combat formation - the 5th Battle Squadron - which had been created for the Queen Elizabeth Class vessels. In November 1915 it consisted of HMS *Barham*, squadron flagship, HMS *Queen Elizabeth* and HMS *Warspite*. The remaining members of the class - HMS *Malaya* and HMS *Valiant* - would join in 1916. At the beginning of December, while steaming in formation during a Grand Fleet exercise, HMS *Warspite* was in collision with the *Barham*. Signal flags on the *Barham* instructing the 5th Battle Squadron to do eight knots were misinterpreted as 'do eighteen knots'.

A view from *Warspite*'s foretop of a Queen Elizabeth Class sister ship while steaming in pursuit of the German High Sea Fleet in early 1916. *Franklin Collection.*

As a result the *Warspite* came charging on behind the much slower *Barham*, her bows hitting the squadron flagship's stern. Heavy seas made for a horrifying accident - *Barham's* stern descending into a chasm...*Warspite* carried high upon a mountain of sea...*Warspite*'s plunging bow twice slamming hard into her sister ship's rising stern...then momentarily grinding against it; a horrifying metallic crunch. Sub Lieutenant Bertie Packer gave a graphic description of what this collision felt like below decks in a letter to his father.

> *The ship bent and jumped like an india-rubber thing, engines full steam astern and our cable going out with a run and a rattle. I thought we'd caught a mine.*

A marine bugler sounded 'Collision Stations' as steam poured through the corridors and water 'swished in the for'd' threatening to drown defaulters in the ship's cells whom Sub Lieutenant Packer immediately released.

His letter added: 'Our bow was split like a pea-pod...'[7]

The *Barham* had ripped away the *Warspite*'s port anchor and the latter's bows were

An inspection of *Warspite*'s torn bows, following her collision with HMS *Barham*. *Franklin Collection.*

so badly crushed it seemed she might sink. However, with her crew working throughout the night to keep damaged compartments shored up, she managed to limp back to Scapa Flow through stormy submarine-infested seas, taking it very carefully at ten knots. Miles from any docking facilities, some ingenuity was employed in inspecting the battleship's bows to ascertain the extent of the damage. Hundreds of shells from A and B turrets were transferred to the quarterdeck, pushing her stern down into the water and lifting her bows. It was decided the damage could be shored up enough for *Warspite* to sail south to Devonport for major repairs. With yet another reprimand for a serious mishap ringing in his ears, the hapless Captain Phillpotts set course for Plymouth six days after the accident. Met by tugs at the breakwater, *Warspite* was shepherded through the snaking, deep channel of Plymouth Sound. Threaded very carefully through the Devil's Narrows, nudged into the dockyard, she was settled gently into a gigantic dry dock.

Warspite returned to Scapa on Christmas Eve, denying her crew an extended shore leave. The combat readiness of the Grand Fleet could not be relaxed for a moment.

Another Fool's Errand?

In late April 1916 the Germans sent their five battlecruisers and attendant cruisers and destroyers across the North Sea to pound Lowestoft. In response the Battle Cruiser Fleet and Grand Fleet tried to trap them, making a mad dash to get between the Germans and home. Despite the best efforts of British light cruisers from Harwich to delay them, and lead them into a position where they could be cut off, the Germans avoided a major action. Lowestoft suffered only four dead and some minor damage to property but the public was still incensed at the British navy failing once again to punish the German raiders.

Pressure for the main battle fleet to move closer to the action was stepped up. The Government tried again to persuade Sir John to make the move but he dug his heels in and refused to budge. Battle Cruiser Fleet commander Vice Admiral Sir David Beatty had for some time been agitating for the 5th Battle Squadron to be added to his force at Rosyth. Jellicoe had resisted. As far as he was concerned the role of the Queen Elizabeths was to act as heavy cavalry for the Grand Fleet. If a part of the British dreadnought battle line looked like it might weaken, the 5th Battle Squadron would use its speed and heavy guns to stiffen it. Likewise, if the enemy looked likely to break, it would be ordered to charge, hammering the weak point swift and hard.

Following the Lowestoft raid, Jellicoe was faced with two difficult choices; either to move the entire Grand Fleet south or to send the 5th Battle Squadron to join Beatty's force. He saw his opportunity to act without losing face when the 3rd Battle Cruiser Squadron came north to Scapa Flow to carry out some badly needed gunnery practice. Beatty was to be allowed to have the 5th Battle Squadron, but only while the 3rd Battle Cruiser Squadron was in the north.

After the monkish existence of barren Scapa Flow, the sailors of the 5th Battle Squadron turned a hungry gaze on the Firth of Forth, as their vessels sailed into their new temporary home on 22 May 1916. In place of the bleak, uninhabited Orkney landscape here was civilization and all the, often dubious, diversions a sailor could

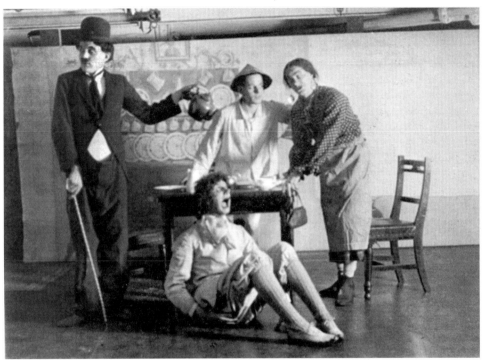

The boredom of barren Scapa Flow was relieved by the performance of amateur dramatic shows, at which *Warspite*'s crew proved to be the best in the fleet. *Franklin Collection.*

desire. The Scottish capital of Edinburgh was just minutes away. The crews of the warships made excellent use of this playground - cinemas and pubs for the junior officers and ordinary ranks, hotels for discreet philandering by senior officers. Those who preferred to keep body and mind pristine for battle took bracing country walks along the banks of the wide river, pursued games of golf on nearby links or tested themselves against each other in robust sports.

Midshipman Richard Fairthorne joined *Warspite* on the day of her arrival at Rosyth, finding that the sight of the battleship at anchor on the Forth sent his spirits soaring. He had just come from the dull routine of serving aboard the ancient cruiser *Leviathan* on the boring West Indies Station. Midshipman Fairthorne was

A group of fresh-faced Midshipmen shortly after joining *Warspite* at Rosyth in May 1916. *Franklin Collection.*

delighted there was no prospect of the 'indescribable tedium' of coaling.

Nearly sixty years later Fairthorne wrote that, on boarding the *Warspite* '...one sensed at once that she was a happy and efficient unit.'[8] The *Warspite* was an immaculate vessel, all spick and span, with the brass polished to blinding perfection, the paintwork pristine and wooden decks unblemished. Another new arrival aboard the *Warspite* was Surgeon Lieutenant Gordon Ellis. On 30 May Surgeon Lieutenant Ellis went ashore for a walk in the early evening, returning to Hawes Pier for a boat back to the battleship at around 7.30p.m.

While waiting for his ride he saw a light cruiser flotilla leader anchored off South Queensferry hoisting 'a long string of flags, which appeared to be a steaming signal.'[9] In fact shore patrols had also been sent into Edinburgh to recall people and a football match organized by the *Warspite* was abandoned, its participants hurrying back to the ship.

Radio intercepts that morning had revealed the High Sea Fleet was raising steam to come out. Possibly another raid on the east coast of England was in the offing, but the level of activity at the main German base of Wilhelmshaven suggested something bigger brewing. Accordingly, shortly before 6.00p.m. while Surgeon Lieutenant Ellis was still on his walk, the Admiralty sent instructions to Jellicoe and Beatty to take their full forces to sea and converge in the North Sea, east of the Long Forties.

Beatty's flagship, the battlecruiser HMS *Lion*, had sent a familiar message to the warships at anchor on the Forth: 'Raise steam for twenty-two knots and report when ready to proceed.' This was followed by: 'Proceed out of harbour 9.30pm.' All visible lights darkened, the menacing shapes of the ten battleships and

Surgeon Lieutenant Gordon Ellis.
Ellis Collection.

34

battlecruisers slowly slid out under the Forth Bridge.

HMS *Lion* led the Battle Cruiser Fleet, with *Princess Royal, Tiger, Queen Mary, New Zealand* and *Indefatigable* following on. In the 5th Battle Squadron *Warspite* was third in line behind *Barham* and *Valiant*, with *Malaya* last. The *Queen Elizabeth* was in a Rosyth dry dock for an extensive refit following bombardment duties in the Dardanelles.

As soon as the Forth Bridge was cleared the 5th Battle Squadron increased to twenty knots, keeping that speed up throughout the night and heading more or less due east. Aboard the *Warspite* there was no feeling among the crew of going to meet a date with destiny, rather one of dull routine. Midshipman Fairthorne - new to all this and therefore excited - was amazed at how calmly the crew of *Warspite* went about their business.

His new shipmates explained they found it hard to believe this would be anything other than another wild goose chase. One of *Warspite*'s gunners enjoyed the freedom of the sea:

> We sailed along through the night zig-zagging to avoid submarines. Eventually dawn broke and it was a wonderful sight - all these ships twisting and turning, with the battlecruisers ahead and we astern of them.[10]

The seventh *Warspite* had several mascots during her life, none more exotic than this lemur which lived in the foretop and may well have dodged enemy shrapnel up there during Jutland. *Franklin Collection.*

The Germans were trying to spring a trap. Their battlecruiser force, under Vice Admiral Franz von Hipper, was making speed parallel to the Norwegian coast, with the express purpose of luring Beatty's force out to play. The main High Sea Fleet, under Vice Admiral Reinhard Scheer, would then appear as Hipper's ships turned the British south. The Germans hoped to have a substantial part of the Royal Navy at their mercy, obliterated by their overwhelming force of sixteen dreadnoughts, five battlecruisers and seven pre-dreadnoughts. What the Germans were most anxious to avoid was any intervention by the immensely powerful Grand Fleet. Strange then, that they allowed themselves to walk right into its arms.

By the afternoon of 31 May 1916, *Warspite* and her sister ships of the 5th Battle

Admiral Beatty's flagship, the battlecruiser HMS *Lion*, viewed from *Warspite* in the Firth of Forth shortly before Jutland. *Franklin Collection.*

Another view of HMS *Lion* from *Warspite*. *Franklin Collection.*

Another of Beatty's battlecruisers, HMS *Tiger*, again pictured from HMS *Warspite* on the Forth shortly before Jutland. *Franklin Collection.*

Squadron were trailing behind Beatty's impatient battlecruisers. At around 2.30p.m., the cruiser HMS *Galatea*, far out in front of the fleet, sent a general signal: 'Cruiser in sight bearing N.E., probably hostile.' Not long after, a signal from *Galatea* to Beatty's flagship, HMS *Lion*, reported five plumes of heavy smoke on the horizon. A copy of this signal was brought to the Spite's bridge where it was realized they could only be German capital ships. 'It was pretty plain there was something serious doing,' *Warspite*'s Executive Officer, Commander Humphrey Walwyn later recalled of this moment.[11]

Captain Phillpotts decided *Warspite* should go immediately to Action Stations. Having ensured the Actions Stations order had been passed - that all watertight doors were closed, all fragile objects and potentially fatal loose items secured or stowed

HMS *Warspite* leaves Scotland astern as she sails out with the rest of the 5th Battle Squadron, headed for the mighty clash at Jutland in May 1916. *Franklin Collection.*

away, the wooden weather-decks dampened to decrease the likelihood of fire - Commander Walwyn made his way back to the bridge to report to the Captain. As he climbed up he looked for signs of the enemy, but could only see the *Valiant* and *Barham* ahead and *Malaya* behind.

The Battle Cruiser Fleet was well beyond reach of the protection afforded by the squadron's 15-inch guns. The gap had earlier increased to ten miles, because a signal from HMS *Lion* instructing the 5th Battle Squadron to turn south-east towards the enemy cruiser sighting had been missed, due to funnel smoke obscuring the flags. As a result the four battleships had proceeded east for another ten minutes before realizing the Battle Cruiser Fleet had made off in another direction. They then followed with all haste. Had the gap between battlecruisers and battleships not been so wide thousands of British sailors might not have lost their lives.

Commander Walwyn decided it was time to go to B turret. On his way down he went to his sea cabin and put on his custom-made Gieves and Hawkes life jacket, his flash hood and protective gloves. It would be the last time he ever saw his cabin, for a German shell would soon blow it to pieces.

Inside B turret Commander Walwyn found everyone in excellent spirits. Their good cheer was provoked by the prospect of some action after so many frustrating sweeps into the North Sea with nothing to show for them. They wanted to load the guns immediately. Commander Walwyn told them to calm down and await 'the usual routine orders'.

A Running Fight

Ahead of *Warspite* and the 5th Battle Squadron the opening shots of the first big fleet action involving the Royal Navy since Trafalgar, nearly 111 years earlier, were being traded. For the Germans it was the long awaited *Der Tag* (The Day) when their much smaller and younger fleet, with a history of barely thirty years, would be pitted against the Royal Navy's several centuries.

Among *Warspite*'s gunners the desire for battle was also high:

> *We were looking forward to a chance to have a crack at the enemy. We were keen. This was the day we were waiting for.*[12]

But the German Navy had one crucial advantage over the British – by starting from scratch the Kaiser's fleet had been able to build dry docks wide enough to enable construction of broad-beamed battleships and battlecruisers which were, for their size, much tougher than the Royal Navy's equivalents. The British – advanced in so many ways – were restricted by older dry docks built to more modest dimensions, allowing length but not the width which made the German ships so tough.[13] Unfortunately for the British battlecruisers, unwisely leaving their heavyweight fast battleship protectors trailing ten miles behind, Winston

The 5th Battle Squadron steams hard to try and catch up with Beatty's impatient battlecruisers at Jutland. *Goodman Collection.*

Churchill's description of a battle 'between egg shells striking each other with hammers' would prove tragically accurate.

At 3.58p.m. the five German battlecruisers – *von der Tann, Moltke, Seydlitz, Derfflinger* and *Lutzow* – opened fire, answered instantly by the British battlecruisers. The May haze was soon thickened by gun smoke mixed with dirty clouds belching from the funnels of warships at full speed.

Aboard *Warspite*, Signal Boy John Chessman, high up in the crow's nest, could hear the thunder of guns but see nothing of the fight. He later wrote:

> *Although out in the open sea there was maximum visibility and a bright sun shone down warmly on a sea smooth as a pond, the eastern horizon was shrouded in a sea mist, and, even with the aid of a telescope, no movement was discernible.*[14]

Calamity on an epic scale was to descend with terrifying speed on the rearmost

British battlecruiser – HMS *Indefatigable* – which rolled over and blew up after being hammered by the *von der Tann*, leaving two survivors from her 800 crew. When the 5th Battle Squadron later carved through her remains, sailors aboard the four fast battleships cheered, believing a German vessel had gone. The idea that a British capital ship had succumbed so easily was unthinkable.

Twenty minutes after battle was joined, the 5th Battle Squadron battleships could at

Ensigns flying, *Warspite* would face great peril during the Jutland encounter. *Franklin Collection.*

last weigh into the fray. Their initial targets were to be three German scouting cruisers – *Frankfurt*, *Pillau* and *Elbing* which had fallen behind the battlecruisers.

In *Jutland The German Perspective* V.E. Tarrant comments:

> *Konteradmiral Bodicker, on the bridge of Frankfurt, observed the masts of the four battleships gradually rise above the Western horizon, which he soon identified and reported to Hipper as being battleships of the Queen Elizabeth Class.*

The first sighting of the Queen Elizabeths caused a mixture of fear and professional fascination – back in their base ports the Kaiser's officers had speculated endlessly about the *Warspite* and her sisters, somewhat in awe of the eight 15-inch guns. Now they were about to find out what it felt like to be on the receiving end of Mr Churchill's and Admiral Fisher's monsters. In their official history of the battle, the Germans lamented the British fleet appeared to be 'as many headed as the hydra'. They had blown apart HMS *Indefatigable* only to see her replaced by four more powerful super dreadnoughts.

With their fire controlled by the directors high up on masts, most of the sailors in *Warspite*'s turrets followed instructions unable to see what their guns were aimed at. In B turret, Commander Walwyn was at least able to see something, if not very much, through the observation hood: 'I made out five columns of smoke in the mist, and that was all I could see, no masts or anything else.'

The *Spite*'s gunners strained at the leash but were still not allowed to fire:

> *Eventually the order to load had been passed. That meant that the shells and the cartridges had to come up from the bottom of the ship where there were shell rooms and magazines. It was all mechanical – the shell came up first, then the rammer operator pushed the shell into the gun followed by four quarter charges of cordite. We stayed in this position until the order to bring the guns to the ready was passed.*

The battlecruiser HMS *Indefatigable* which was blown apart at Jutland. *Goodman Collection.*

The experience of being inside the huge metal box that was a 15-inch turret was a peculiar mixture of invulnerability and claustrophobia.

> *There are three ways of getting out – one is out through a manhole at the top of the turret, another exit is through a manhole at the bottom. It is also possible to leave the turret by going down through the trunking down to the magazines and shell rooms.*
>
> *While you are in these turrets you are naturally cut off from anything going on outside except you are in telephone communication with the bridge and the gunnery control towers. It is a feeling of being fastened in a big box.*
>
> *The atmosphere is good and the crew numbers some sixteen people. Everyone has their individual jobs which they attend to and work as a team. At Jutland the guns being loaded, the next order passed was 'Guns to the Ready'. When the guns are brought to the ready you simply wait for the bang – when it happens the gun comes back three feet and then it goes out again. With a good turret crew you can actually fire about one round per minute.*[15]

The initial range was extreme and, as Commander Walwyn observed, most shots appeared to miss:

> *Opened fire on light cruisers, range about 21,000 yards. Could see the fall of shot well but could not see at all what we were firing at.*
>
> *Fired a few rounds by director and saw* Barham *and* Valiant *were firing too; light cruisers were getting clearer now. Suddenly saw the number two column of smoke break into a bright flame; this dropped astern and at first I thought she was hit but later I thought it was a smoke box, as it looked like an enormous calcium life buoy, bright flame and huge white smoke cloud drifting astern.*

Down below decks at his post in the Forward Aid Distributing Station, Surgeon Lieutenant could 'feel the shock to the ship with full charges for each salvo.'

Warspite made a fast turn to starboard and now Commander Walwyn caught his first glimpse of the five German battlecruisers:

> *They were steaming the same way as we were and going very hard. A mass of black smoke, and I could only see their masts and the tops of their funnels above the horizon....*

He also saw the mountainous stern wave kicked up by their propellers 'showing up white and very high.'

On sighting the 5th Battle Squadron, *Derfflinger's* Gunnery Officer, Georg von Hase knew a testing time was ahead for his battlecruiser.

> *There had been much talk in our fleet of these ships. They were ships of the line with the colossal armament of eight 15-inch guns.*

He added, perhaps recalling his foreboding at the time: 'They fired a shell more than twice as heavy as ours.'[16]

The 5th Battle Squadron switched fire to the German battlecruisers at 23,000 yards, with maximum elevation on the guns. *Barham* and the *Valiant* concentrated on the *Moltke* while *Warspite's* and *Malaya's* guns were initially laid on the *von der Tann*, the rear-most German battlecruiser. Their shells fell short.

Commander Walwyn was disappointed: '...I could not make out what was the matter.' But he had to turn away in some pain from the observation hood when the blast from *Warspite's* A turret blew salt water and dust into his eyes. German shells were also creating their fair share of turbulence, falling short, but tight together, and ricocheting spectacularly right over the *Warspite*. They passed a few feet from Sub Lieutenant P.E. Vaux, a gunnery officer in the foretop. Another new member of the crew, Vaux had served aboard HMS *Lion* at the battles of Heligoland Bight and Dogger Bank and was meant to have gone to the destroyer *Ardent*. However, he somehow missed his berth on her and was sent to *Warspite* instead. It was a stroke of good luck which he would come to appreciate after Jutland, as *Ardent* was destroyed during the battle.

'We had a rather thrilling time in *Warspite*,' he later remarked in a letter to his brother. 'To start with it was extremely nice, with the odds in our favour and a very interesting spectacle to boot.'[17]

Vaux was fortunate in being able to see the action, but for many of *Warspite's* 15-inch gunners there was no sight except the mechanisms of their gigantic weapons.

> *...they were kept firing as quick as possible. It was just a normal routine to the men in the turret having done it so often in practice. Things just clicked.[18]*

At this stage only the *Barham* suffered a hit, which caused modest damage. Commander Walwyn, back at his viewing position, saw her straddled by enemy fire. It now occurred to him that this mad dash in pursuit of the German battlecruisers might open out into something more daunting.

> *I realized we were steering south and it crossed my mind whether we should meet the High Sea Fleet.*

The Germans had now straddled the *Warspite* with heavy shells, but had yet to hit her. Their accuracy may have been affected by the fact that they were zig-zagging hard to avoid the British battleships' return fire.

Then, success for the *Spite's* gunners with a hit on the *von der Tann*, which cheered Commander Walwyn tremendously:

> *I distinctly saw one salvo hit No5 and she turned away six points to port and went away in a cloud of black and white smoke.*

Commander Walwyn was entranced by the awful beauty of war, which made even the enemy's attempts to kill him fascinating: 'It was a wonderful and rather horrible sight to see the constant orange flicker of flame along the line when they fired.'

However, for the British battlecruisers ahead, the true horror was hitting home.

The Royal Navy's mighty 15-inch guns made the Germans recoil with fear at Jutland. *Goodman Collection.*

Warspite and the other Queen Elizabeths were just too far back to distract *Derfflinger* and *Seydlitz* from concentrating a deadly barrage of killer blows on HMS *Queen Mary*, which had been shooting with deadly accuracy and inflicting real pain on the enemy. The *Queen Mary* exploded, her wreckage falling all around HMS *Tiger* and HMS *New Zealand* as they raced through the smoke and offal. The dead battlecruiser's stern poked above the water, screws still turning. Some of her seventeen survivors clung to this surreal tombstone. For their part, the members of *Warspite*'s crew who saw more evidence of a destroyed vessel assumed, again, that she must be German. But, above the North Sea, a mushroom cloud of smoke nearly 1,000ft tall was dissipating and with it the legend of absolute British naval invincibility established by Horatio Nelson.

Having left the heavy protection cloak of the 5th Battle Squadron trailing too far behind, Beatty was discovering reckless bravery provided a paper thin shield for inadequately armoured and internally protected British vessels, especially facing better constructed opponents blessed with superb gunners. The final bitter truth of the *Queen Mary*'s demise was that her own fantastic shooting was largely in vain, as defective British shells used at Jutland frequently broke up on the outside of the German armour without causing significant harm.

Sixteen minutes later the British met the vanguard of the High Sea Fleet. Aboard the cruiser HMS *Southampton*, Commodore William Goodenough, commanding 2nd Light Cruiser Squadron, was greeted, despite overcast weather in the south-east, with first their heavy smoke on the horizon, then tall masts, and finally the ships themselves. A series of coded wireless transmissions to Beatty culminated at 4.37p.m. with the urgent declaration: 'Have sighted the enemy battlefleet bearing approximately SE. Course of enemy N.' Collision course.

Now Beatty very sensibly laid aside his lust for personal glory. He did the only logical thing to save his ships from destruction and attempt to lure the enemy to theirs – he ordered a turn to the north, leading the Germans into the jaws of the Grand Fleet which was now fifty miles away. As the Battle Cruiser Fleet ships reversed

HMS *Queen Mary* blowing up at Jutland, a sight the crew of HMS *Warspite* cheered, for they believed they were seeing a German battleship's destruction. *Taylor Library.*

course at 4.45p.m., German shells were falling short and now they piled on the speed again to try and stay ahead of the enemy fire. Eight nautical miles astern of the Battle Cruiser Fleet, the 5th Battle Squadron continued to hurtle south towards the main German force, still engaged with the enemy battlecruisers.

The Queen Elizabeths were plainly unable to see the signal flags on Beatty's flagship giving the instruction to turn north. As the British battlecruisers approached from the south it was noticed for the first time that two ships were missing from the Battle Cruiser Fleet line.

Commander Walwyn counted Beatty's warships off in order:

I suddenly saw our battle cruisers coming close by about four cables in the opposite direction and I realized they had turned back. I saw Queen Mary *and* Indefatigable *were adrift but never for a moment realized they had gone.*

Then Beatty's ships were momentarily between the 5th Battle Squadron and the Germans, preventing the Queen Elizabeths from firing for fear of hitting their own vessels. Another attempt to signal the turn north was made by Beatty but towering shell splashes surrounding HMS *Lion* hid the message. *Warspite* was herself deluged with a number of near misses. Commander Walwyn confessed: 'One salvo came very close, just short, smothering us with spray, and I am afraid I ducked....'

Then, like a curtain being torn aside, suddenly there it was – the whole High Sea Fleet. Squadron commander, Rear Admiral Hugh Evan-Thomas, instantly ordered an about turn. At 4.58p.m. the 5th Battle Squadron swung away from certain destruction but instead of turning one by one where they were, they followed each other around, enabling the Germans to range on the turning point. As the *Warspite* curved around on her reverse course, all her turrets swung to train on targets on the other beam.

Admiral Beatty, who rashly left behind the protection of the 5th Battle Squadron at Jutland.
Taylor Library.

Now the full impact of danger facing the British battleships hit home. Commander Walwyn was again in awe of the terrible majesty of war:

Very soon after the turn I suddenly saw on the starboard quarter the whole of the High Sea Fleet; at least I saw masts, funnels, and an endless ripple of orange flashes all down the line, how many I didn't try and count, as we were getting well strafed at this time, but I remember counting up to eight. The noise of their shells over and short was deafening... Felt one or two very heavy shakes but didn't think very much of it at the time and it never occurred to me that we were being hit.

This moment is described graphically in a letter written after the battle by Royal Marine Captain R.A. Poland who commanded *Warspite*'s Y gun turret.

Captain Poland wrote:

...as we turned we got our first hit (the only one I actually saw). It got us very low down right aft and threw up a big cloud of grey smoke and shook the ship all over.[19]

Malaya, having seen her sisters straddled by very accurate fire at the turning point, cut the corner, curving inside the others and escaping any hits. But the *Warspite* wasn't taking punishment without giving something back, for she and *Malaya* were hitting the leading German battleships hard. Commander Walwyn was delighted to see one of the enemy enveloped in flame and thought the vessel was surely doomed. He said:

> *I distinctly saw two of our salvos hit the leading German battleship. Sheets of yellow flame went right over her mastheads and she looked red fore and aft like a burning haystack; I know we hit her hard.*

During the run north, while *Warspite* and *Malaya* fired on the leading battleships, *Barham* and *Valiant* continued to engage the German battlecruisers.

Under the fire of the 5th Battle Squadron, the *Seydlitz* had her starboard waist turret wrecked while the aft waist turret was turned into an inferno. Half her guns were put out of action. The *von der Tann* also shuddered to more 15-inch hits, scaring the wits out of her crew. *Lutzow* and *Derfflinger* also felt the devastating weight of the 15-inch guns, the former soon unable to act as flagship for Hipper as all her wireless communication gear was shot away. The dreadful battering was so severe it seemed to make Hipper himself punch drunk and incapable of giving decisive orders.

Maximum Peril

From his well protected position behind inches of thick armour inside *Warspite*'s B turret, Commander Walwyn had so far been able to witness the most spectacular clash of battle fleets in history in comparative safety. However, damage to the battleship's stern was now causing Captain Phillpotts some concern. He knew that if his ship faltered in the middle of this running battle she would be ripped apart by the pack of German wolves snapping at her heels. He therefore decided he had no option but to extract Commander Walwyn from his position and send him aft to investigate the damage and oversee emergency repairs. From this moment on Commander Walwyn would be exposed to considerable personal danger, involved in a desperate fight to keep the *Warspite* fighting and floating despite an increasing amount of heavy damage. For a few seconds after receiving the Captain's message, Commander Walwyn contemplated whether he should exit via the hatch in the top of the turret or go down through the shell room. Personal safety recommended the latter, but '...I realized I ought to get there quickly and decided to go over the top of the turret.' The hatch was opened by one of the gunners who melodramatically bowed. Commander Walwyn nervously clambered out and found himself the lone star of this theatre of war.

> *...directly I was on top they banged the hatch to. I didn't waste much time on the roof as the noise was awful and they were coming over pretty thick.*

The shock of *Warspite*'s own 15-inch guns going off a few feet away, while German heavy shells roared in overhead, their impact spraying tons of shrapnel-laced water, cannot be downplayed. Commander Walwyn later did his best to shrug it off in his action report:

> *As I got down the starboard ladder of B, both A and B fired and made me skip a bit quicker....*

He found no way in. All the doors were securely shut as he had ordered:

Ran down the port superstructure ladder and tried to get into the port superstructure all clips were on, so I climbed up over 2nd cutter. Just as I got up one came through the after funnel with an awful screech and spattered about everywhere. I put my coat collar up and ran like a stag, feeling in a hell of a funk.

Commander Walwyn's nerve nearly went. A German 12-inch shell had hit a fresh meat store, propelling a sheep carcass into some grating where it became wedged, giving the appearance of a badly mangled human corpse. Luckily Commander Walwyn found a door slightly ajar because some marines were watching the action. Once inside he ordered them to slam it tight shut. Inside the huge hull Commander Walwyn found himself cut off from the bedlam of battle.

Went right down to the mess deck and all along port side; all was quiet and could see nothing wrong at all.

Meeting a grinning sailor who seemed to have nothing better to do, Commander Walwyn sent him to the Captain with a message that nothing was wrong aft.

However, *Warspite* had been hit under the waterline – the shell impact Captain Poland had seen from Y turret. This would later send her on a suicide run straight at the German battle fleet.

As a portent of the moment of maximum peril about to hit their battleship, some of *Warspite*'s sailors were to look on in horror as the Germans obliterated a trio of foolhardy British armoured cruisers. The British ships – HMS *Defence*, HMS *Warrior* and HMS *Black Prince* – decided they would descend upon the gravely injured German cruiser *Wiesbaden*, which lay dead in the water after a mauling from passing British battlecruisers. Unfortunately, as the three British cruisers set about the *Wiesbaden*, the German battle fleet plunged out of the haze, its leading elements pouring a withering fire on the Royal Navy squadron.

The *Warspite* skirted this calamity, Sub Lieutenant Vaux watching the destruction of the *Defence* from *Warspite*'s foretop:

She was about a quarter of a mile on our engaged side when she blew up – I saw her very plainly first on fire for'ard and then a huge flame about twice the height of the mast, no noise, and nothing at all left of her, a ghastly sight.

The *Warrior* and *Black Prince* were left in a sad state, but continued to float and fight. However, unless the *Warrior* was blessed with a miracle the German battle fleet would pass so close she would surely be next to explode.

The strange tranquillity inside *Warspite*'s heavily armoured hull was rudely interrupted by a German 12-inch shell ripping through the side armour of the boy sailors' mess deck. Commander Walwyn saw a 'terrific sheet of golden flame' followed by 'stink, impenetrable dust, and everything seemed to fall everywhere with an appalling noise.' Surgeon Lieutenant Ellis, in the forward aid distributing station, was directly below the impact point: 'There was a loud crash as it exploded and mess tables and stools seemed to be being thrown about all over the place judging from the noise and clatter.' Senses reeling, Commander Walwyn called a nearby battle damage team into action. They played their water hoses onto a fire which went out easily but the dreadful stink remained.

Several of the fire crew were sick due to the sweet sickly stench, but there was no signs of poison gas. The shell hole was clean and about the size of a scuttle; big flakes of armour had been flung across the mess deck wrecking everything.

Smoke poured through holes in the deck and Commander Walwyn suddenly realized the ammunition magazine for the anti-aircraft guns was nearby and might explode. He immediately gave orders to stand by to flood the middle deck position. But before this was necessary water from severed fire mains pouring through holes in the deck doused the fire. While a damage control team struggled with closing off the damaged water mains other sailors scrambled about in the wreckage retrieving souvenir bits of shrapnel. Commander Walwyn told the fire hose teams to turn their jets of water on them 'to make them take cover below again'.

Surgeon Lieutenant Ellis was meanwhile attending to his first casualty – the only wound victim of the shell in the boy sailors' mess – a stoker hit in the neck by a piece of shrapnel. He stopped the bleeding by packing the wound with strips of gauze. In his diary, he later noted that another sailor blown down a ladder by the impact of the same shell escaped injury.

Going aft again, Commander Walwyn discovered serious damage to the Captain's and Admiral's accommodation. Commander Walwyn was surveying other areas of damage and ordering sailors evacuated from compartments that seemed in danger of flooding, when a shell burst in the Captain's lobby. On arriving at the latest scene of carnage he found his own day cabin had been 'completely removed overboard.'

Next Commander Walwyn saw his first casualties of war.

Three stokers were dead in voice pipe flat, one having his head blown off and another badly smashed to pieces, rather a horrible sight...

Then he came across a damage control team that had suffered dead and wounded.

A shell had come in further forward and hit X turret barbette armour, killing several of No.5 fire brigade in engineers' work shop and wounding a lot more.

The Wireless Transmitting room had also had its door blown off and the young sub lieutenant working inside had been killed. Another shell-hit momentarily put out all internal lights but candles proved adequate in the circumstances. As he made his way forward again, the broken glass of lightbulbs crunched under Commander Walwyn's feet and jagged shards of armour plating also made walking difficult.

Commander Walwyn now came across two stokers involved in an act of sheer stupidity:

The body of a 12-inch shell was found above engineers' work shop, unexploded. The filling was sticking out like a chock of wood and a couple of stokers were trying to chip the fuze out. I luckily stopped this little effort.

The shell the stokers were meddling with had knocked a door down on top of a chief stoker and killed him, wrecked the bandmaster's cabin before embedding itself at the top of the ladder leading down to the engineering workshop. But, despite all the damage he had encountered, and the shock to his own frail human senses, Commander Walwyn reckoned the tough battleship was still in good enough shape to carry on fighting. He sent someone to telephone Captain Phillpotts with the message that things were under control.

The Paymaster, who was wandering about 'using appalling language as to when the Grand Fleet was going to turn up', stopped by to have a good humoured chat. As the two officers enjoyed a grim chuckle at their potentially serious predicament, a 12-inch shell destroyed the Warrant Officer's galley. A Warrant Officer stoker standing beside the Commander remarked: 'There goes my **!!**! dinner!'

Making his way via the 6-inch battery deck on the port side to see what damage the shell had caused, Commander Walwyn was relieved to find very little. The gunners seemed 'very cheery'. Moving along the starboard side of the mess deck, Commander Walwyn found some of the 6-inch battery support crews bunched up together and ordered them to spread out to reduce casualties.

Needing a breather after these exertions, Commander Walwyn decided to go up to the port side battery deck to see if he could see any of the battle through the 6-inch gun controller's observation hood. A high explosive shell hit the ship on the port side aft just as the Commander was taking his look and, blinded by a terrific flash, he was knocked over by the shock of the impact, his eyes full of water and dust. A sailor came to his rescue, thinking he was wounded, but Commander Walwyn was only bruised. Picking himself up, he decided to inspect the damage down below as the ship appeared to be receiving more heavy hits.

Crossing to the starboard side of the ship Commander Walwyn heard a shell burst above in the 6-inch gun battery.

> Sheet of flame came through slits of sliding shutters. Told them to open the shutter with a view to going up the escape to see what had happened... .

But fires were still burning above so Commander Walwyn ordered the shutter closed again. The disturbing sound of mortally wounded sailors groaning in agony could be heard.

As Commander Walwyn dashed forward to try and gain access he was told the superstructure of the battleship was ablaze but decided external problems would have to wait until he saw the extent of the damage to the battery.

> A fragment from the shell bursting by the starboard 6-inch gun had come through the roof of the battery deck and actually hit the after 6-inch cordite case containing four full charges.

When the shell fragment struck, a sailor had been standing by ready to load a gun with a cordite charge half out of the protective case in his arms. In addition to the whole of the No 6 six-inch gun crew being dreadfully burned, together with some members of the neighbouring gun, there was a danger the fire could spread along the whole battery. Luckily a crucial protective door was shut and so the fire was contained while it was brought under control. Despite being badly burned himself, the ship's fifty-six-year-old Roman Catholic padre, Father Pollen, heroically persisted in pulling casualties away from the flames.

As her crew dealt with the consequences of this latest hit, more shells were slamming into *Warspite* and the noise of battle was extraordinary.

> At this time I thought our 6-inch were firing but I realized afterwards it was only hits on us. The noise was deafening and rather nerve shattering. You could not hear yourself speak and had to shout in anybody's ear.

Amid this cacophony Commander Walwyn remembered he'd better investigate the

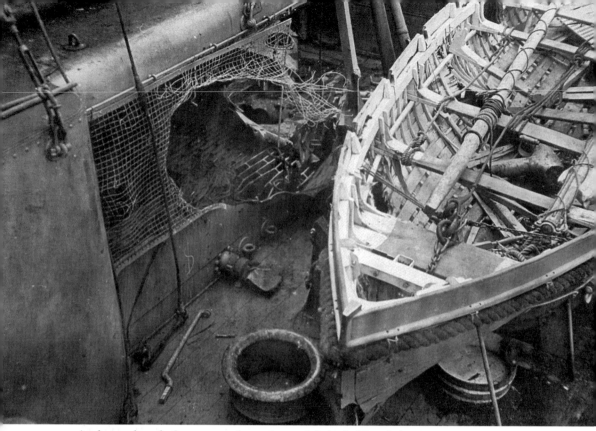

As she raced north, German guns began to punch holes in *Warspite*'s superstructure. *Franklin Collection.*

burning superstructure.

Climbing out to the upper deck using the six-inch battery deck escape ladder, he found 'the whole place ablaze'. Worst of all, the firefighting teams couldn't do anything about it, as the water mains had been cut.

Through the observation slits in the ship's conning tower Commander Walwyn could see signalmen and messengers who feared they would be roasted alive.

With their mouths agape calling 'put the fire out!' Commander Walwyn thought they looked like chicks trapped in a thrushes nest. Somehow Royal Marines and midshipmen managed to get hoses connected to a steam main and pulled up water that way. As a hose spurted into life, Commander Walwyn was accidentally knocked over by the force of its water jet.

Picking himself up, he decided to take a quick survey of the battleship's exterior:

The upper deck and superstructure looked perfectly awful, holed everywhere. I think at this time the firing had slackened but the noise was still deafening, shells bursting short threw tons of water over the ship.

Treating the burns casualties from the six-inch gun battery was a grisly business. Surgeon Lieutenant Ellis and the Principal Medical Officer with their staff treated eleven cases, including Father Pollen, suffering from

...very severe and extensive burns of the face, body and limbs. They were so badly

burnt that one could do very little to relieve them of their pain and shock, injections of morphine seeming to have little, if any, effect on them.

Specially treated bandages were tried, but laying them on the burns was so excruciating for the injured men that they tore them off. Instead an oil was used but still they suffered greatly. Surgeon Lieutenant Ellis:

It was no easy job either, as they required constant attention and watching to guard against them hurting themselves through moving about.

The medical staff '...could not keep them still even with repeated hypodermic injections of morphine.'

Using a ragged shell hole in the hull on the boy sailors' mess deck as his window, Commander Walwyn tried again to catch sight of some action. Even with a crew of more than 1,000, only around two dozen could actually see what was going on and then the fog of war restricted their clarity of vision to flashes in the smoke.

Unsurprisingly Commander Walwyn was little the wiser after his look at the scene of battle. It '...looked red, lurid and beastly, heavy firing all round and splashes everywhere...'

It did, however, appear to him that *Warspite* had slowed down. Going aft to see how the battle against flooding was progressing, he found the centre engine room deluged with 'a fair amount of water' as shell hole plugs were washed away. Any handy items of wooden furniture or fittings were fair game for ongoing attempts to plug these holes, including mess stools, hammock bins and candle boxes which carpenters adapted to the emergency at hand. With very few, if any, of the crew knowing what was happening Commander Walwyn was forever being buttonholed by sailors anxious for news of how the battle was going. He told them he couldn't really help.

'Everybody was very cheery, and anxious for news which I couldn't give as I hadn't the faintest idea what was happening.' Such was the feeling of being divorced from events beyond their own compartments, Commander Walwyn saw some members of the crew playing cards, seemingly without a care in the world. On the other hand, he was bothered by a pair of very anxious sailors. 'Two stokers came to me when I was very busy and begged me to take watches. letters etc., found on men who had been knocked out.' The Commander was not pleased at this distraction.

It struck me as so incongruous, as if it mattered a damn as we might all of us go at any minute. I told them so but they were so insistent about it... .

Commander Walwyn passed them on to a senior rate.

Overall the Commander was very impressed with the crew's resilience.

Men everywhere were simply splendid, and all so cheery and although I confess it was mighty unpleasant and unnerving I myself had plenty to do, but for those who merely had to wait it must have been a thousand times worse. The noise was so perfectly appalling, and you couldn't hear at all between decks and the worst of it was knowing nothing.

There was always room for humour, particularly when a sailor fell down a shell hole in the main deck and cut himself. According to Commander Walwyn this raised 'a good laugh'. Later the sailor would claim this injury as a 'war wound', displaying the appropriate stripe on his uniform until it was 'forcibly removed'.

Called to the bridge by the Captain, Commander Walwyn was a frightful sight, wet through from head to foot and covered in dirt.

Captain Phillpotts was direct to the point of rudeness in his interrogation of his second in command. As Commander Walwyn went though his damage report the Captain cut him off mid-sentence.

'I don't care a damn about the damage,' he snapped. 'Can we join the line?'[20]

Unaware of the state of play in the battle, Commander Walwyn felt the Captain must have thought him a bit of an idiot. He later confessed that, had the Captain been killed or badly wounded, and he had been asked to take control, he would not have had a clue what to do. Pressed to give a verdict by Captain Phillpotts, he stated: 'If she gets another heavy hit the port side I don't think she will stand it.'

Captain Phillpotts was seething during his interrogation of Commander Walwyn because of another mishap his capricious battleship had inflicted upon him. She had fallen victim to a lethal steering problem at exactly the wrong moment.

As the 5th Battle Squadron joined the Grand Fleet and turned into line, the *Warspite* narrowly avoided being squashed between the *Valiant* and *Malaya*. Turning hard, her steering jammed because it had already been damaged by the shell which hit near the port wing engine room. The after bulkhead of the centre engine room – to which the steering engine was fixed – had buckled. This had created a 'hot bearing' so that, when the wheel was rotated too quickly during the turn to avoid *Valiant*, the steering jammed. Like a car driver missing his turning on a roundabout, Captain Phillpotts decided it was better to go around again and keep moving than stop and reverse course while under fire from the entire German fleet. Control of the guns was immediately devolved down to individual turrets, it being impossible for the control tops to function in such wild circumstances. Captain Poland of Y turret later commented:

> *My 2nd officer was howling for permission to fire at something, but I refused until there was something visible to fire at.*[21]

It was a frustrating interruption to the rhythm of *Warspite's* main guns which had been doing a lot of damage to the enemy. One of the gunners noted:

> *Suddenly for no reason at all we stopped firing. The trainers and gun layers looked into their telescopes and someone said 'this ship is running around'. Then someone said 'she is still turning around...she is going in circles '. And the word was then passed from the bridge that the rudder was jammed. That was the reason we were turning and the ship had stopped firing.*

The silence of temporary inactivity provided the same gunner with an opportunity to listen to the action outside:

> *I kept hearing bangs which I thought might be our 6-inch guns firing, and repelling torpedo attacks, but it didn't turn out to be*

Captain Phillpotts, pictured here aboard *Warspite* with a faithful friend, was fuming with frustration when the *Warspite* ran out of control at Jutland.
Franklin Collection.

that. It later transpired that the bangs I had been hearing were shells hitting the ship.[22]

While Commander Walwyn may not have noticed the turns, fully absorbed in supervising damage control and firefighting, Surgeon Lieutenant Ellis and the Principal Medical Officer in the forward aid distributing station most certainly had.

...the ship suddenly took a list to port, and instead of righting herself as she would have done had it been an ordinary turn, kept heeling over indefinitely.

The two men feared the end was nigh:

...as it persisted we concluded that she had been hit heavily somewhere, by a torpedo possibly, and that it was the beginning of her going right over... but after an appreciable length of time the list stopped, and she gradually got back onto an even keel again.

In the centre of *Warspite's* crazy circles was the badly damaged HMS *Warrior* which duly received salvation, German gunners deciding the out of control British super dreadnought was a much juicier target.

Warrior's crew believed the *Warspite's* actions were a deliberate act to save them from certain death and were, for the rest of their days, grateful to the battleship. An officer in a nearby British cruiser saw the enemy's barrage switch to *Warspite*:

As she continued to plunge forward towards the Germans the tornado lifted from Warrior, *hovered as it seemed in space and fell with a crash about* Warspite.

In the fire storm which enveloped *Warspite*, Signal Boy Chessman was wounded by small bits of shrapnel, his trousers shredded and flesh lacerated. He was amazed at his miraculous escape:

To stand in the centre of a metal storm and to be cut as I was without a single piece lodging must surely indicate I was born of a miracle.[23]

In the foretop, still recovering from the shock of witnessing the *Defence* blowing up, Sub Lieutenant Vaux felt as if he would die at any moment. He saw,

...about four or five German dreadnoughts firing at us for about twenty minutes and hitting us about once a minute. Why we weren't sunk is a perfect mystery, personally, after seeing the Defence *go. I thought we should go every minute. I was simply soaked with salt water from the splashes of their shells that fell short.*

The enemy shells thudded into *Warspite* with such a deafening noise that the Captain's orders could not be heard on the conning tower. *Warspite's* gun flashes had also blinded the Navigating Officer. Captain Phillpotts was forced to scream orders down the voice tubes. He told the engine room to steer with the screws. This they did, and after two circles, the battleship did an 'S' which prevented another circuit but threatened to take her back towards the Germans. Captain Phillpotts ordered the engines stopped and the ship was stationary for ten minutes, continuing to weather gunfire. Her steering gear was then repaired well enough for her to get underway again. Lady Luck truly rode with *Warspite* at Jutland.

Fortunately for the *Warspite* the German ships broke contact because they were forced to turn away by the Grand Fleet finally bringing its substantial weight of fire into play. The British fleet could focus its full power against the Germans in a vast arc of death while they were in line astern and could only bring a small proportion of their guns to bear. *Warspite's* Midshipman Bickmore recalled as each Grand Fleet battleship turned into line, he saw her 'breaking into a ripple of flame from end-to-end...'24

The smaller ships caught between the two battle lines reverberated to shock waves from the big guns.

Still standing on the bridge, a little dazed from his experiences keeping the *Warspite* afloat, Commander Walwyn was at last able to absorb something of the bigger picture:

> There was a heavy pall of smoke everywhere, terrific rumbling of heavy firing and the whole horizon lit by orange flashes everywhere, everything blurred and beastly. I saw Agincourt *a long way off firing like blazes and remember thinking she was going pretty hard but that's all I ever saw of the Grand Fleet.*

Agincourt was instrumental in saving *Warspite*, which was fitting for a warship which took the name of the cancelled sixth Queen Elizabeth Class battleship.

The Grand Fleet thundering down from the north had regarded the battlecruisers as merely the opening act for their main performance and Beatty's vessels had proved to be boxers with glass jaws. The demise of yet another battlecruiser – HMS *Invincible*, the victor of Battle of the Falklands in 1914 – in a horrific explosion, reinforced this harsh truth before the whole Grand Fleet.

The light was fading fast as night came on, and the smoke and haze of battle was obscuring visibility. German telescopic sights – so deadly earlier – were increasingly affected by dampness in the air. Despite their problems, German gunners were lucky to have the British warships silhouetted against the sun setting in the west while the High Sea Fleet was hidden in the gloomy east.

The Battle to Keep Afloat

Warspite slipped away from an enemy which believed it had dealt her a death

The massive broadside of HMS *Agincourt* helped to save HMS *Warspite* from destruction.
Goodman Collection.

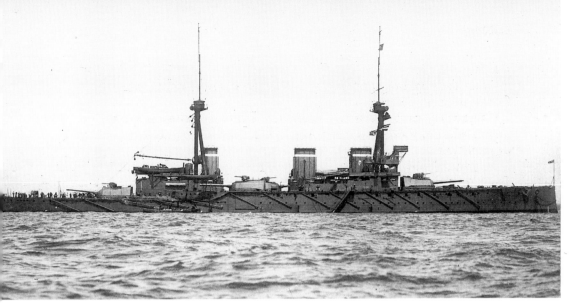

The battlecruiser HMS *Invincible*. *Goodman Collection.*

blow. But, despite her moment of maximum peril, the battleship had survived. Commander Walwyn went below again and was making another inspection of the damage on the port side when he received a message from the Captain asking: 'What speed can we go?' Commander Walwyn replied: 'Sixteen knots'. This was probably needed for an exchange of signals between Captain Phillpotts, still desperate to get back into the battle, and Rear Admiral Evan-Thomas, aboard *Barham*. Evan-Thomas decided not to risk *Warspite* any further and ordered her home to Rosyth. Having been cocooned from the damage caused by German shells to the *Spite*, the 15-inch gun crews were shocked at what they found on being allowed out of their turrets.

> When the ship got out of range of enemy guns, the order was passed by telephone to us saying crews could stand easy but remain in the vicinity of the turrets. This meant you could come out and walk around the top of the turret. When I got out I was amazed. There were fires under the bridge where the lifebelts had caught fire, there were fires in the 6-inch battery where the cordite was alight. The funnels were holed – every boat in the ship had a hole in it. The ship looked really bad.[25]

Ahead of the *Spite* in the night lay the battle to keep afloat, her engine rooms in danger of flooding. Leading this battle for survival, Commander Walwyn also faced the unpleasant job of clearing corpses from damaged areas. Rounding up a dozen sailors to help him, Commander Walwyn was worried even he might quail in the face of it. But no, he had become hardened. The corpses they retrieved were,

> badly knocked about but absolutely 'dry' and not bleeding at all. The thing that struck me was they were not nearly so frightening as I thought they would be somehow.

About dusk, having checked his services were not needed for a while, Surgeon Lieutenant Ellis ventured up to the quarterdeck:

> We were moving through the water slowly, at almost six knots, heading back towards Rosyth and there was no other ship in sight, or noise of firing anywhere. There was still a dull red glow from the sun left in the sky, low down, but it was very hazy,

and impossible to see any distance. The sea was still calm but there was just enough breeze to make its surface tumbly. As regards the ship it is difficult to say what one's feelings were on looking at her.

Only a few hours before she had been one of the cleanest and smartest looking ships in the fleet, her decks spotlessly white, and her light grey paint, freshly put on only recently, gleaming every where in the sunshine. Now her decks were filthy, littered with debris and in places torn up by shells, one of the quarterdeck ladders had been blown away, her funnels had ragged holes in them, the small iron ladder on X turret had been bent and twisted and broken away from its lower supports, whilst the side of the turret was covered with marks from glancing hits, and her general appearance was in about as absolute a contrast to what it had been before as well could be.

Starting to feel a little numbed, Surgeon Lieutenant Ellis was glad to see the ship still flew her colours:

A ragged White Ensign still flew from her ensign staff – which had been struck once and broken, so that it was now much shorter – however, at the main masthead there was flying the Union Jack.

Overnight a 6-inch gun section and two of the 15-inch gun turrets were kept manned, just in case.

The agony of the burns victims being treated by Surgeon Lieutenant Ellis and the Principal Medical Officer showed no signs of abating, one of the men dying before daylight. At 2.30 a.m. Surgeon Lieutenant Ellis took a break and went to the ward room. He settled himself in an armchair, which had suffered one of its legs blown off when a shell passed through. He lit up a relaxing cigarette. Surgeon Lieutenant Ellis had been sleepy at midnight but this had passed and he was now wide awake. After another spell tending to the casualties, he still found himself unable to sleep and decided to see if some fresh sea air would send him off. Emerging onto the forecastle deck he found:

It, like the quarterdeck, was covered with debris of all kinds – bits of broken woodwork from boats, part of a damaged life-saving raft, half of a lifebuoy with the name of the ship on it and any amount of small odds and ends. The deck was holed by the starboard 6-inch gun, which had been struck by fragments of shell all over it. The spray shield was full of holes, the breech mechanism destroyed, and the barrel pitted all along its length, whilst from the muzzle, which was trained starboard, there blew out in the breeze the tattered remains of what had once been its canvas blast screen. The latter gave the gun a ludicrous appearance which it possibly was far from feeling – if guns have any feeling.

Several other members of the crew were standing about chatting nearby but Surgeon Lieutenant Ellis decided not to join them and returned to his battered chair in the ward room.

Limping Home Through U-boat Waters

As 6.00a.m. on 1 June came around, *Warspite* was about to enter a danger zone off Scotland where German submarines traditionally lurked to attack British warships leaving, or returning to, Rosyth. Captain Phillpotts stood his crew by for an attack.

They were completely frazzled by this time, their nerves shot to ribbons, many having worked through the night to keep the ship afloat. Commander Walwyn got the hands up and to work at daylight, with the threat from U-boats prompting him to get the ship's carpenters repairing the only wrecked small boat capable of salvage – the 1st cutter. Mess tables and stools were also brought onto the upper deck to build rafts.

At 7.00a.m. Captain Phillpotts sent for Commander Walwyn and said he was convinced a submarine attack would come very soon and everything possible should be done to prepare for it. Commander Walwyn decided to get the upper deck 6-inch guns at the ready. These weapons had been too exposed to man during the battle but now were an excellent means of attacking any U-boats unwise enough to show themselves.

In the ward room a concerted attempt had been made to get things back to normal. On entering for breakfast, Surgeon Lieutenant Ellis found:

> the sight of white tablecloths amidst the somewhat dishevelled surroundings, and individuals, did look a little incongruous.

Under his feet he could sense the *Warspite* had not enjoyed the rough weather:

> One could feel she was sluggish owing to her flooded compartments...any sea was bound to put the strength of her superstructure to a severe test.

At just after 9.30 a.m. a U-boat fired two torpedoes which passed down either side of the battleship. Commander Walwyn reckoned: '...one missed across the bow, the other followed up astern alongside the starboard side.

The *Warspite* increased her speed to twenty-one knots and zig-zagged away as vigorously as she could. Lookouts had already been doubled and officers not on watch or otherwise engaged were ordered onto the upper deck to watch out for periscopes and torpedo tracks. Below decks Surgeon Lieutenant Ellis heard about the torpedo near miss from a sailor who stuck his head around the curtain of the Principal Medical Officer's cabin to say it passed 'only about some ten feet off.'

Surgeon Lieutenant Ellis observed:

> This was a new complication and had the effect of making me feel I wanted to go up on deck at once – for what reason I don't know – but the PMO went on writing with his usual imperturbability so that for sheer shame I felt bound to stay also.

With evidence the threat was indeed high, Commander Walwyn ordered the wounded brought closer to the upper deck and watertight doors shut at all times. Having finished his reports and supervised the move of the wounded, Surgeon Lieutenant Ellis finally got to the upper deck.

At 10.00a.m. a 6-inch gun opened fire at what looked like a U-boat off the port quarter, which had just fired a torpedo. Despite firing eight rounds *Warspite*'s gun hit nothing. Commander Walwyn observed: 'McDonald swore he saw a conning tower and so did the gun-layer.'

Surgeon Lieutenant Ellis had followed the German torpedo track:

> It had come from astern, and, as we watched, the periscope and top of the conning tower of the submarine from which it had been despatched emerged above the surface about half a mile distant on the port quarter. The gun's crew of the port 6-inch on the forecastle deck immediately fired in its direction, and the shell pitched sufficiently close

for the spray to hide all sight of it. It probably wasn't hit, but at any rate when the spray subsided it was no longer visible... .

By this stage everyone's nerves were very raw. The thought of being picked off so close to home, was more than some could stomach – they showed their anger by turning on each other, two officers almost coming to blows over a petty matter. Commander Walwyn later reflected that the forenoon was 'about the worst part of the whole show...'.

Not long after, a submarine periscope was seen right under the battleship's bows. Despite *Warspite's* delicate condition an attempt to ram the U-boat was made – the 6-inch guns opened up too. But it was all in vain, as the target, U-63, disappeared unharmed.

Commander Walwyn later explained:

About 11.45a.m., submarine came up on the port bow; if we had not been steering from the engine room we might have got her, but it took a certain interval for the orders to get through. The foremost 3-pounder could not get sufficient depression on to fire as she passed.

Surgeon Lieutenant Ellis also observed this attack from *Warspite's* upper deck: 'He dived in such a hurry that his tail came up out of the water.'

After the first submarine encounter, *Warspite's* speed had been increased to nineteen knots and then to twenty-one knots. Now she put tremendous strain on her battered structure to make twenty-five knots; an enormous boiling of water behind the battleship as her propellers dug in, smoke billowing everywhere from her punctured funnel.

At 8.00 a.m. the *Warspite* had sent a signal requesting some escort vessels to deter submarines – these duly came after the final submarine attack. They turned out to be torpedo boats from Rosyth and Commander Walwyn was not impressed by their screening attempts: '...their speed was not up to it and they dropped astern.' Surgeon Lieutenant Ellis found their arrival comforting: 'The chances of us seeing the Forth Bridge had, up to then, been a question of some doubt in my mind.'

As the *Warspite* finally reached the Firth of Forth, Commander Walwyn could relax and, far from being on the receiving end of insults from railway workers, he was quite touched by the reception his battered warship got. 'I am bound to say I heaved a sigh of relief as we passed the bridge, and the cheers from the troops made one feel quite gulpy.'

Maybe they were jeers, not cheers, and the Commander misunderstood.

Shedding Tears & Licking Wounds.

The *Queen Elizabeth* was immediately moved to allow *Warspite* to be docked down. She would be under repair for nearly two months.

The dockyard workers and railwaymen may well have initially expressed a nation's anger at the Jutland result but, as *Warspite's* fourteen dead and eighteen wounded were brought ashore down the gangways, people surely realized the injustice of their reaction.

The *Warspite's* male voice choir added to the emotional impact of the scene by assembling on the upper deck to sing a sombre 'Comrades in Arms' as farewell to dead shipmates. There were sobs and tears on all sides. Of the burns cases two more

Despite her fragile condition, the *Warspite* still made a game bid to ram a German U-boat which was unwise enough to attack her as she sailed back to Rosyth. *Specially commissioned painting by Dennis C. Andrews.*

died in hospital, but the rest survived. *Warspite* officers who had no accommodation due to their cabins being blown apart went to live temporarily aboard HMS *Dreadnought* and HMS *Queen Elizabeth.*

Surgeon Lieutenant Ellis was given the opportunity of a decent night's sleep in a comfortable cabin which seemed to have 'every conceivable luxury', including a box of chocolates donated by the officer who had vacated it for his benefit. But, even now, he found he could not sleep. The next morning he went to look *Warspite* over as she lay in dry dock. He found the sight of the battleship which had carried him safely on a rollercoaster ride through the Battle of Jutland an emotional experience:

> *I felt I just loved her. And I think now that there is no other ship in the world like her...may her name always be honoured.*

The Germans were, however, claiming to have sunk the *Warspite*. While the 150 holes in her bore testimony to the ferocity and accuracy of the German gunnery, she had obviously lived to fight another day.

According to Captain Donald Macintyre, in *Jutland*, the battlecruiser *Invincible's* death, was mistaken for *Warspite's* destruction. In reality *Warspite's* casualties and damage were minimal and good evidence of her solid construction. But, like many others fretting in the vacuum created by the British failure to swiftly release a detailed account of the battle, the family of *Warspite's* Midshipman Fairthorne feared for the worst. They didn't want to believe their son's ship was gone, but they had no information to contradict the German claims.

Midshipman Fairthorne recalled:

> *At home my family, on opening the morning newspaper of 3 June, had been*

confronted with several versions of the encounter, one of which was the German claim to have sunk the new battleship Warspite. *Luckily I had the foresight to send a telegram of reassurance when the Marine postman went ashore, so they were kept in suspense only till that afternoon.*[26]

In Plymouth – home port of the *Warspite* – the news of Jutland had a devastating effect. Aside from lingering anxiety over the *Warspite's* fate, hundreds of families in the city had suffered the loss of a husband, son or brother on the destroyed *Indefatigable* and *Defence*. Both warships were Devonport manned ships and the *Indefatigable* was built at the Plymouth dockyard. The *Defence* had been a Plymouth-based warship since 1909.

Telegrams from sailors aboard ships which had not been sunk arrived before official confirmation of the casualties. Carrying their own confused accounts of the action, and ship losses, these telegrams further increased confusion and distress. Plymouth's

newspapers reported tragic scenes. Crowds of worried relatives gathered at the dockyard, outside the office of Commander-in-Chief Plymouth, and at the *Western Morning News* building in the city centre. Once reports based on an official Admiralty communique were placed in the windows of the *Western Morning News* building, the effect was immediate. Seeing the names of lost ships and their men confirmed in black and white, wives and mothers broke down and were escorted away by relatives. A few sad souls remained late into the night, lingering outside the newspaper offices hoping for more news which might hold out some hope that a loved one had survived after all.

On the morning of 3 June the *Western Morning News* revealed:

> *At a late hour last night it was reported that a woman fell dead in a Plymouth street upon being informed that a ship in which two of her sons were serving had been lost.*

When a statement finally emerged from the Admiralty it was downbeat and lame. The incurably reticent Jellicoe – an inveterate hater of the press – failed to amplify his strategic victory. Further communiques did, however, try to convey the fact that the Royal Navy had retained overwhelming strategic control and the Germans had turned and fled.

Surgeon Lieutenant Ellis found emotion welled up inside him when he went to look the battered battleship over in dry dock at Rosyth. *Ellis Collection.*

Winston Churchill, who had resigned as First Lord of the Admiralty a few months earlier, partially came to the rescue on 3 June by writing a fresh communique to the press. He paid full tribute to the success of the super dreadnoughts he had created by saying: 'The fast division of Queen Elizabeths seem to have vindicated all the hopes reposed in them.'[27] However, estimates of German losses the Admiralty was giving out were not to be borne out by the truth. It was claimed the Germans had lost two battleships, two battlecruisers, four light cruisers, nine destroyers and a submarine.

As the battleship lies in dry dock at Rosyth, a dockyard worker stands by the hole in *Warspite*'s stern which betrays the entry point of the shell which damaged her steering and caused her to run out of control at Jutland. *Franklin Collection.*

In fact German losses were one battleship, one battlecruiser, four light cruisers and five destroyers. The total British vessels lost were three battlecruisers, three armoured cruisers and eight destroyers. In terms of casualties, the Royal Navy lost 6,097 killed (most of them on the battlecruisers) while the Germans suffered 2,551.

The amount of damage done to the tougher German capital ships was considerable and effectively removed the High Sea Fleet from the stage for a long time. The Grand Fleet was ready for battle again on 2 June – such was the overall British materiel and strategic superiority.

But no one could dispute that the Battle Cruiser Fleet's daring, combined with its overall poor gunnery and vessels too vulnerable to risk a fight with battleships, had

Rosyth workers begin the task of repairing the *Warspite* after Jutland. *Franklin Collection.*

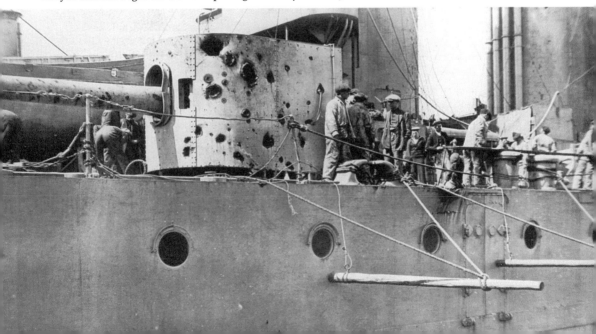

proved to be the Royal Navy's Achilles heel. It was equally clear the four Queen Elizabeth Class battleships helped save the Battle Cruiser Fleet from complete annihilation. Their good shooting with 15-inch heavy guns, plus their speed and protection, had enabled them to hold off the entire German fleet.

The Grand Fleet had arrived too late but deployed superbly and in such a manner that it opened up a trap into which the Germans nearly fell. Macintyre summed it all up bluntly. He said the British battlecruisers were designed to pursue and bring 'an unwilling enemy to action.' He continued:

> *The Germans, on the other hand, had succeeded in building ships that were almost unsinkable by gunfire, a skill which they showed they had not lost in the Second World War. That the British shells were found wanting in action, breaking up on impact instead of penetrating as they were designed to do, only stressed the superiority of German ship design, from a defensive angle.*

The Germans were 'forced, nevertheless, to pay deep respect to the shooting of the Queen Elizabeths of the 5th Battle Squadron.' Macintyre added:

> *When Jellicoe's battle squadrons came partially to action, a few minutes of their cannonade only was sufficient to make Scheer turn tail.*[28]

Later, while the Grand Fleet formed a wall between the Germans and their bases, it proved easy to penetrate due to poor British night fighting skills. During the day the failure of British scouting cruisers and Beatty's battlecruisers to pass proper reports on enemy positions to Jellicoe also denied him crucial information which could have made the British trap tighter.

King George V -'The Sailor King' – who had fought so hard over the naming of the *Warspite* and her sisters with Winston Churchill, found himself joining forces with his old antagonist in the aftermath of Jutland to soothe the fleet's wounds.

A message, released to the press 3 June, paid tribute to the Royal Navy's bravery at Jutland and commended it for achieving a strategic victory. The King remarked that the Germans, in turning away from a full confrontation, had stolen the chance of 'gaining a decisive victory.'

During a later visit to Rosyth, King George used the *Warspite* as a backdrop to address massed ranks of Jutland veterans. 'You drove the enemy into his harbours,' he told his sailors.[29]

That much at least was true. But it was no consolation for a British fleet accustomed to thinking it ruled the waves. The Royal Navy had gone looking for a victory on the scale of Trafalgar and for a number of reasons been denied it. There would be bitter recriminations for many years, with Jellicoe and Beatty – Grand Fleet and Battle Cruiser Fleet – blaming each other.

Within the Grand Fleet Beatty was widely regarded as a self-aggrandizing egotist who let Jellicoe and the nation down by being cavalier with his ships and losing touch with the 5th Battle Squadron. The King appeared to make his displeasure – and that of the Grand Fleet – felt when he later went aboard *Warspite*. He had spent two hours aboard, surveying repairs to the damage, when his chief guide – Beatty – provoked his anger. Eager to get the King over to HMS *Lion* for lunch, Admiral Beatty suggested the tour should be cut short.

Admiral Beatty and the King pose for a photograph during the post-Jutland visit to *Warspite*. The King was not amused by Beatty's attempts to interrupt his inspection of the battleship. *Franklin Collection.*

King George V - 'The Sailor King' - made a special effort to inspect repairs of *Warspite's* battle damage during a morale-boosting visit to the Grand Fleet after the battle. *Franklin Collection.*

According to *Warspite*'s Paymaster Cadet G.H. Bickmore, the King rounded on Beatty and snarled: 'I didn't come here to have lunch with you. Let it wait!'[30]

The bravery of the *Warspite* was not in doubt and the King had rightly allowed no one, not even an Admiral, to stop him seeing the scars of war she bore. Her exploits at Jutland – particularly her alleged sacrificial shielding of the *Warrior* from German heavy guns – made her a legend in the eyes of the British people once the full facts of the battle were known.

The sailors of the *Warrior* paid due tribute to *Warspite* by sending a deputation to her with gifts. According to one newspaper report of the time, the *Warrior*'s sailors found themselves rebuffed.

Take 'em mates, said the sailors of the Warrior. *You saved our lives.*

Take 'em back, came the reply. *We didn't save you. We couldn't help chasing our tail. The helm was jammed!*[31]

No doubt the *Warrior*'s sailors would not take no for an answer and pressed their gifts on the *Warspite*'s matelots. For God must have smiled on the *Warrior* to make *Warspite* run out of control at that precise moment. The *Warspite* had proved to be a lucky ship in battle even if she couldn't help being accident prone.

Notes

1   Max Arthur, *The True Glory.*
2   Ibid.
3   J.J. Hazelwood, Sound Archives, Imperial War Museum.
4   Geoffrey Penn, *Fisher, Churchill and the Dardanelles.*
5   Winston Churchill, *World Crisis.*
6   Andrew Gordon, *The Rules of the Game.*
7   Joy Packer, *Deep as The Sea.*
8   From an account published in *Nautical Magazine,* December 1973.
9   Ellis Papers, Imperial War Museum.
10 J.J. Hazelwood, Sound Archives, Imperial War Museum.
11 Phillpotts Papers, Imperial War Museum.
12 J.J. Hazelwood, Sound Archives, Imperial War Museum.
13 Mark Simmons, *WARSHIPS IFR* magazine, June 2000.
14 Chessman Papers, Imperial War Museum.
15 J.J. Hazelwood, Sound Archives, Imperial War Museum.
16 von Hase, *Kiel and Jutland.*
17 Vaux Papers, Imperial War Museum.
18 J.J. Hazelwood, Sound Archives, Imperial War Museum.
19 In a letter to his brother published in *Naval Review,* 1985.
20 Commander Walwyn in the Phillpotts Papers, Imperial War Museum.
21 In a letter to his brother published in *Naval Review,* 1985.
22 J.J. Hazelwood, Sound Archives, Imperial War Museum.
23 Chessman Papers, Imperial War Museum.
24 Bickmore Papers, Imperial War Museum.
25 J.J. Hazelwood, Sound Archives, Imperial War Museum.
26 From an account published in the *Nautical Magazine,* Dec 1973.
27 *Western Morning News,* 3 June 1916.
28 Captain Donald Macintyre, *Jutland.*
29 *The Great War.*
30 Bickmore Papers, Imperial War Museum.
31 *Western Morning News,* June 1916.

Chapter Four

ARMISTICE & MUTINY

No Triumph in Victory

With the sour aftertaste of Jutland still strong in its mouth, the Royal Navy was, in the summer of 1916, hungry for another chance to engage the German fleet.

But, with capital ships decisively flawed in both attack and defence, and despite holding the strategic upper hand, the British were forced to follow caution. Sweeps in search of the enemy could be mounted, but for some time there would be anxiety about what might happen when battle was next joined.

The fact that shells for the Royal Navy's big guns were defective, plus adequate

A view of HMS *Warspite*'s A and B turrets as the battleship steams at speed. *US Naval Historical Center.*

flash and armour protection fatally lacking in some vessels, was kept secret from the population at large and knowledge of it within the Service was restricted.

It was hoped the munitions flaw could be counterbalanced by sheer weight of fire power. One thing was certain – fragile battlecruisers would be kept at a safe distance. Where necessary the improvement of armour plating over ammunition magazines and flash protection was taken in hand. The shells problem would not finally be solved until the spring of 1918 with the issue of new munitions.

Luckily the Germans had been too badly battered at Jutland to pose much of a threat for several months and that allowed a breathing space.

The effects of Jutland were also swiftly felt in dockyards where new ships were being constructed for the Royal Navy. Battlecruisers ordered in the wake of the Battle of the Falklands victory of December 1914 suddenly looked a dreadful waste of resources. One of the vessels ordered in the warm afterglow of this South Atlantic triumph was the gigantic HMS *Hood*, lead vessel of a class originally conceived as a speedier version of the battleship *Warspite* and her sisters. The *Hood* was laid down at John Brown on the Clyde on 31 May 1916. However, with faith in battlecruisers blown apart at Jutland that same day, work on her was immediately halted. *Hood* was laid down again that September but with thicker belt armour. Ultimately, after further changes, she was completed in May 1920 carrying belt armour twelve inches thick, displacing 42,670 tons (standard), and packing eight 15-inch guns. With such protection, and a mighty punch, plus a top speed of thirty knots, she was every inch a racier version of the *Warspite*.

Three sister ships were laid down in October and November 1916, but in the spring of the following year intelligence sources revealed Germany had given up constructing capital ships. Cancellation of *Hood*'s sisters was confirmed shortly before the war ended in November 1918.

After concluding post-Jutland repair work and trials on the Firth of Forth, the *Warspite* had returned to Scapa Flow at the end of July 1916.

In mid-August the Grand Fleet put to sea in pursuit of the High Sea Fleet. It had been spotted by a British submarine which managed to torpedo the German

HMS *Hood*, a speedier version of the Queen Elizabeth Class super dreadnoughts. *Goodman Collection*

HMS *Warspite* digs her bows in during a vain attempt to run down the High Sea Fleet. *Franklin Collection.*

The battleship's restored upper works. *Franklin Collection.*

battleship *Westfalen* and send an accurate sighting report. However, the Germans eluded the rapidly closing British trap because of an error by their scouting Zeppelins which mistook Royal Navy cruisers and destroyers speeding north from Harwich as part of the Grand Fleet. The German battleships and battlecruisers hared off southwards hoping to have a portion of the Grand Fleet at their mercy. Subsequent signals from the scouting Zeppelins informed Admiral Scheer that the bulk of the Grand Fleet was in fact closing from the north. Fearing a trap, he decided to head for home without further delay.

During the voyage back to Scapa from this frustrated dash south, *Warspite*'s steering curse struck again and she had to pull out of line in considerable difficulty. The reason for this was a mystery for the problem soon righted itself.

Misfortune struck again when *Warspite* managed to ram HMS *Valiant* amidships on returning from some night shooting. *Warspite*'s bows were stoved in again while *Valiant*'s oil tanks were cracked open. *Warspite* was out of action for more than a month.

An inquiry into the accident apportioned blame equally – *Warspite* should have kept a sharper look out, but so should *Valiant*. Captain Phillpotts and the Commanding Officer of *Valiant* were declared equally guilty by an inquiry but the *Spite*'s Commanding Officer escaped a reprimand.

In November 1916, Jellicoe was promoted to First Sea Lord and command of the Grand Fleet passed to David Beatty who was not given the most enthusiastic reception when he arrived at Scapa Flow. The resentment over Jutland was still keenly felt. Aboard *Warspite* and the other battleships the sailors greeted him with silence until ordered to start cheering.

The 5th Battle Squadron soon lost a member, for in early 1917 Beatty chose HMS *Queen Elizabeth* as his flagship. Captain Phillpotts had already said farewell to the

Warspite, leaving her in December 1916 to become First Sea Lord's Naval Assistant to Jellicoe.

Ever the astute politician, Beatty implemented a decision which found favour with the government by bringing the Grand Fleet's main base to the Firth of Forth. The Forth was not, however, a comfortable place to base so many large vessels, so battlewagons were often sent north on extended detachment to Scapa where they had plenty of room for intensive gunnery practice.

It was after just such a gunnery practice session in the summer of 1917 that HMS *Warspite* was rocked at her Scapa Flow anchorage by a cataclysmic explosion which completely destroyed HMS *Vanguard*. Forlorn boats plied back and forth in a hopeless search for the living, under a vast towering column of smoke, but there were only two survivors from the 700 or so people aboard the St Vincent Class battleship at the time. All Grand Fleet warships including *Warspite*, made urgent checks of their magazines to ensure they wouldn't suffer the same fate at the hands of faulty cordite.

Eight months later *Warspite* suffered a severe fire in her port wing engine room. An oil pipe had split and the blaze started when fuel dripped onto a hot steam pipe. Attempts were made to douse the fire with water hoses but it didn't go out until a brave sailor switched off the oil supply at source. Hit by this latest episode of bad luck, *Warspite* faced another four months of repairs.

As the German army was trying, and failing, to achieve a decisive breakthrough during the Kaiser Offensive of Spring 1918, the High Sea Fleet made an ill-starred foray into the North Sea. The German intention was to savage a convoy off the coast of Norway and lay waste to the Royal Navy escort. The German force was emphatically not looking for an encounter of any description with the Grand Fleet. However, not only did the target convoy evade them, but the battlecruiser *Moltke* lost

The 5th Battle Squadron lost one of its members, when Admiral Beatty chose HMS *Queen Elizabeth* to be his Grand Fleet flagship. The official German naval surrender took place aboard her in November 1918. *Goodman Collection.*

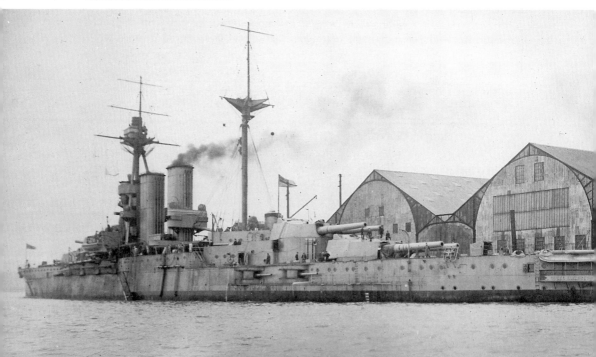

HMS *Warspite* at Scapa Flow. *US Naval Historical Center.*

The *Warspite* was rocked at her moorings when the battleship HMS *Vanguard*, pictured, blew up due to faulty ammunition. *Goodman Collection.*

one of her props, a turbine exploded and an engine room was flooded. Under tow from the battleship *Oldenburg*, the *Moltke* was also torpedoed by a British submarine. *Warspite* and the rest of the Grand Fleet put to sea and made speed to the south-east but, as usual, it was a chase in vain, for the entire High Sea Fleet escaped to Wilhelmshaven not long after the *Moltke*.

Even as hundreds of thousands of German soldiers were deserting their trenches to walk home, and the U-boats were being called in to avoid provoking the Allies, the high command of the High Sea Fleet decided to make a suicidal gesture. Orders were given in late October 1918 to prepare for a final showdown with the Royal Navy. The Germans were going to strike out for the Thames estuary, sinking whatever merchant vessels could be found. Hopefully, this would draw the Grand Fleet into battle. The aim was to inflict such losses on the Royal Navy that Germany's position in looming peace talks would be strengthened.

However, this mad scheme never came to anything as the sailors of the High Sea Fleet mutinied and the Kaiser's once proud battleships and battlecruisers came under the red flag of communism instead of the Imperial Ensign.

Ten days after celebrating the 11 November Armistice, *Warspite* and the rest of the Grand Fleet put to sea for a rendezvous with the enemy. The High Sea Fleet had been ordered to surrender and, as at Jutland, it was the German battlecruisers which the Grand Fleet encountered first – the *Seydlitz, Moltke, Hindenburg, Derfflinger* and *von der Tann*. The Grand Fleet formed two lines either side of the Germans, battle flags flying, guns loaded and ready to fire. Commander Randolph Pears gives a very vivid description of the event:

> *The crews at battle stations, gas masks and asbestos suits were issued, the ships cleared for action. The Grand Fleet's last appearance at sea was an unforgettable occasion, a show of strength never to be again approached.*

The crews of 221 Royal Navy warships, six American battleships and three French ships felt no sense of triumph. The fight had gone out of the Germans and their ten battleships and five battlecruisers looked bedraggled. They were also toothless, their guns having been disabled in Germany before sailing. The British cruiser *Cardiff* led the 'dirty uncared-for ships' between the two parallel lines of Allied naval power.[1]

A young officer aboard the American battleship USS *New York* looked on in pity:

> *The low sun glances from their shabby sides. Their huge guns, motionless, are trained fore and aft. It is the sight of our dreams – a sight for kings! Strangely enough, the German surrender lacked the thrill of victory. There was the gaping wonder of it, the inconceivable that was happening before our very eyes – the great German fleet steaming helplessly there at our side – conquered... The one prevalent emotion so far as I could ascertain, was pity.[2]*

The German fleet was ordered to drop anchor outside the anti-torpedo nets in the Firth of Forth while the full scope of British and Allied naval might slid by in complete silence. Then the defining moment came for Beatty, as his flagship, HMS *Queen Elizabeth*, passed between the lines of Allied ships at anchor, a wave of cheering following her majestic victory passage.

Just over a week after the German fleet sailed into captivity, the US Navy's 6th Battle Squadron said farewell to the Grand Fleet and, more particularly, *Warspite* and

The German battlecruiser *Moltke*, was one of the first German ships to be encountered by the Grand Fleet on the day of the surrender. *K. Smith Collection.*

Germany's answer to *Warspite* and her sisters was the battleship *Bayern*, carrying 15-inch guns. Entering service too late to see a fleet v fleet action, the *Bayern* is pictured here interned at Scapa Flow after the First World War. *M. Welsford Collection.*

The German battlecruiser *Derfflinger* traded shots with the 5th Battle Squadron at Jutland and sank the battlecruiser *Queen Mary*. She is pictured here interned at Scapa Flow after the surrender of the High Sea Fleet. *M. Welsford Collection.*

the 5th Battle Squadron which it considered its sister formation.

The Americans had sent more than 350 vessels to European waters including the battleships USS *Texas*, USS *Nevada*, USS *Arkansas*, USS *Florida*, USS *Wyoming* and USS *New York* which had been America's chief representatives when the High Sea Fleet sailed to captivity. The USS *Delaware* had already gone home. Now, it was the remainder's turn to proceed between long lines of warships at anchor on the Forth, the decks of the British vessels packed with wildly cheering sailors sending the Americans off in good style. They received a guard of honour for the first twenty miles home from the 5th Battle Squadron, with the *Valiant* and *Warspite* to port and *Barham* and *Malaya* to starboard. The ships cheered each other all the way out to May Island, culminating in a huge roar as *Warspite* and other Queen Elizabeth Class battleships peeled away on either side.

Seven months later, after sailing to Scapa Flow, which was to be its permanent prison because no neutral country would provide a harbour for it, the High Sea Fleet scuttled itself. This act of suicide was prompted by a breakdown in the peace negotiations at Versailles which made the German sailors fear a renewal of hostilities might mean a massacre in the confines of Scapa. With the German fleet lying on the seabed, the Royal Navy was once again the ruler without peer of the Seven Seas. Having in excess of 1,300 warships of all types, Britain's fleet was as big as the world's other navies put together.

Surviving the Culling of the Fleet

Warspite was created as the ultimate offensive weapon of the battleship era. After the First World War, during which submarines and aircraft had emerged as effective deliverers of destruction, she would be reshaped to improve her defences against them. The perfect balance of *Warspite*'s design meant she survived difficult post-war years when many of her contemporaries in the Grand Fleet were cleaved from the Royal Navy's pennant list with alarming speed.

Britain had been drained of her riches by the war and this relative poverty coincided with the introduction of measures designed to preserve world peace by preventing naval arms races. Only *Warspite* and her sisters of the Queen Elizabeth Class, plus the five Royal Sovereigns, would survive the culling of the Grand Fleet's main striking force. The rest of the Royal Navy's capital ship inventory was composed of three battlecruisers built at the end of the war – HMS *Hood*, HMS *Repulse* and HMS *Renown*.

Between 1920, when *Hood* was completed, and the late 1930s, when Britain finally responded to a renewed German threat by ordering the King George V Class vessels,

The *Warspite* celebrates the end of the war. *Franklin Collection.*

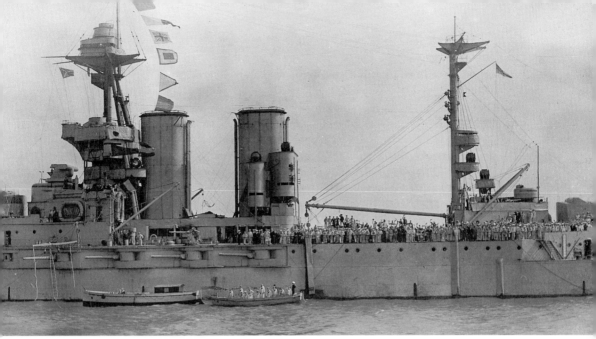

In the summer of 1918, sailors line the *Warspite*'s rails and say farewell to a US battleship which served with the Grand Fleet. After the Armistice of November 1918, the rest of the US Navy's battleships went home after a big send off from the 5th Battle Squadron. *US Naval Historical Center.*

the only battleships built were HMS *Rodney* and HMS *Nelson*. These ships were constructed to bring the Royal Navy's much depleted tonnage up to a limit agreed at the 1921-22 Washington Conference on naval arms. At this summit, attended by representatives of the British, American, Japanese, French and Italian fleets, it was agreed limits should be imposed on all the leading naval powers.

Victory had therefore ushered in crushing reality for the Royal Navy – it could not live beyond its means and so had to divest itself of most of its power. That was also the reality for Britain as a whole, and the 1920s was a period of social upheaval which sometimes found HMS *Warspite* embroiled in unconventional roles. The Grand Fleet had been replaced with the Atlantic Fleet and, from 1919 until May 1921, *Warspite* was a member of its 2nd Battle Squadron.

In May of 1920 *Warspite* loitered off Ireland during the death throes of British rule in the South, standing by to send parties of armed sailors ashore to support the Army. She later ferried Royal Marines from Plymouth to Ireland.

Making regular spring cruises to the Mediterranean while part of the Atlantic Fleet, *Warspite* first entered Valetta Harbour, Malta, in the spring of 1924.

That summer she paid off for her first major refit, after duty as Cowes Week Guardship and taking part in a massive Royal Review of the fleet off Spithead. The two year refit saw *Warspite*'s displacement rise to 31,300 tons, with the addition of torpedo bulges and a quartet of new 4-inch anti-aircraft guns (replacing the 3-inch high angle guns and boat deck 6-inchers). A couple of 2-pounders were also added plus armour protection increased but half her torpedo armament was taken away. *Warspite*'s funnels were also trunked into one and her bridge platforms modified.

As she approached the end of her refit in 1926, *Warspite* was earmarked to become flagship of the Commander-in-Chief Mediterranean Fleet.

Bertie Packer, had left the *Spite* in January 1918 but rejoined her in February 1926, while she was still in dry dock at Portsmouth. Glad to be back on his old ship, he decided to show her off to his new wife. She later wrote of her husband's guided tour:

> The big battleship looked grotesque to me, out of her natural element, cluttered with wire hawsers and tangled ropes, and stained with red lead as if she were bleeding from innumerable wounds... .The dockyard mateys at work on the huge disabled hull looked like lilliputians scrambling over the tethered body of some mighty beached leviathan.[3]

On 31 March 1926, HMS *Warspite* took on ammunition but it was almost a month before she left Portsmouth bound for sea trials off Scotland. As *Warspite* curved around the south-west peninsula the weather was fine, but storm clouds lay ahead. She was off Rothesay by 26 April 1926, and then headed for the Clyde, carrying out speed trials on the way and managing twenty-four knots.

On Saturday 1 May a national coal strike was called, followed on 3 May by a

By 1926 the battleships HMS *Orion* (above) and HMS *Erin* (below) had been sent for scrap, as part of the massive culling of the Royal Navy's frontline warships under the Washington Treaty. *HMS Orion: Franklin Collection, HMS Erin: Goodman Collection.*

General Strike. *Warspite* was ordered to get ready to quell trouble. She arrived at Greenock early on 3 May and was immediately asked to send landing parties ashore. They were split between oil tanks, pipe lines and torpedo factories along the Clyde and Bertie Packer headed a detachment tasked with guarding docks in Glasgow itself. The sailors patrolled twelve hours out of twenty-four which was a hard routine but the battle lines between dock workers and the authorities remained fairly placid. A week went by and the *Warspite* heard HMS *Hood* would take over guard duties so she could finally go to the Mediterranean. At this point things started to turn sinister, with *Warspite*'s sailors intercepting several groups armed with petrol cans trying to sneak in to burn down warehouses. Bertie Packer described this as 'a bit of fun' and told his wife: 'We stalked them but they ran like the devil leaving full petrol tins behind.'[4]

Four days later the *Spite* handed over to the *Hood* and headed south.

In December 1927 Captain James Somerville was made the *Spite*'s Commanding Officer, his first association with a vessel which fifteen years later would be his flagship while shadow boxing the Imperial Japanese Navy. But, even under the stewardship of this lucky officer, misfortune returned to haunt *Warspite*. After nearly two mishap free years she struck an uncharted rock in the Aegean while acting as flagship of Vice Admiral J.D. Kelly, Second-in-Command of the Mediterranean Fleet. Ordered home for repairs in dry dock at Portsmouth, *Warspite* was back in the Mediterranean as fleet flagship by the beginning of 1929, her crew now including young Midshipman Richard Raikes. He joined 'a very very happy ship'. However, life for midshipmen aboard *Warspite* in the late 1920s was still about learning the hard way.

> *You were lower than the low as far as the Navy was concerned. You were at everyone's beck and call. The sailors knew that you knew nothing. The officers knew that you knew nothing. You were kicked around but you were supported in the most remarkable way by the lower deck. They were on your side.*

To Midshipman Raikes the Royal Navy's capital ships looked fantastic, rather than obsolete. It was a very exciting life for a teenager.

> *At the end of one of the dog watches the C-in-C would hoist a signal saying 'Midshipman's Manoeuvres'. This meant in every ship a Midshipman took over as Officer-of-the-Watch... if anyone got out of station because someone got it wrong, up would go a signal in the flagship to indicate the Midshipman. Your name was then spelled out in flags for the whole fleet to see and be amused by. We in* Warspite *conned the whole fleet. Needless to say your Captain is close to you during such manoeuvres. I was only seventeen – an awesome responsibility. I think everyone succeeded. I cannot remember anyone really failing.*[5]

The *Warspite*'s time as Mediterranean Fleet

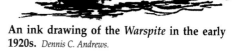

An ink drawing of the *Warspite* in the early 1920s. *Dennis C. Andrews.*

flagship ended in the spring of 1930 and she was ordered home to join the Atlantic Fleet. She carried the out-going Mediterranean Fleet Commander-in-Chief, Admiral Sir Frederick Field, who was to be the new First Sea Lord. One night during the voyage back to Britain he dined with the Midshipmen. Richard Raikes recalled:

The Admiral's chief claim to fame was that he was a member of the inner circle of conjurers. The Admiral turned up immaculate in evening dress for this dinner. At the end of the evening he turned to the Sub Lieutenant and said 'it's been worrying me all evening' and produced a billiard ball from inside the Sub's uniform. Not content with that, he produced three more billiard balls. Now where the hell had he hidden them all through dinner in his immaculate uniform?

Also aboard the *Warspite* was an eight-year-old lad called Frank Page whose father, Petty Officer Victor Page, had arranged his passage home on the battleship as a special treat. Seventy years later Frank Page still treasured the memory of his voyage on the *Warspite*.

I slept in a cabin and had my meals in the Petty Officers' Mess and was generally made a fuss of. The ship's carpenter made me a model picket boat of wood complete in every detail like the real ones with the brass funnels. I used to attend the cinema shows aboard the Warspite *but sat behind the screen as it was cheaper. By doing so I could afford a bar of chocolate to enjoy while I watched the back-to-front film.*

My visit to the battleship's diving equipment store was a bit of an ordeal, as I was made to wear a pair of diving boots, or, to be more accurate, disappear into them. Wearing the helmet was the last straw. I vaguely recall another exciting, but slightly frightening, experience was being in one of the 15-inch turrets when the guns fired. I remember being very sick with all the fumes and noises.

Having safely delivered Frank Page and Admiral Field to the United Kingdom, *Warspite* sailed into an explosive crisis which would create a mutiny conjured up by a less than magical decision about ratings' pay.

Mutiny in Scotland

In the immediate aftermath of the First World War, Royal Navy personnel received a kind of victory bonus known as the 1919 pay rate. By 1931, with the down-turn in the global economy really starting to bite, the decision was taken to reduce the wages of the Navy's 1919 pay rate personnel to 1925 pay rate levels. This was part of a programme of pay cuts applied across the board to all three armed forces and indeed to public sector workers in general. However, the effect within the Royal Navy was felt to be more severe than elsewhere. Although allowances would be retained to take the edge off the impact, it would still create widespread discontent in the fleet, including aboard HMS *Warspite*.

Confirmation by the Admiralty of the pay cuts was delivered in mid-September in a special communique to home ports which the various ships of the Atlantic Fleet missed, having sailed north from their south coast naval bases to Invergordon. The Atlantic Fleet at the time consisted of HMS *Rodney*, HMS *Nelson*, HMS *Valiant*, HMS *Warspite* and HMS *Malaya*, plus the battlecruisers HMS *Hood* and HMS *Repulse*, four cruisers and a host of escorting destroyers. Rumours of the pay cuts spread like wild fire through the ships during the voyage north. The buzzes below decks would soon be given flesh by wireless reports. Once the warships were at Invergordon the official signals on the pay cuts were also received and posted on ships' noticeboards. It was possible for sailors from all the ships to exchange views on the pay cuts in the Royal Naval canteen ashore during weekend leave and, with alcohol fuelling hot tempers, there were calls for some sort of 'industrial action'. *Warspite*'s Chief Petty Officer blacksmith Sidney Ramell fully sympathized with the sailors affected:

> *It was my opinion right from the word go that it was a disaster to cut sailors' pay by a shilling a day. It was such a ferocious blow to them. It was like dropping an atomic bomb among them. They couldn't believe it because, in those days, our sailors were terribly badly paid. Our fellas were like tramps and down-and-outs if you compare what they got with the money and amenities the American navy had.*[6]

Late on the Sunday afternoon a shore patrol found the canteen packed with militant sailors and doors locked. It appeared a crowd was being addressed by a junior rating. The shore patrol Lieutenant gained entry by asking a sailor inside to unlock the door. On entering he received a robust greeting – sailors shouted at him to get out and a beer mug was hurled, striking him a glancing blow. In the hurly-burly the rabble-rouser disappeared, the Lieutenant was pushed out of the canteen and the door locked behind him.

Norman Clements, who was a Royal Marine serving aboard *Warspite*, witnessed the incident: 'I was walking past and heard a commotion. They were singing the Red Flag in there.' According to Marine Clements a bottle, not a glass, was thrown:

> *I think one of the Navy shore patrol said 'we'll stop that' and that was when the bottle was thrown. Anyway they all came aboard quietly. I don't know what happened*

HMS *Warspite*, pictured here in the Mediterranean after her 1924-26 major refit, survived the drastic reduction of British fleet along with her Queen Elizabeth Class sisters. *Goodman Collection.*

to whoever threw the bottle.[7]

That evening large crowds of militant sailors gathered for heated discussions on the forecastles of ships.

On the Tuesday morning the Atlantic Fleet was due to sail for more exercises. HMS *Warspite* and HMS *Malaya* had already left for some gunnery practice on the Monday and overnight were anchored respectively off Lossiemouth and Nairn. *Warspite* returned to Invergordon along with the *Malaya* on the Tuesday to be greeted with the incredible sight of the fleet still in harbour after junior ratings on many ships refused to turn to.

Marine Clements saw unusual signals being traded:

> *We were just entering harbour and the* Hood *was the nearest to us. They just spelled out our name and we enquired what it was all about.*

The unrest soon infected *Warspite* but the Royal Marines on the battleship were singularly uninterested in taking part. Marine Clements explained:

> *We carried on doing normal duties like cleaning the flats and the galley. We never downed tools. I just don't think a Marine would do that.*

Throughout the Warspite, according to Marine Clements, the level of protest was low:

> *There were no major speeches made on the* Warspite. *They was all arguing amongst themselves, some of them saying they wanted to get back to Portsmouth and sort it out from there. There was no violence whatsoever. No one tried to tell men they were being silly. We didn't know what was happening on other ships. As far as we could tell all they were doing was spelling ship names out and coming out onto the upper decks and making a din. There was no threats or intimidation.*

Chief Petty Officer Ramell said the displays of disaffection were low key:

> *The Chief Bosun's Mate came and told the Commander that ratings were refusing to budge. They told him they would keep their messdeck clean and that was it. I just carried on as usual. You can take it from me that anyone with a rate on their arm was frightened to talk about their feelings of sympathy in case someone went and squeaked. Notices aimed at organizing protest meetings were strictly barred from being posted anywhere inside the* Warspite.

However, there was no serious effort by the officers to stop the mutineers communicating ship-to-ship from the upper deck. Commander's Writer Robert Tyler described a holiday atmosphere:

> *They did exactly what they wanted to. The men sat on the upper deck playing uckers, dominoes, darts and kept brewing up tea by the gallon. But there were no organizers or protest leaders on our ship. We were totally apart from all that. There were no incidents of representatives going to see the Captain and certainly no sabotage on my ship, nothing whatsoever. In the* Warspite *the officers were quite in sympathy with us.*

But the *Warspite* was still a ship of war and the Captain decided to make it quite clear to his crew that their 'down tools' would have to end. Chief Petty Officer Ramell recalled:

> *The Captain cleared lower deck and said 'we are going to go back to Portsmouth.' He added 'I am sure you are all pleased to hear that news and in the meantime you will carry on as usual'. That put the men right up there in the sky. The so-called mutineers*

were quite sure of themselves and said that any monkey business would bring problems.
At Portsmouth, as soon as the gangways were thrown across from *Warspite*, those who had been involved in the protest trooped off as they pleased and no one tried to stop them.

According to the official Admiralty statement released to the press, news of pay cuts had created 'unrest among a proportion of lower ratings.' This, the Admiralty admitted, led to a suspension of Atlantic Fleet exercises. However mild this statement was, it caused a run on the pound. Five million pounds in gold was withdrawn from the Bank of England on the Wednesday. The following day ten million was withdrawn and another eighteen million on the Friday. This forced Britain off the Gold Standard, with the value of the pound dropping by four shillings.[8]

The distinguished naval historian N.A.M. Rodger has pointed out that the tradition of mutiny has been a valuable safety valve in the Royal Navy for centuries.

When other methods failed, mutiny provided a formal system of public protest to bring grievances to the notice of authority. It was a sort of safety-valve, harmless, indeed useful so long as it was not abused.[9]

Mutinies did not provoke severe punishment provided they did not take place at sea, or when the enemy was close at hand, and so long as there was no violence and nothing overtly offensive to naval tradition. Seen in that light Invergordon was certainly well within the accepted boundaries and would not have been at all unusual in the Royal Navy of the Georgian era.

Around forty ratings directly involved in the disturbances at Invergordon were dismissed the Service and another 400 who had taken part in discontent elsewhere were also thrown out of the Navy. According to Chief Petty Officer Ramell, aboard *Warspite* three men were 'given the push'. He went on: 'I didn't know them, but they weren't picked at random.'

But once the immediate aftermath was past, the whole affair was instantly forgotten with no rancour existing at all between officers and men of *Warspite*.

As a result of the mutiny the Atlantic Fleet became the Home Fleet, a title that would be retained through the Second World War.

To nineteen-year-old Midshipman Raikes aboard *Warspite*, who received so much help in his everyday chores from the lower deck, the trouble at Invergordon was a puzzle. Because of his good relations with the ordinary sailors he never felt threatened in the slightest.

I can remember the surprise of the whole thing and the extraordinary friendliness of it all. There was no animosity at all. They just refused to do what they were told. It was as simple as that.

A young officer on a gunnery course at the Greenwich Naval College, destined to serve on *Warspite* during the Second World War was astounded by the reaction of one of his peers. 'As I was at the Staff College, I was not in contact with any lower deck ratings at that time at all,' said William Lamb.

My reaction when I heard about the mutiny was shock, almost incredulity. I was very struck by the attitude of the commandant of the college. He felt his generation had failed the Navy in allowing the situation to arise. It impressed me to see a senior and respected officer admitting that a particular group of his contemporaries in uniform had been carrying out their job not as well as they should have.[10]

At the time of Invergordon, Andrew Cunningham, who would sail aboard *Warspite* as his flagship in the Mediterranean during the Second World War, was Commodore of Chatham Barracks.

He wrote of the mutiny:

Looking back on the results and writing from my own personal views and experiences at the time, I have no doubt that many of the officers had fallen out of touch with, and were most ignorant of, the problems and difficulties affecting the men in their home lives. This applied particularly to the senior officers and the officers in the big ships.[11]

Cunningham believed the pressing need to get to grips with rapidly evolving complexities of the ships, and constant exercises, led to the human element being neglected. In the approaching global conflict officers like Cunningham, who realized Invergordon should be a lesson in management rather than a sign of Bolshevism, would be able to use first class fighting men to offset second class warships.

Notes

1   Commander Randolph Pears, *British Battleships 1892-1957*.
2   A.A. Hoehling, *The Great War at Sea*.
3   Joy Packer, *Deep as the Sea*.
4   Ibid.
5   Sound Archive, Imperial War Museum.
6   Sound Archive, Imperial War Museum.
7   Sound Archive, Imperial War Museum.
8   David Divine, *Mutiny at Invergordon*.
9   N.A.M. Rodger, *The Wooden World*.
10 Sound Archive, Imperial War Museum.
11 Viscount Cunningham of Hyndhope, *A Sailor's Odyssey*.

Chapter Five

RECONSTRUCTION

Stripped Down, Built Up

Returning to the Mediterranean, HMS *Warspite* led an uneventful existence until March 1933 when she was in collision with a Romanian steamer in the mouth of the Tagus River. The battleship was rammed on her starboard side in thick fog but suffered no lasting damage. Still, it was a reminder of how accident prone she could be. In Germany a new Chancellor took full control of government the same month as *Warspite*'s collision – Adolf Hitler. Aside from being determined to rebuild the Fatherland's fleet as part of a rearmament process, he was also intent on seizing by force that which he believed was unjustly taken from Germany by the Treaty of Versailles.

Against such a background, it was fortunate the Royal Navy's dire need for modernization was finally recognized, and funds set aside at least for reconstruction of battleships if not yet for the building of new capital vessels. It was proposed that all the Queen Elizabeth Class vessels should be completely rebuilt. *Warspite* was the first, to be closely followed by *Valiant* and *Queen Elizabeth*. However, *Malaya* would only receive partial modernization and *Barham* was left in a virtually obsolete condition. This, and the failure to rebuild the Royal Sovereign Class battlewagons, would seriously handicap the conduct of the Royal Navy during some of its most crucial moments. The Queen Elizabeth Class rebuilds proved remarkably successful. At £2,363,000 *Warspite*'s reconstruction gave the Admiralty a virtually new ship for

HMS *Warspite* finally leaves Portsmouth in January 1938 after her major rebuild.
Goodman Collection

Sister ship HMS *Valiant* in 1935, two years before her own major reconstruction.
Goodman Collection

not a lot more than her original cost. The battlecruiser *Renown* was similarly reconstructed and also proved effective.

Warspite returned to the Atlantic Fleet in May 1933 and paid off into reserve two days before Christmas. Her major rebuild started the following March at Portsmouth Dockyard where she was dismantled down to her frame. Most sorely needed were modern boilers and an upgrade to her main armament. Admiralty boilers and geared turbines were fitted and her guns received an extra ten degrees of elevation – to thirty degrees – raising her range from 23,400 to 32,300 yards. Because they were virtually inoperable in anything but a calm sea, both the after and forward 6-inch guns in the batteries were taken off, leaving four guns on each side. The battleship's last pair of torpedo tubes was removed. New fire control equipment for the 15-inch and 6-inch guns was also installed.

The new propulsion machinery was lighter and saved nearly 1,500 tons in weight. This was used to improve deck armour forward of A turret and over the ammunition magazines, giving better protection against bombs and plunging shell fire. *Warspite* received a new pattern funnel which took up less space, enabling the fitting of a pair of eight-barrelled 2-pounder weapons – known as pom-poms or Chicago Pianos – each side. On two of her 15-inch turrets a pair of four barrelled .50 calibre machine-gun mountings were sited, to boost her close-in anti-aircraft defences. *Warspite's* existing 4-inch guns were replaced with more modern versions in twin high angle mountings.

The slimmer funnel also allowed the construction of a large hangar. An aircraft catapult was installed, running across the entire beam of the ship between the hangar and the after gunnery control position. A pair of electrically powered cranes were fitted, one each side of the battleship, to enable aircraft to be hoisted back aboard after completing scouting or gunfire observation missions. While a maximum of four aircraft could be carried, in reality only two ever flew from *Warspite*. From 1938 until the end of 1941, she carried two Swordfish floatplanes which were to prove their worth many times in the Second World War. Walrus flying boats were carried between early 1942 and May 1943 when the aircraft handling gear was removed.

Warspite's ability to sustain and survive damage was improved by sub division of engine rooms and boiler rooms – giving strength to the hull and watertight integrity, something else her crew would be grateful for during the forthcoming war. Proper repairs to the Jutland damage which had been merely plated over were now possible. One problem caused by First World War damage – her unreliable steering – would remain with *Warspite* for the rest of her fighting life.

The most striking alteration to *Warspite*'s silhouette was the removal of her tripod mast and tiered command platforms to be replaced by a slab-sided tower block bridge. This was needed to provide protected accommodation for the new command and control equipment and make her better able to serve as a flagship.

In October 1936 *Warspite* began sea trials under Admiralty supervision, but still in contractors hands, to see how well she had emerged from rebuild. The speed trial results looked promising. *Warspite*'s maximum deep load displacement had been raised to 36,096 tons yet she could still manage twenty-four knots – an incredible achievement, bearing in mind her original designed top speed was around twenty-five knots.

In March 1937 *Warspite* was handed over to the Royal Navy and embarked on further sea trials, sailing out of both Portsmouth and Plymouth. During a hard turn to starboard on a high speed running trial, her steering jammed, despite a new steering engine having been recently fitted. However, it seemed to cure itself during more speed trials the following week off Cawsand, near Plymouth. Returning to Portsmouth in mid-March, *Warspite* embarked on test-firings for her 15-inch guns.

By the end of June 1937 the *Warspite* had embarked her full 1,200 strong crew. The main draft of 1,000 men marched into Portsmouth Dockyard on 29 June, having arrived by special train at the nearby Harbour Station. One of those marching in that day remembered:

> My first view of the Warspite *was of her being tied up at Middleslip Jetty and she looked great and special, being painted Med Fleet grey. By contrast the rest of the ships, like the carrier* Courageous, *were painted Home Fleet grey and looked rather drab.*[1]

The *Warspite*'s crew was now drawn from Chatham Division and her commanding officer was Captain V.A.C. Crutchley VC who won his medal during the Zeebrugge raid of the First World War. A fair but strict Commanding Officer, Captain Crutchley could be trusted to drive both ship and crew hard to get the best out of them. Everybody aboard the *Warspite* was keen to give their utmost, to ensure she would be fighting fit for her forthcoming deployment to the Mediterranean. She was destined to be the flagship of the Mediterranean Fleet's Commander-in-Chief, Admiral Sir Dudley Pound. The final trials were exhausting, particularly when things didn't go smoothly and, by June 1937, with departure day fast approaching, the crew was starting to feel a little bit worn down. The sailors were really looking forward to their last weekend home leave, especially as they faced a couple of years away. However, when leave was posted, they were appalled to discover they would be due back aboard the *Warspite* at 7.00a.m. on the Monday.

This meant sailors leaving their homes the night before to ensure they got back and therefore missing precious time with their families. The fact that they were assigned to a Portsmouth ship had already curtailed any possibility of the odd evening at home.

In a pale echo of Invergordon, some of the ratings gathered to air their grievances on a messdeck. Seaman Gunner William Nichol was approached to see if he wanted to join the meeting:

> *People were discontented about their weekend leave. I didn't take part as I didn't want to know. It wasn't a mutiny, just some people moaning.*

News of it reached the Captain who promptly assembled those sailors not turned in for the night on the battleship's quarterdeck. After listening calmly to their grumbles he told them they knew the correct way to represent them to the proper authorities. It was decided to do nothing about the gathering despite its 'unlawful character' under naval regulations. However, some of the people involved decided to air their complaints in public by contacting a newspaper, and so the Admiralty was forced to take action.

An official inquiry was convened and it was decided blame lay on both sides. The decision to finish leave at 7.00a.m. on the Monday was unwise, but the sailors should have complained in a proper manner without offending naval regulations with their unauthorized gathering or going to the press. The *Warspite*'s Executive Officer and two divisional officers were taken off the ship while three ratings were dismissed from the Service. Nine others were dispersed to other ships. A rating aboard *Warspite* at the time gave his own assessment of how this minor situation could have been easily avoided:

> *Looking back, the men concerned had been working the dogwatches to get the ship ready to sail for the Mediterranean by 5 July. After her three year special refit there was certainly a lot of cleaning up to do to get her fit for Flagship duty. I think a bit of give and take on the officers' part was needed. Of course what made it a mountain out of a molehill was those men contacting the newspapers.*

One of *Warspite*'s sailors remembered that one enterprising matelot – a habitual offender, allegedly nicknamed 'Ali Babar' in reference to his wicked ways – was at the time of the so-called 'mutiny' trying to make a tidy profit out of bootleg railway tickets.

> *Somehow or other he managed to steal some books of railway warrants. His price list was five shillings for Edinburgh, down to one or two shillings for places in the south-east of England. The lads were only too willing to take advantage of these cut price bootleg tickets. But 'Ali' slipped up. A married man, he went home every night, stealing a dockyard matey's bike to do so. He always dumped the nicked bike back in the dockyard the following morning so no long-term harm, beyond temporary inconvenience for some poor dockyard worker, was done. One evening on his way home he stopped off to do some shoplifting and was caught trying to make off with a pound*

of sausages. Duly arrested he was taken before the magistrate the next morning. A Corporal and two Marines were sent to bring him back to the Warspite *to collect his kit and then go off to jail. His locker was opened by a senior rating and lo and behold the missing railway warrants were revealed. That was the end of 'Ali Babar' for a good while.*

While thieving from the civilian population, including butchers and dockyard workers, and even hi-jacking naval travel warrants from those in authority, might have been sins which the *Warspite*'s sailors could live with, any sailor who stole from a shipmate would get into instant hot water. With everyone living so much on top of each other, dishonesty could have a corrosive effect unless it was stamped on immediately.

A member of the battleship's crew, Donald Auffret, who would see service during the Second World War observed:

A sailor might be the biggest rogue outside his ship but aboard ship you can literally leave money lying around and it'll be there when you come back. And it just has to be that way, not only with money but in possessions, clothing, even your particular sleeping space. You'd never dream of slinging a hammock in someone else's sleeping space. And, besides slinging their hammocks on particular mess decks assigned depending on their working departments and ranks, the sailors also took their meals there. You all mostly sat at the same place at the mess table to eat your meal. Overall, you respected each other's privacy, such as it was. If you were all writing letters, it was obvious you were all crowded together but you wouldn't dream of looking to see what someone else was writing. There was a lot of unwritten laws and also some long-standing traditions. Rum was a great tradition in the navy. It wasn't just an alcoholic drink – rum was currency. If you wanted the carpenter to do a little job for you, you wouldn't offer him money, because money wasn't acceptable. Offer him your tot of rum the next day and you'd get the job done.[2]

It was a traditional system which worked well.

Hammocks were as widely used in the Royal Navy of the late 1930s as they were in Nelson's day and many of Warspite's sailors thought them better than having a bunk. One of Warspite's gunners explained the advantages: 'In my mess we all slept in hammocks. They were great because when the ship rolled you would stay central.' Then, as today, sailors had limited space for personal property. 'Each one of us had a locker into which went the contents of our kitbags but they were quite large.'

Regardless of sleeping conditions and personal space, food was paramount when it came to the morale of the crew as one *Warspite* sailor made clear.

Good wholesome traditional grub was very important to keeping our spirits up – even if it could get a bit samey – and meals were the social event of the day. Before the Second World War the menu was the same on all ships in the fleet – kippers for Monday breakfast, smoked haddock for Thursday...fried egg and rashers cooked at 4.00a.m...corn dog stew...an apple for duff on Saturdays or rice pudding. Mid-week could be you might get figgy duff and custard...the ward room was not immune from such repetition.

D. Auffret said of *Warspite*'s living conditions:

> *The living conditions were quite reasonable aboard the* Warspite. *The food was quite good. There was quite a bit of space. It was quite a nice ship...the idea of bunks and things like that didn't occur to you. It was marvellous sleeping in a hammock especially in rough weather – the ship swung but the hammock didn't.*

The same sailor believed personal hygiene was important to making life bearable:

> *...living in a confined space, the only way that life can be tolerable is for everybody to be clean; you get very short shrift in the Navy if you are dirty. In fact I've seen people taken to a bathroom and scrubbed with hand scrubbers ...* ·

With the beginning of July 1937, *Warspite* was due to carry out her acceptance trials – the final running in of the ship's crew, machinery and weapons. They should have been a formality. However, niggling doubts remained about the *Warspite*'s steering and, as any defects discovered could still be swiftly put right by the dockyard, Captain Crutchley decided to put the battleship through a most severe test. During a series of violent manoeuvres the steering jammed yet again and, as the *Warspite* was re-entering Portsmouth, turbine gearing on one of the shafts gave out, forcing her to go up harbour on one propeller. Six months of additional sea trials and remedial work on the ship followed.

The solution was to slow down the two outer propeller shafts and so reduce vibrations. While this action helped it would not prove to be the end of *Warspite*'s difficulties in that respect.

The delays to *Warspite*'s arrival in the Mediterranean had not endeared the battleship to Admiral Pound. Mechanical problems were one thing, but hearing about trouble over leave enraged him – it was not the sort of conduct he expected from the crew of a vessel destined to be his flagship. Nine days after finally leaving the United Kingdom on 5 January 1938, Pound's errant flagship entered Valetta Harbour in Malta, where the Mediterranean Fleet had its main base.

In early February, when he went aboard the *Spite* for the first time, Admiral Pound decided to let the crew have a piece of his mind, using A turret as a platform to launch his reprimand. Seaman Gunner William Nichol said the crew became determined to show Pound he was wrong about the *Warspite*.

> *The slagging off he gave the* Warspite *when we got to Malta so angered us that we worked ourselves up to be the top gunnery ship. We were determined after that to really make the grade and show him it wasn't the entire crew, only one or two, who had been troublemakers.*

The *Warspite* was to come good at a time of increasing international tension, when it was becoming clear that Hitler was on the path to war.

In contravention of the Versailles Treaty, in March 1936 Hitler sent German troops to occupy the de-militarized Rhineland and Britain and France did nothing to stop him. A year earlier the Germans had discarded the Versailles restrictions on their armed forces and started a process of rearmament which included construction of battleships and increasing numbers of submarines. In March 1938 Austria was subsumed into the Greater Reich, again with no substantial action from foreign powers. As Hitler's troops were annexing Austria, *Warspite* took part in a huge exercise off Gibraltar, involving both the Mediterranean Fleet and ships of the

Mediterranean Fleet Flagship HMS *Warspite* returns to Malta, with HMS *Hood* following her into harbour, after intensive gunnery exercises in August 1938. *Sutherland Collection.*

Atlantic Fleet. Following this her crew was given some leave on the French Riviera and then the battleship returned to Malta.

The Italians and Germans were also fanning the flames of conflict by becoming heavily involved in supporting the Fascist side in the Spanish Civil War. When she sailed to the Mediterranean *Warspite* carried red, white and blue identification stripes on her turrets to make sure both sides in the civil war were aware she was a British ship and should not be attacked.

In late August 1938, amid the continuing international tension, *Warspite* led the Mediterranean Fleet, including HMS *Hood*, to sea for more intensive exercises. The *Warspite*'s improved 15-inch guns were fired continuously under simulated battle conditions, maintaining incredible accuracy. This performance went some considerable way towards redeeming *Warspite* in Admiral Pound's eyes.

Within a few weeks the threat of war for which the exercise had prepared the fleet seemed about to become reality as Hitler threatened to seize Czechoslovakia.

Back in Britain 'weekend sailor' H. Banks had been sent by the Tyne Division of the Royal Naval Reserve on a gunnery course at Chatham where he was caught up in the crisis. 'On the second to last day of the course, we were told that the Royal Navy was to be mobilized and we could be drafted to warships.'

In the Mediterranean the autumn cruise programme was abandoned and the Mediterranean Fleet headed for its war base in Egypt. In 1936 the Anglo-Egyptian Treaty had given Britain the right to station troops in Egypt and also have a naval base at Alexandria. This was needed because it was likely any war with Germany would also be against its close ally, Italy and Malta was thought too vulnerable to the depredations of Italian air power for capital ships.

As British Prime Minister Neville Chamberlain met with Hitler at Munich in late

September, prepared to agree to anything to avoid war, the Mediterranean Fleet's shells were fused and plans for a bombardment of Tobruk – one of Italy's main ports in North Africa – were finalized. It was then however, that Chamberlain's misguided Munich Agreement which gave Germany the Czechoslovakian Sudetenland for 'peace for our time', temporarily pulled Europe back from the brink. The Mediterranean Fleet's shells were de-fused...for now.

H. Banks was sent home from Chatham: 'Back home we came, having profited by the princely sum of £5 for having been mobilized.' Another mobilization was not far away; and it would send him to sea

Souvenir postcard made up for a member of HMS *Warspite*'s crew to mark the Summer 1938 cruise.
Sutherland Collection.

***Warspite* as viewed from an American warship in harbour at Villefranche during the earlier Spring 1938 cruise. Note the markings on her turret to warn participants in the Spanish Civil War that she is a British warship and should not be attacked.**
US Naval Historical Center.

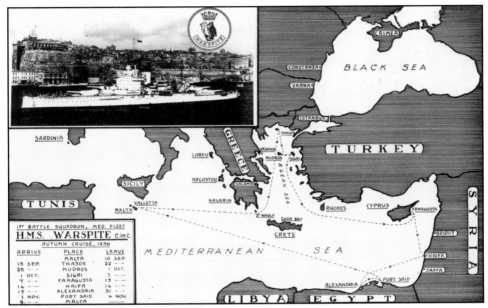

Souvenir postcard made up for a member of HMS *Warspite*'s crew to mark the Autumn 1938 cruise. *Sutherland Collection.*

HMS *Warspite* at sea with the Mediterranean Fleet in late 1938. *Foster Collection.*

The *Warspite* at Malta in late 1938. *Foster Collection.*

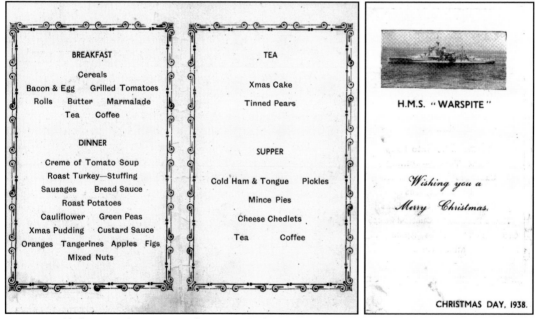

BREAKFAST	TEA
Cereals	
Bacon & Egg Grilled Tomatoes	Xmas Cake
Rolls Butter Marmalade	Tinned Pears
Tea Coffee	

BREAKFAST

Cereals

Bacon & Egg   Grilled Tomatoes

Rolls   Butter   Marmalade

Tea   Coffee

DINNER

Creme of Tomato Soup

Roast Turkey—Stuffing

Sausages   Bread Sauce

Roast Potatoes

Cauliflower   Green Peas

Xmas Pudding   Custard Sauce

Oranges   Tangerines   Apples   Figs

Mixed Nuts

TEA

Xmas Cake

Tinned Pears

SUPPER

Cold Ham & Tongue   Pickles

Mince Pies

Cheese Chedlets

Tea   Coffee

H.M.S. "WARSPITE"

Wishing you a

Merry Christmas.

CHRISTMAS DAY, 1938.

Christmas Dinner menu for 1938, the last Festive Season the battleship would spend at Malta. *A. Jones Collection.*

aboard the *Warspite*.

With the threat of war temporarily diminishing, *Warspite* was to spend Christmas at Malta rather than Alexandria. She would never spend another Christmas there, as the island would be unsafe by the time the Festive Season of 1939 came around.

A Legendary Partnership Begins ... and is Interrupted

In June 1939 Dudley Pound went home to Britain to become First Sea Lord and

Souvenir postcard made up for members of HMS *Warspite*'s crew to mark the Spring 1939 cruise. *Sutherland Collection.*

was succeeded by Vice Admiral Sir Andrew Cunningham. The hand-over between Pound and Cunningham took place on *Warspite* in Alexandria when the rest of the fleet was at sea. Following the change of command *Warspite* joined the fleet for exercises which were again taking place against a background of high tension. Hitler's troops had occupied the whole of Czechoslovakia in early March 1939 and Germany had also annexed the port of Memel in Lithuania.

The Führer was now determined to take the Polish port of Danzig which, like Memel, had been taken away from Germany as part of the peace settlement following the First World War. In late March an attempt was made by German troops to seize Danzig, but they were withdrawn after Britain and France finally found some backbone and told Hitler it would mean war. The Germans decided they would

HMS *Warspite* at Malta, with *Rodney* or *Nelson* in the background. *Wyles Collection*

HMS *Hotspur* **transfers mail to HMS** *Warspite* **in the Mediterranean shortly before the outbreak of war. In April 1940 HMS** *Hotspur* **would take part in the First Battle of Narvik, while** *Warspite* **distinguished herself in the Second Battle of Narvik a few days later.** *Topham/Keystone.*

go back when their military was stronger. Emboldened by the way in which a fascist alliance had achieved victory in the Spanish Civil War that spring, in late May 1939 Germany and Italy signed their so-called Pact of Steel which promised military co-operation for ten years.

Meanwhile Italy had annexed Albania at the beginning of April. Britain and France decided to respond to this threat by underwriting the security of Greece and Romania which feared Mussolini would move against them next.

The dockyard at Malta was still the fleet's main maintenance and repair facility because there were problems with the support services at Alexandria.

Anti-aircraft defences were woeful, there was no support airfield for the carrier aircraft to fly to for maintenance and repair when not at sea, warship berths were limited and storage areas – particularly for ammunition – were scarce or non-existent. Docking and repair facilities had to be improved radically if Alexandria was to truly become a war base for the *Warspite* and the rest of the fleet. The biggest ship that Alexandria's Gabbari dock could take was a cruiser. Cunningham set about implementing improvements including deep-water berths and storage facilities. The Admiral had also been involved in discussions about transferring a floating dry dock capable of taking battleships from Portsmouth to Alexandria.

With time before hostilities so obviously running out, Admiral Cunningham was very keen for his flagship to take an opportunity for a docking period at Malta in July. The following month, as German troops began their final preparations for the invasion of Poland, *Warspite* set sail from Malta on an important mission to Istanbul.

Cunningham embarked on a round of high level social visits aimed at fostering a feeling of friendship between Britain and Turkey and was later involved in official talks with Turkish leaders.

Meanwhile the crews of *Warspite* and escorting destroyers enjoyed amazing hospitality ashore, including plenty of beer and a troupe of dancing girls at a party hosted personally by the British ambassador.

On 6 August the *Warspite* and her escorts left the Bosphorus. Cunningham observed: 'Our mission had been an important one, and from what we heard later it undoubtedly did a lot of good.'[3]

Turkey was to stay neutral during the Second World War. *Warspite* made a call at Cyprus and then headed for Alexandria, carrying out some 15-inch gunnery practice on the way.

Back in Britain Royal Naval Reserve sailor H. Banks had, early in 1939, managed to find a good job as a conductor with South Shields Corporation Transport. 'I believe I was the first person employed by them to be called up, on Wednesday August 23 to be exact.'

A relief conductor was lined up, the 'weekend sailor' said goodbye to his wife, family and friends and, after reporting for orders to HMS *Satellite*, the drill ship berthed on the Tyne in North Shields, he headed south.

> *I was in Chatham Barracks, 300 miles away that same night and next morning I went through the mobilization routine again wondering if this time the balloon would really go up.*

In late August Hitler had signed a non-aggression pact with Stalin, so paving the way for Russia and Germany to divide up Poland. This shrewd move also guarded Germany's flanks and rear if she made any moves towards the north or west. In the meantime, the Royal Navy wasted no time in sorting out reinforcements for its Mediterranean Fleet warships to bring them up to fighting strength. The draft for *Warspite*, including H. Banks, was swiftly processed at Chatham and put on a ship across the English Channel. H. Banks remembered:

> *After a very rapid train journey across France, we embarked onboard HMS Shropshire, a County Class cruiser, at Marseilles which took us to Alexandria, stopping only at Malta to pick up mail. The cruiser arrived at Alexandria on Thursday, 31 August. The* Warspite *was at sea.*

The next day Germany invaded Poland from the west while Russia steamed in from the east.

On 2 September, *Warspite* and the Mediterranean Fleet returned to harbour to await the official declaration of war. Britain honoured her commitments to Poland's security and, on the following day, declared war on Germany. A signal was sent from the Admiralty to Cunningham aboard *Warspite*. It read: 'Total Germany'. A messenger took the signal to the Admiral in his day cabin where he was discussing the possibility of bombarding Tobruk with his staff officers. Cunningham reportedly read the signal then asked the bearer: 'Not Italy?'[4] Italy was staying out of the conflict until she saw which way the cards fell. The bombardment of Tobruk would have to wait.

One of the sailors who had seen the signal come in was Albert Cock, who had just passed for Leading Telegraphist.

> *We were excited by the prospect of war as we had been training like mad. Before hostilities, although much of the signals traffic needed deciphering, some of it was in plain language. Once the war started it all came by cipher. But, even though we were at fighting pitch and eager, Italy was not in the war so it became a sort of 'Phoney War'.*

At the outbreak of hostilities the impact aircraft would have on naval warfare was not appreciated by the Royal Navy. It had never faced massed aircraft attack and many officers found it hard to believe a battleship could be sunk by aerial bombing. HMS *Warspite* would soon find out exactly what it felt like to be under attack from the air and an officer who was shortly to join Cunningham's staff aboard her was to bring some valuable insights into the new threat.

William Lamb was, by September 1939, on the staff of the Royal Navy's gunnery school at Portsmouth.

> *The declaration of war was no surprise at all. My job at that time was to be Officer -in-Charge of the Anti-Aircraft firing range. It was an interesting job because, on the whole, I think insufficient attention had been given in the training of people to use close-range AA weapons. The big guns were the important ones and the small ones mattered less. There was a feeling of nakedness in our close-range AA gunnery abilities so I felt I was in a job where there was a lot to do. When it came to close-range, the main weapon was the Chicago Piano, an eight-barrelled 2-pounder gun. It was used to fill the air with explosive little shells and hope some of them might find an aircraft target.*

It was a weapon *Warspite* would be calling on a great deal in the conflict.

The French Navy soon agreed to cover the western Mediterranean while the Royal Navy took the eastern end. The battleship FNS *Lorraine* was based at Alexandria with a quartet of cruisers and a trio of destroyers to help out. The Anglo-French forces presided over a placid arena. But, while it might have been very quiet in the Mediterranean, the Royal Navy's Home Fleet faced the daunting task of containing Germany's formidable force of modern heavily armed battleships. The Home Fleet had settled in well at its Scapa Flow war anchorage but disaster struck in mid-October 1939. A U-boat skippered by Kapitän Leutnant Gunther Prien sneaked in through patchy defences and sank the battleship *Royal Oak* at her moorings, with large loss of life.

Following this calamity, reinforcements were needed for home waters and, at the end of October, HMS *Warspite* was called back to join the Home Fleet, where operations against the Germans would soon land her in Prien's sights.

Notes

1   A *Warspite* veteran writing in *Anchors Aweigh*, the journal of the *Warspite* Association.
2   D. Auffret, Sound Archive, Imperial War Museum.
3   Cunningham, *A Sailor's Odyssey*.
4   S.W.C. Pack, *Cunningham The Commander*.

Chapter Six

TO NARVIK

Hunting Nazi Raiders

After some maintenance work in Malta dockyard, *Warspite* next called at Gibraltar where she received new orders to sail for Nova Scotia. It was feared German surface raiders had broken out into the Atlantic so *Warspite* was to escort Convoy HX9, composed of thirty ships, leaving Halifax on 18 November 1939. During the four days *Warspite* was at Halifax taking on stores and ammunition for the escort mission, Able Seaman Gunner H. Banks had an opportunity to get ashore.

> *Of course, having come from the Med, none of us had suitable clothing for the climate, which was very cold. On top of that the pay of an Able Seaman did not allow me to afford Canadian prices. We were definitely the poor relations as far as the Canadians were concerned.*

Warspite joined her slow convoy out of Halifax and hit heavy weather. Royal Marine Arthur Jones, a gun layer in Y turret, was surprised to find he was invulnerable to it. 'It was dreadful weather, the merchant ships were really wallowing and the *Warspite* was burying her bows but I never felt seasick once.'

Six days into her first, and only, transatlantic crossing *Warspite* was diverted away from the convoy to try and intercept the battlecruisers *Scharnhorst* and *Gneisenau*, which had just sunk the British Armed Merchant Cruiser *Rawalpindi*.

Boy Seaman Ray Emmington in X turret was tasked with a job not many would want.

> *On northern patrol we closed up at dawn and dusk and this is where an odd job arose. The 15-inch shell had a fuse fitted in its base set differently at night and day. So, as we closed up, I had a heaving line tied to my leg and had to claw my way in the barrel with a special spanner to set the fuse. When the job was done, I was pulled back out of the barrel. Another boy looked after the left gun. The 15-inch gun barrel is more than fifteen inches diameter, in fact the explosion chamber was eighteen inches, so it was easy for a small boy to do the job. We came out faster than we went in.*

Warspite battered her way through the Denmark Strait seeking to encounter the enemy but made no contact. At the scene of the *Rawalpindi*'s last know location she found no survivors. Seaman Gunner Nichol scanned the horizon from his trainer's position on one of the 4-inch anti-aircraft guns. 'All we found was an empty lifeboat, he said ' Sweeping down the western side of Scotland, *Warspite* met only friendly ships. Marine Jones recalled one of these encounters:

> *We went to action stations because someone had spotted a destroyer which failed to respond to any Aldis lamp signals. The Skipper, realizing it couldn't be easy for such a small warship in that weather, told them to signal her again. This time the destroyer replied, so she was obviously one of ours and we didn't need to open fire.*

In the atrocious weather the German ships had slipped through the Home Fleet's fingers. They were aided by intercepts of coded British naval signals the Kriegsmarine was finding easy to break, enabling them to steer clear of Royal Navy hunting units.

Calling in at the Clyde, which had become the main Home Fleet base while Scapa's defences were improved, *Warspite* was expecting to head for Portsmouth. However, as HMS *Nelson* had just been put out of action by a German magnetic mine, it was decided *Warspite* should replace her as Home Fleet flagship. By the following March the Orkneys were secure again and *Warspite* found herself back at the old familiar anchorage of Scapa.

Able Seaman Banks was introduced to the 'Dummy Fleet'.

Practically every major ship was duplicated by merchant vessels with wooden superstructures and guns. They were exact replicas of the real Royal Navy ships, but in later years it was found the enemy knew all about the fakes. That might explain why they were never attacked during numerous air raids.

Royal Marine Arthur Jones found Scapa was as bleak and unwelcoming for the young

HMS *Warspite* at Scapa, 1940. *Specially commissioned painting by Dennis C. Andrews.*

HMS *Warspite* in Norwegian waters, 1940.
Specially commissioned painting by Dennis C. Andrews.

servicemen of the Home Fleet as it had been for their forebears in the Grand Fleet of the First World War.

It was very primitive. There was a canteen ashore and you got there by using a drifter which took you in and landed you on the mud. You had these tickets to exchange for chocolate bars, sweets, toffee and you took your own glass for beer which was five pennies a pint. That was the beginning and end of entertainment ashore at Scapa Flow.

During this period *Warspite* was sent on many fruitless patrols of Arctic waters which numbed her crew. Able Seaman Banks:

At this time my job was range-taker in A turret. Often, due to the very bad weather, it was impossible to gain access to the turret, which in my case was in the forecastle - for the uninitiated, the sharp end. Instead we had to descend four decks and climb up into the turret via a ladder in the trunk. Before doing so, it was necessary to get permission from the Officer of the Turret so that the guns did not train round during our ascent, as this could result in a rather nasty mess, to say the least. Naturally permission was never given during an alert, and unless you could get in via the upper deck, then your relief just had to wait, though I cannot remember anyone waiting for more than a few minutes. On the other hand, if the ship was at action stations there would be no relief.

Norway was retaining neutrality but feeding the Nazi war effort by allowing the export of Swedish iron ore via the Arctic port of Narvik. If this wasn't galling enough, the British were certain German vessels were using Norwegian territorial waters to avoid interception while slipping out into the Atlantic. The British response was an operation to mine Norwegian territorial waters. But, even as this was being mounted in early April 1940, German troops invaded Norway and Denmark. Narvik was one of several Norwegian ports where German forces were landed, with 2,000 mountain troops carried 100 miles up the Vestfiord and Ofotfiord by ten large destroyers.

While all this was unfolding, *Warspite* was on her way back to the Mediterranean, where she was to be flagship again. However, she suddenly found herself redirected to Norwegian waters. On her way to rendezvous with the Home Fleet, *Warspite* weathered her first German dive bomber attack which was ineffective, but demonstrated the worth of her extra anti-aircraft defences.

In the meantime, having finally realized the Germans were in possession of Narvik, a flotilla of British destroyers was sent up to disrupt them and sank two of the German warships during a battle on 10 April. The remaining eight German destroyers remained at Narvik because of lack of fuel and some were almost

HMS *Icarus,* **one of** *Warspite's* **hunting pack of destroyers at the Second Battle of Narvik.**
Goodman Collection.

unseaworthy due to battle damage. Their fuel and ammunition resupply tanker was intercepted and blown up by British destroyers.

Having a significant force of German destroyers – in fact almost a third of the Kriegsmarine's entire destroyer force – trapped in the confines of Narvik was just too good an opportunity to miss. The Royal Navy decided to attack them with overwhelming force. A hunting pack of destroyers – HMS *Cossack*, HMS *Eskimo*, HMS *Bedouin*, HMS *Forester*, HMS *Hero*, HMS *Icarus*, HMS *Kimberley*, HMS *Foxhound* and HMS *Punjabi* – was assembled around HMS *Warspite*.

The leader of this force was to be Vice Admiral William 'Jock' Whitworth –

Another member of the Narvik hunting pack - HMS *Hero.* *Goodman Collection.*

Battleship *Warspite* storms up the Norwegian fjords, her 15-inch guns blazing.
Specially commissioned painting by Dennis C. Andrews.

commander of the Battle Cruiser Squadron – who swapped his flag from HMS *Renown* to HMS *Warspite* in the early hours of 13 April. The night of 12-13 April was bitterly cold, with an uncomfortable swell and ice coating the battleship's decks. Deep inside her hull the fuses of 15-inch shells were altered to non-delay. The sheer weight of the one ton shells meant if they weren't set to explode instantly on contact, they might go off after coming out the other side.

At 5.00 a.m. on 13 April the *Warspite* started her journey to Narvik, with three destroyers steaming ahead of her using minesweeping gear to clear the way.

Others were posted evenly around her, all of them eager to attack the enemy. With oppressive clouds pressing down, and snow flurries swirling off the steep sides of the fiords, visibility was around ten miles at best. Signalman Donald Auffret, whose action station was the wireless office on *Warspite*'s bridge, remembered:

> As we came to the entrance of the fiord we could see the mountains on either side, all grey, with snow and it looked a very, very grim place.[1]

On the battleship's forecastle, while they were waiting for something to happen, the crews of A and B turrets relieved tension with an enthusiastic snowball fight. Soon the gunners were called back into their turrets, shells were rammed up the guns and the *Warspite* accelerated, the vibrations of her engines clearly felt underfoot. As the battleship gathered pace a U-boat carefully stalking her, collided with a rock and was temporarily exposed. HMS *Eskimo* chased the submarine off with a shower of depth charges.

A Swordfish floatplane from the battleship was launched to scout ahead and soon reported two enemy destroyers not far away. They greeted the plane with a storm of anti-aircraft fire but failed to score any hits.

Skimming over Narvik, the Swordfish sighted another German destroyer in harbour and then flew up the Herjangsfiord to the north. Petty Officer Pilot Frederick 'Ben' Rice spotted something interesting: 'We got up the top of the fiord and my Observer said that we may as well turn around and go back. I replied "hang on, there's a U-boat".'

This dramatic find was U-64 moving away from a jetty at the small settlement of Bjerkvik. Petty Officer Rice put his ungainly aircraft into a dive.

> With floats on a Swordfish you couldn't carry a torpedo. What we carried was 250lbs armour piercing bombs, two 100lb bombs and an anti-submarine bomb. I decided to use the two armour-piercing bombs.

As Petty Officer Rice released the bombs, his Wireless Operator/Gunner, Leading Airman Pacey, hosed the German submarine down with machine-gun fire. The U-boat replied with a 37mm anti-aircraft gun mounted on its conning tower. One of the Swordfish bombs hit at the base of the conning tower, making short work of the submarine, as she sank by the bows in less than thirty seconds, drowning a dozen of her crew. This was the first U-boat to be sunk by a British naval aircraft in the Second World War. Petty Officer Rice was glad the majority of the enemy survived:

> Thirty-eight men managed to escape from the U-boat. I learned after the war that it was lucky anyone got out at all. Fortunately they had her watertight doors shut. She sank with her stern sticking out of the water – those that were in the front compartments didn't make it.

At 12.25p.m. one of the enemy destroyers the Swordfish sighted earlier emerged out of the mist ahead of the British warships. Immediately doing an about-turn, this vessel – the *Hermann Künne* – was fired on by HMS *Foxhound* but escaped back into the mist unharmed. The Swordfish now saw the *Koellner* tucked behind a corner of the Ofotfiord at Djupvik, preparing to torpedo whatever came around it next. Forewarned by the spotter aircraft, which circled above, *Bedouin* and *Eskimo* came past Djupvik with their guns and torpedo tubes trained to starboard. Their weapons soon turned the *Koellner* into floating wreckage while the German ship's own shells and torpedoes found no target. Not long after *Warspite*'s great bulk nosed around the corner, her 15-inch turrets also trained to starboard, guns at minimum elevation. Some foolish members of *Koellner*'s crew who had stayed behind now fired her remaining torpedoes. Arthur White, a junior rating on HMS *Eskimo*'s A turret gun crew, saw *Warspite*'s devastating response:

> There was rushing noise just like a bloomin' express train. It put the fear of Christ in us. We wondered what the hell it was. All of a sudden this destroyer and the cliff behind blew up.[2]

Two full broadsides of eight 15-inch guns and four 6-inch salvos slammed into the unfortunate German warship. Royal Marine gun layer Arthur Jones, who had been switched to No3 gun in the starboard 6-inch battery got a good view:

> One of our 15-inch shells ricocheted up the side of the mountain and, through my telescopic range-finder, I saw it hit this line of German sailors who had abandoned their ship after the earlier fight.

As a member of the A turret gun crew, Able Seaman Banks was partly responsible for this carnage and recalled:

Warspite *had immediately turned to starboard, suspecting the enemy's intention would be to torpedo us as we passed. As we did so we saw the enemy torpedo tracks but, due to us turning towards them and presenting a much smaller target, they missed. In the next few seconds all hell was let loose. Both A and B turrets fired and we couldn't miss from that range. Imagine if you can, four 15-inch shells each weighing a ton, packed with high explosive, hitting a thin skinned destroyer.*

The *Koellner* was ripped asunder, her remains rapidly sliding beneath the cold dark waters.

As *Warspite* and her destroyers approached Narvik, the rest of the German warships were either raising steam or unable to move due to damage sustained on 10 April.

With the *Kunne* retreating after her brief encounter with the British force, and the frightening sound of *Warspite*'s heavy guns bouncing off the fiord side, the most battle-worthy German destroyers – *Ludemann*, *Zenker* and *von Arnim* – made haste to leave Narvik port. The four German destroyers made a charge, weaving back and forth, while the British twisted to and fro, the surface of the water erupting with shell fountains and crisscrossed with launched torpedoes. Frost on the sights together with the swirling snow and mist made aiming difficult and, although there was much sound and fury, no projectile made an impact. Now, from around three miles behind her own destroyers, the *Warspite*'s big guns fired again, the fiord trembling to their mighty roar. Terrifying as it was for the Germans to find themselves retreating while dodging and weaving to avoid 15-inch shells, again no hits were scored. *Warspite*'s aiming difficulties were compounded by her own guns enveloping the gunnery director tower with thick cordite smoke. According to Signalman Auffret, the battleship was causing more damage to herself with the back blast of her own guns than the enemy could inflict.

We were firing directly over the bow, the turrets were trained almost fore and aft and consequently all the blast was coming back aboard. One of the forward hatches was blown off and all the blast was actually going down into the cable deck where it caused quite a considerable amount of damage.

The battleship was forced to take evasive action when torpedoes fired at her screen of destroyers came dangerously close, one exploding right underneath but causing no damage. According to Able Seaman Banks it was around this time the old steering gremlin made its presence known.

She gave a repeat performance of the Jutland problem. However, this time it was in the confines of a fiord, not the open sea. But it was remedied quickly enough to prevent us running ashore.

The Germans were running out of space and their ammunition was nearly all gone. It would be pure slaughter once they were hemmed in at Narvik and *Warspite* closed to point-blank range. Into all this mayhem came Swordfish from HMS *Furious*, gamely trying to emulate the bombing success of *Warspite*'s floatplane. Diving in from 2,000ft, they managed near misses on *Kunne* and *Arnim* but suffered two of their number shot down. The *Thiele*, *von Arnim*, *Zenker* and *Ludemann* tried to buy more time for themselves by retreating up the Rombaksfiord which ran off to the east. The

Another painting of HMS *Warspite* and her destroyers at Narvik, with HMS *Cossack* depicted leading the battleship into action. *US Naval Historical Center/E. Tufnell.*

Kunne headed north up the Herjangsfiord.

The *Giese* struggled to raise enough steam to leave Narvik harbour while the *von Roeder* was unable to move at all. The *Kunne* was hotly pursued by HMS *Eskimo* and, after the German vessel was beached and her crew fled, the Tribal Class destroyer blew her up with torpedoes.

Back at Narvik, the *Giese* now tried to make a run for it and was badly knocked about by the guns of the British destroyers. Meanwhile the *Warspite* was lobbing shells into Narvik at the *von Roeder*, but failing to score any hits. The battleship's gunners now got a target they couldn't miss – the mortally wounded *Giese* drifting into their path. The *Warspite* swiftly demolished the German destroyer which was abandoned by her crew. Turning her guns back to the *von Roeder*, *Warspite* scored a hit but had to break off fire when *Cossack*, *Kimberley* and *Foxhound* stormed into Narvik harbour guns blazing. The defiant *von Roeder* managed to hit *Cossack* with four 5-inch shells before being silenced, leaving the British destroyer in such a bad way she ran aground. As *Foxhound* approached the *von Roeder* to put a boarding party aboard, the German destroyer exploded, blown up by her own crew.

In the Rombaksfiord, the other German warships were being run to ground with ruthless efficiency. *Eskimo* led the chase, plunging into a smokescreen laid by the retreating Germans, closely followed by *Hero*, *Bedouin*, *Icarus* and *Forester*. With all their shells now gone, the Germans made one last desperate bid to stave off the inevitable. The *Thiele* ran herself aground as she turned to launch torpedoes at *Eskimo*, one of them managing a lucky hit which spectacularly blew off the British destroyer's bows. Arthur White on *Eskimo*'s A turret saw it coming:

> As we went through, the chap that gives me the shells says 'here Knocker look at those lines of bubbles coming' and I said 'you so-and-so bloody fool they're bloody

torpedoes'. There were four lines of them and there was another one coming along, a fifth one with his nose out the water and he'd gone mad, he was a maverick and he was going all over the place.

The remaining three German destroyers ran themselves aground at the head of the Rombaksfiord and were abandoned by their crews after scuttling charges were set. The *Warspite* nosed into the Rombaksfiord but found her services were not needed.

Her Swordfish was now recovered. Petty Officer Rice found his plane had sustained damage from U-64's anti-aircraft gun:

When we landed alongside my air gunner says 'we're sinking, that German must have pierced one of the floats'. Fortunately we managed to get swiftly over to the crane and were picked up right away.

The din of battle suddenly died away, except for the crack of a German mountain howitzer on the shore trying to hit the stranded *Cossack*.

Admiral Whitworth could have put ashore landing parties from his ships, but, even with the heavy guns of *Warspite* behind them, they would have found it difficult to hold Narvik against 2,000 elite German mountain troops. The enemy troops were for the moment demoralized and in total disarray, but it wouldn't take them long to rally and any land battle would be very much on their terms. British troops were on their way, but were at least two days away. Any fierce battle in Narvik would also inevitably lead to heavy civilian casualties. Most alarming for the British Admiral was the revelation, from a captured German naval officer, that U-51 had been at Narvik when the attack began. This vessel had dived and managed to sneak away. Even now she might be preparing an attacking run against the *Warspite*. In addition German aircraft were seen nosing around and, in the confines of the fiord, the battleship

Black smoke rises from German shipping ablaze in Narvik Harbour. *Taylor Library.*

would have been unable to manoeuvre to avoid bombs. *Warspite* withdrew with a protective screen of destroyers gathered around her. She returned several hours later to take aboard the wounded from the crippled British destroyers, and additional German prisoners. Throughout this delicate overnight operation *Warspite*'s gunners and lookouts were at maximum alert for either aircraft or submarine attack. But she was lucky and nothing materialized.

Carrying 200 wounded and eight German prisoners of war, the *Warspite*'s crew got to meet their enemy face to face for the first time. Able Seaman Banks remarked:

> *They didn't have two heads, nor had they horns or cloven hooves. They were just seamen like ourselves, doing a job they had been ordered to do.*

But the ordinary sailors and marines on *Warspite* had been specifically ordered not to consort with the enemy. 'The six German ratings were in the cells and the two officers were kept in officers' cabins,' said Marine Arthur Jones.

> *We were warned against fraternization with the enemy. So, naturally, there were hordes of matelots giving cigarettes and nutty to the Germans locked in the cells. They were just ordinary sailors and they seemed alright.*

Some of them were, however, the picture of Nazi arrogance, as Signalman Auffret recalled:

> *Our cell place was directly underneath the cable deck and they looked at the damage and had a sort of look on their faces. They thought they'd inflicted it. They were very cocky. The feedback we got from the sentries guarding them was that they thought this defeat at Narvik was only a temporary thing. Germany would win in the next six months anyway so they weren't too bothered about being taken prisoner. I was amazed at that because it never occurred to me that my side could lose the war.*

German prisoners after the Second Battle of Narvik, waiting to be taken to HMS *Warspite* against a background of sunken German naval vessels in Narvik Harbour. *Wyles Collection.*

'The One That Got Away'. While U-64 was sunk by *Warspite*'s Swordfish, U-51 managed to slip away from Narvik unharmed. *Specially commissioned painting by Dennis C. Andrews.*

Warspite was lucky throughout the whole Narvik operation for she made an easy, and very tempting, target for a U-boat.

In *The German Navy in World War Two* Edward P. von der Porten reveals that Lieutenant Commander Herbert Schutze, one of the German Navy's top submarine commanders, had *Warspite* at his mercy as she left the Vestfiord after the Narvik battle.

'Two destroyers and the battleship itself were saved when the torpedoes failed again.' Von der Porten also wrote that, on 19 April, Gunther Prien – the legendary killer of the *Royal Oak* – 'found the *Warspite* and fired two torpedoes at her.'

They failed to hit but one exploded near the battleship, bringing a swarm of depth-charging destroyers down on Prien. In all, von der Porten reports in his book, thirty-nine attacks on British and Allied warships and merchant vessels during the Norway campaign were failures. According to von der Porten the *Warspite* was subjected to a total of four U-boat attacks.

Of German U-boat torpedo problems, Macintyre observes in *Narvik*:

> The magnetic pistols in the warheads were failing to function correctly owing to the differences in the earth's magnetic field in those northern latitudes from that in German waters. Furthermore the depth-keeping mechanism of the torpedoes themselves was unreliable.

All in all the capture of Norway in May 1940 was not a happy experience for the German Navy. While it might have managed to sink the old British carrier *Glorious* and her escorting destroyers, the Kriegsmarine's losses were heavy; five cruisers in addition to the destroyers sunk at Narvik. Throughout the war the German Navy was to be badly handicapped by a lack of destroyers. *Warspite* and her hunting pack can be held directly responsible for that.

Warspite stayed on in Norwegian waters to act as flagship for a task group sent up to Narvik to carry out a bombardment. This was meant to soften the Germans up before the British launched their own amphibious assault on the area. Joining *Warspite* in this bombardment were the cruisers *Effingham*, *Enterprise* and *Aurora*, with the carrier HMS *Furious* launching her aircraft to make another spirited, if lame, attempt at area bombing. The bombardment was conducted in atrocious weather conditions, with visibility obscured by snow storms. Very few of the German positions could be seen and firing on the town itself was barred to prevent civilian casualties. Hopes that the enemy might even surrender were, to say the least, forlorn.

Map: John Pearce.

After returning to Scapa Flow, *Warspite* made a brief stop at Greenock to load up provisions. Narvik was a famous victory and, by the time *Warspite* reached the United Kingdom, news had been released to the British public, as Signalman Auffret discovered when he went on leave.

> The day after we arrived back I went up to Glasgow. In those days you still had the full name of your warship on your cap rather than just H.M.S. I was sat in this train carriage and these Scottish civilians passengers were nudging each other and pointing and remarking at the name *Warspite* on my cap tally.

The name *Warspite* was on everybody's lips but even more glory lay ahead of her as she headed south to the Mediterranean to become Admiral Cunningham's flagship again.

Notes

1 Sound Archive, Imperial War Museum.

2 Sound Archive, Imperial War Museum.

Chapter Seven

CALABRIA, TARANTO & MATAPAN

Point Blank in Alexandria

With Italy so far electing to stay out of the war, and the German fleet firmly focused on waters nearer to home, *Warspite* was able to sail back to Alexandria via Gibraltar and a safe west-east passage across the Mediterranean.

Italy entered the war on 10 June 1940, when it was becoming clear France would soon fall to Germany. Admiral Cunningham took his fleet to sea the following day, with *Warspite* leading a sweep along the southern coast of Crete and then off the coast of Libya. There was no sign of Italian warships or aircraft but, when the British

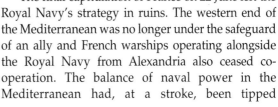

returned to Alexandria on 14 June, they were warned that mines had been laid off the port in their absence.

The final capitulation of France on 22 June left the Royal Navy's strategy in ruins. The western end of the Mediterranean was no longer under the safeguard of an ally and French warships operating alongside the Royal Navy from Alexandria also ceased co-operation. The balance of naval power in the Mediterranean had, at a stroke, been tipped

Admiral Cunningham, who used HMS *Warspite* as his flagship during the battles of Calabria, Taranto and Matapan.
Goodman Collection.

HMS *Warspite* pictured in the early part of the Second World War.
US Naval Historical Center.

decisively in Italy's favour.

Not only was the Royal Navy's Mediterranean Fleet lacking in destroyers, submarines, minesweepers and fighter aircraft, its major ships were slow and old. The British had one key advantage as Admiral Cunningham noted:

> Our ships might be old, and there was much that we lacked. Nevertheless we had our personnel, and, through them were able to forge a weapon that was as bright and as sharp as highly-tempered steel.[1]

But, even if the mettle of British sailors was undoubtedly superior to Italian matelots, the enemy fleet had fast and powerfully armed modern ships, and plenty of them. Italy's two Andrea Doria Class battleships were nearing the end of extensive reconstructions in the summer of 1940 and by August two formidable Littorio Class battlewagons – armed with 15-inch guns – would enter service.

Italian confidence was boosted by the notion that the French fleet would soon be in Axis hands and British naval power in the Mediterranean would collapse once Hitler struck across the English Channel. If the Italians had acted swiftly and aggressively with their fleet between June and November 1940 they could have used superiority in numbers and their more modern warships to deliver a killer blow. However, a series of ill-judged political appointments in senior ranks of the Italian Navy (passing over more daring and skilled naval officers) was combined with a rigid diktat that the fleet had to be kept intact 'at all costs' to create a crippling caution. Meanwhile the German Navy, in contrast to the timid Italians, and despite having its hands full fighting the Royal Navy in the Atlantic, was putting forward wild schemes including the capture of Gibraltar and the Suez Canal. They were plainly beyond its resources and would have needed significant participation and sacrifice by the Italians, which was unlikely.

Admiral Cunningham realized as he contemplated the challenges facing him that taming Italian naval power could only be attempted after neutralizing the vexing question of the French vessels at anchor in Alexandria. How could the British fleet embark on offensive operations against the Italians and leave behind warships which might switch sides? On 29 June Cunningham was instructed by the Admiralty to seize the French ships at Alexandria. This operation was required to go ahead on 3 July, at

The French battleship _Lorraine_, which _Warspite_ came close to firing on in Alexandria Harbour during tense negotiations between Admiral Godfroy and Admiral Cunningham in July 1940 following the fall of France. _Goodman Collection._

the same time as the Royal Navy's Gibraltar-based Force H, commanded by Vice Admiral Sir James Somerville, moved on Oran in North Africa to demand the surrender of other major units of the French Navy. The French Squadron at Alexandria – Force X – was under the command of Vice Admiral Godfroy who seemed an honourable man. He would probably have liked to carry on the fight were he not under orders to obey the terms of the Armistice to the letter. After tense discussions aboard *Warspite*, the French finally agreed to discharge oil from their warships and disarm their weapons. This agreement was secured, and held, despite great bitterness over events at Oran where Force H bombarded the French warships and killed 1,297 sailors.

A Free French Naval Force fought with distinction on the Allied side, but it did not welcome any vessels from Alexandria into its ranks until spring 1943. For Admiral Cunningham in July 1940, securing the neutralization of a potentially serious problem in the heart of his most important base allowed him to focus on the real task at hand. Now he went in search of an encounter which would allow the British to stamp their authority on the Mediterranean. Cunningham would be given the domination he needed by the breath-taking gunnery of HMS *Warspite*.

Victory With a Single Shot

The island naval fortress of Malta was a dagger held to the jugular of Italian supply convoys to North Africa. While it could not host a major battle fleet, throughout its long siege it was home to submarines, destroyers, small attack boats and bomber aircraft which did their best to wreak havoc in enemy shipping lanes. From the moment Italy entered the war, Malta was therefore subjected to intensive bombing to try and wipe it off the map, although neither Hitler nor Mussolini ever grasped the necessity of occupying the island. A major part of the Royal Navy's role during the war in the Mediterranean was ensuring convoys reached Malta with vital supplies to sustain it. But, when Cunningham took his fleet to sea after settling the French issue, he was going to meet two convoys carrying badly needed stores and personnel from Malta to Alexandria to consolidate the British naval base.

The Admiral hoped to safeguard the convoys by drawing Italian naval forces onto his fleet which was split up into three packets he hoped might look tempting to the enemy. *Warspite* was with five destroyers while the battleships *Royal Sovereign* and *Malaya* were in company with the aircraft carrier HMS *Eagle* and ten destroyers. The third group was made up of five cruisers and a destroyer.

The three task groups left Alexandria on 7 July, hoping to get early warning of any Italian moves from a picket line of British submarines strung across the central Mediterranean. At 5.15a.m. on 8 July one of these boats – HMS *Phoenix* – spotted and reported a strong Italian force which included two battleships about 200 miles east of Malta. That afternoon a reconnaissance aircraft reported two Italian capital ships, half a dozen cruisers and two dozen destroyers at sea, steering north-west about 200 miles from Benghazi. Cunningham decided he had to put his own force between the Italians and their main base at Taranto.

The British fleet was by this time under constant air attack from Italian high level

The Royal Sovereign Class battleship HMS *Royal Sovereign*, lead ship of the class of super dreadnoughts built immediately after *Warspite* and her sisters. However, they remained inferior to the Queen Elizabeth Class battleships throughout the Second World War and were almost a liability. *Royal Sovereign* struggled to keep up with the action at the Battle of Calabria in July 1940. *Goodman Collection.*

bombers. Their accuracy was poor, but the show they put on was impressive. British warships would be lost in a forest of bomb splashes and eye-witnesses thought them doomed, only to see them emerge unharmed. However, the cruiser HMS *Gloucester* was hit and her bridge destroyed. With her captain and twelve sailors killed, she also had to be steered from the aft position.

By the morning of 9 July the British naval force was concentrated to the south-west of Greece, with the enemy less than 150 miles away. It was a fine day for a battle – visibility up to twenty miles, a calm sea and above 'a sky dappled with thin cloud.'[2] The enemy force was now identified as a pair of Cavour Class battleships (with 12-inch guns) half a dozen heavy cruisers (with 8-inch guns) ten light cruisers (with 6-inch guns) and more than thirty destroyers. While Cunningham's battleships had more powerful weapons – they were all armed with 15-inchers – the *Sovereign* and *Malaya* were slow and their main guns fell short of *Warspite*'s range by 10,000 yards.

Eagle launched a strike but her aircraft only managed to find and attack a single enemy cruiser without causing any damage. At 3.08p.m. the cruiser HMS *Neptune* signalled she had the Italians in sight. Opening shots were exchanged half an hour

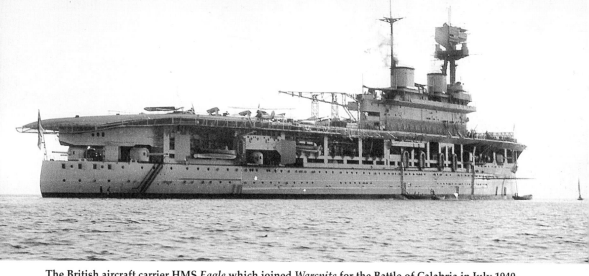

The British aircraft carrier HMS *Eagle* which joined *Warspite* for the Battle of Calabria in July 1940.
Goodman Collection.

later in an unequal duel between Italian and British cruisers.

At twenty-four knots *Warspite* was steaming as hard as she could. But, while she was eating up the miles, behind her *Malaya* and *Royal Sovereign* were making painfully slow progress and lagging ten miles behind. Even though he was badly outnumbered Cunningham felt he had no choice but to push on without his other two battleships to help his hard pressed cruiser force. Shortly before 3.30p.m. *Warspite* was able to come to the rescue, her 15-inch salvos persuading the Italian cruisers to turn tail and flee under protection of a smoke screen. There was now a lull in the action during which the *Warspite* circled to give HMS *Malaya* a chance to catch up. *Royal Sovereign* had become a lost cause. Half an hour later the Italian battleships were sighted – the fleet flagship *Guilio Cesare* and the *Conte di Cavour*, both of which opened fire. They straddled the *Warspite* without effect. Being on the Admiral's staff, Leading Telegraphist Albert Cock got a pretty good view of the action:

I was in the remote control office below the flag bridge and we had our own open

Shells from the Italian battleship *Giulio Cesare* straddle *Warspite* at the Battle of Calabria.
Sutherland Collection.

deck on the side. *The Italians had a greater range and they were putting shells wide and over us. Seeing the Italian shell spouts, I felt excitement mingled with a bit of apprehension but not fear. In fact during my war service I don't think I ever saw actual fear in anyone's face.*

High above the action was the Swordfish piloted by Petty Officer Rice. The *Warspite* was down to just one aircraft at the time, so he had his work cut out:

Our other Swordfish had been flying in support of the Australian cruiser HMAS Sydney but had failed to find the action she was involved in. Rather than bring a full bomb load back to the ship they thought they would go over and bomb the Italians at Tobruk. Unfortunately for them some RAF Blenheims had just carried out a raid so the enemy was waiting for them. They got shot down and ended up prisoners of war for five years. That left just my Swordfish. They used us for spotting the fall of Warspite's 15-inch shots at Calabria. The Italians could do thirty knots but Warspite could only do twenty-four knots, so it was quite a chase. When the Warspite fired back at the Italians, initially her shells were falling short, so we were telling them to correct. They were adjusting by 200 yards but should have done so by 600, so they only got one hit. The Italians did fire on us with their AA but failed to hit my aircraft. Was I scared? No. I was only twenty-four and well trained in how to react when things turned hot.

Warspite had opened fire on the leading vessel – the *Guilio Cesare* – from a distance of 26,000 yards and even though it was only a single hit amidships, it won the battle. Admiral Cunningham later wrote:

The Warspite's shooting was consistently good. I had been watching the great splashes of our 15-inch salvos straddling the target when, at 4.00p.m. I saw the great orange-coloured flash of a heavy explosion at the base of the enemy flagship's funnels. It was followed by an upheaval of smoke, and I knew that she had been heavily hit at the prodigious range of thirteen miles.[3]

According to Leading Telegraphist Cock a ripple of jubilation went through the *Warspite*: 'The whole ship knew within seconds that we had struck the Italian and we were pretty pleased with our shooting.'

In addition to putting some of the *Cesare's* boilers out of action, and halving her

A near miss by Italian high-level bombers as they attempt to hit the *Warspite* and *Eagle* during the Battle of Calabria. *Sutherland Collection.*

A stick of Italian bombs nearly hits HMS *Warspite* at Calabria. *Sutherland Collection.*

speed, the *Warspite's* hit caused over 100 casualties. *Malaya* fired, but her shells fell short while the *Royal Sovereign* was never in the frame to take part. *Warspite's* single devastating hit caused the Italian flagship to turn around and retreat with haste, followed by the rest of the fleet making smoke furiously. Over the next two hours, *Warspite's* Swordfish spotter plane kept above the Italian fleet, reporting back on its disarray as it fled. There was a brief mêlée between British cruisers and destroyers and Italian warships forming a rearguard. *Warspite* and *Malaya* took part in this action but scored no hits – *Warspite's* 6-inch guns fired occasionally on Italian destroyers dodging in and out of the smoke. The main purpose of the Italian withdrawal into smoke was to draw the British over some submarines and close enough to the mainland for their air force to attack. But, when the Italian planes did turn up, the first thing they did was to bomb their own warships. Finally turning their attention to the British, the Italian bombers inflicted a three-hour bombardment but their bombs failed to find the mark. The *Warspite* and *Eagle* were the most obvious targets and received the majority of the attention.

HMS *Eagle* had only two Gladiator fighters to send up but these two quaint looking biplanes managed a good score, shooting down a dozen Italian bombers.

Skirting around the smoke screen, for fear of nasty surprises lurking in it (or under it), by 5.00p.m. *Warspite* and the rest of the British ships were in sight of the Calabrian coastline. They found the Italians had vanished through the Straits of Messina.

Hoping for more action, the British remained around Malta for a day before trailing some convoys back to Alexandria which the fleet duly reached on 13 July. Under intense air attack from high level Italian air force bombers for most of the way, hundreds of bombs fell around the *Warspite* but, incredibly, no hits were scored.

While the Battle of Calabria was seen by many as a frustrating encounter – there wasn't much glory in putting a whole enemy battle fleet to flight with a single shell – it set the tone of the entire naval war between the British and Italians. Cunningham said:

> The one 15-inch hit they sustained from the Warspite *had a moral effect quite out of proportion to the damage. Never again did they willingly face up to the fire of British battleships...* .[4]

But, even though he felt contempt for the Italian lack of fighting spirit, *Warspite's* Signalman Donald Auffret, believed Calabria could so easily have been a defeat for the British.

> In hindsight I think now that had they not disengaged they would probably have made mincemeat of us. They had the firepower there, the number of ships and Warspite *couldn't possibly have survived.*

Inspiring the Japanese

When the Imperial Japanese Navy was looking for a means to deal a devastating blow against the American fleet at Pearl Harbor it would seize upon Admiral Cunningham's next master stroke for inspiration.

For, more than a year before Japan unleashed the 7 December 1941 surprise attack on Hawaii, British naval aviators demonstrated the potency of air-launched torpedoes against battleships trapped in harbour.

The Japanese – never slow to seize upon a good idea and turn it into something brilliant – looked on in admiration at what the Royal Navy did with obsolete Swordfish biplanes and decided they could do better.

The event which would influence the Japanese so much was born out of frustration. After Calabria the Italian fleet resolutely refused to come out. This was a pity, as the Mediterranean Fleet started to receive badly needed reinforcements. Towards the end of July, Cunningham was informed he would be receiving HMS *Illustrious*, a brand new carrier with an armoured flight-deck, *Warspite*'s modernized sister ship HMS *Valiant*, equipped with some revolutionary new kit for detecting the enemy, plus the anti-aircraft cruisers HMS *Calcutta* and HMS *Coventry*. A passenger on the *Valiant* ordered out to the Mediterranean to help Admiral Cunningham hit back at enemy air attacks was Lieutenant Commander Lamb from the anti-aircraft range in Portsmouth:

> *The Med Command felt they needed someone experienced in AA gunnery to improve the performance of the fleet and so I was appointed as Fleet AA Officer. Taking passage to my new appointment in HMS Valiant, I discovered she was one of the first ships to have been fitted with radar, or RDF as it was called in those days. It was a good opportunity to learn about something which was a closely guarded secret.*

Even though the Italian fleet might have made itself scarce, the enemy's aviators showed no sign of letting up, frequently using the cover of night to attack Alexandria. This meant no rest for Royal Navy anti-aircraft gunners even in port, as they had to blast off saturation barrages to keep the Italians at bay. The techniques involved in this were instituted by the new Fleet AA Officer as one of his first jobs:

> *One of things I did on arriving was establish an AA firing-range at Alexandria for ships of the fleet. I also found myself acting for Admiral Cunningham on an inter-service committee concerned with the AA defence of Alex. I discovered there was a difference in outlook between how the RAF wanted to operate and how the Navy thought it should do the job. The RAF had night fighters to try and drive off the attacks but the Royal Navy thought perhaps the fleet should just look after itself. The advent of radar in the Med Fleet did enable us to use the deterrent effect of mass gunfire by giving more accuracy to defence by blind barrage which I duly instituted. This meant every warship would have a responsibility for firing in a particular direction. The ship with the radar would tell them when they should start their blind barrages judging by how far away the target aircraft was at that particular moment. The idea was to fill the air with a mass of gunfire that would deter the Italians from pressing home their attacks effectively. It was most inefficient if you compare the number of aircraft shot down with the ammunition expended, but survival was the important thing. The number of bombs dropped in Alex Harbour was very few and this is not criticizing the bravery of the Italian airmen – our blind barrages were formidable and I believe a very effective deterrent.*

Moonlit nights were a favourite for air raids but, in August 1940, there was a period where there was no moon. Both *Warspite* and *Malaya* were therefore put into the floating dry dock for essential maintenance. *Warspite* had her peacetime light grey

A shot taken from HMS *Warspite* of HMS *Malaya* (nearest), HMS *Ramilles* and the cruiser HMS *Kent* during the August 1940 bombardment of Bardia. *Goodman Collection.*

painted over with a camouflage pattern.

In mid-August the Mediterranean Fleet was used to support the British Army's drive into Italian North Africa by bombarding Bardia, with *Warspite* employing her 15-inch and 6-inch guns against Italian fortifications. Lieutenant Commander Lamb found *Warspite* most 'unsatisfactory' because he was too junior on the Admiral's staff to get a cabin while in port and therefore had to live on another vessel. When he went to sea for operations he lived a refugee life on the flagship:

> I used to embark *Warspite* with a suitcase when the ship went to sea. I had a little nook and corner to live in and used someone else's cabin to wash. I could have slung my hammock but I preferred to lay it out on the deck.

His job meant he came into close contact with Admiral Cunningham, especially during air attacks.

> My detailed function was to watch the high level bombers and tell Admiral Cunningham how the bombs were falling near us so he didn't have to lie down and take shelter on the deck until the last possible moment.

By the end of September 1940 the Mediterranean Fleet had devolved into a highly capable A team – *Warspite*, *Valiant* and *Illustrious* – and a B team composed of the less effective *Malaya*, *Ramillies* and *Eagle*. That month Cunningham used his top team to escort 2,000 troops, embarked aboard the cruisers *Liverpool* and *Gloucester*, to Malta as reinforcements. During this operation a reconnaissance aircraft from *Illustrious* spotted four Italian battleships at sea but, even though he was desperate for a crack at the enemy, Cunningham decided not to seek battle. Delivery of the troops safely was his top priority.

At the end of September *Warspite* welcomed another of her sisters, the unmodernized HMS *Barham*, together with some badly needed additional destroyers.

With this strength in numbers and enough quality warships to make up for the elderly liabilities, Cunningham was in a better position than ever to seek a clash with the Italians. But the enemy still declined to emerge and give him satisfaction.

The idea of a torpedo bomber attack on the main Italian base at Taranto was not a new one – it had been studied by planners in the Mediterranean Fleet since the mid-1930s. In October 1940, Admiral Cunningham decided it was time to put it into action. Commander Manley Power, Cunningham's chief war planner, was responsible for fixing the fine detail of the raid, basing it all on a 'scheme in my head and a few dirty bits of paper in my pocket.'[5] With key staff crammed into Cunningham's cabin aboard *Warspite*, perched wherever they could find space, the plan's pros and cons were outlined and discussed. A reconnaissance flight by a Malta-based aircraft produced firm evidence the Italian main battle fleet was indeed skulking at Taranto and an auspicious date was set aside for the strike – 21 October (Trafalgar Day).

However, an accidental fire aboard HMS *Illustrious* forced a postponement to 11 November, which was chosen because a three quarter moon would give enough light to see the targets. Both *Eagle* and *Illustrious* were supposed to take part but the former had to pull out due to mechanical problems and some of her Swordfish were put on the latter. On 6 November, *Warspite*, in company with *Illustrious*, *Valiant*, *Malaya*, *Ramillies* and escort destroyers, sailed out of Alexandria. They were soon being harassed by the usual Italian air attacks which Fairey Fulmar fighters from *Illustrious* intercepted.

Aboard HMS *Warspite*, Manley Power looked on with detached fascination as the Italian aircraft 'shining like silver in the sky' tried in vain to hit his ship. Even after the air attacks died away the Italians continued to sniff around *Illustrious* which regularly reported to *Warspite* 'shadower spotted' followed by 'shadower shot down'.[6] A reconnaissance flight on 11 November confirmed all six Italian battleships – *Duilio*, *Cesare*, *Littorio*, *Vittorio Veneto*, *Doria* and the *Cavour* – were safely tucked up in Taranto. Cunningham remarked with some relish: 'So all the pheasants had gone home to roost.'[7] *Warspite* and the main fleet stayed in a covering position to the south, while HMS *Illustrious*, with four cruisers and protective destroyers, steamed to a flying off position near Cephalonia. At 8.40p.m. twelve Swordfish aircraft took off followed sixty minutes later by another flight of nine. Meanwhile a diversionary bombardment of the Straits of Otranto was carried out by a separate cruiser force. In *Warspite* Manley Power thought it a perfect evening for a raid: 'A beautiful calm night, bright moon, as still as it could be... No sound except the wash of the bow wave...'

The silence was broken only by,

> *...orders as the guns train to new lookout bearing to keep the crews alive. All night wondering how things are going with the forces we've detached. We drop off for a bit of sleep in turns in various corners. Then the morning. The carrier turns up...two aircraft missing. Aircraft report three enemy battleships torpedoed and some small craft damaged seen burning.*[8]

Cunningham sent his congratulations to *Illustrious* by signal flag: 'Manoeuvre well executed. Resume station previously ordered.'

The *Littorio* had been hit with three torpedoes and sank at her moorings, as had the

Conte di Cavour after one torpedo strike. The *Duilio* received one torpedo hit and went down by her bows. The Swordfish also managed to inflict damage on a cruiser and two destroyers. *Littorio* and *Duilio* were refloated six months later and repaired but the *Cavour* was taken out of the war for good. Cunningham later observed that the Fleet Air Arm had proved itself beyond a doubt:

> *...twenty aircraft had inflicted more damage upon the Italian fleet than was inflicted upon the German High Sea Fleet in the daylight action at the Battle of Jutland.*[9]

Aside from the three battleships put out of action, the rest of the Italian fleet moved to Naples, further away from danger but less able to threaten British convoy routes. As a result of the decreased threat, *Malaya* and *Ramillies* sailed for home waters where they were used to help escort Atlantic convoys.

Even with the success at Taranto this was still Britain's darkest hour, standing alone against fascism and facing seemingly insuperable odds. Luckily more and more people were answering the call to colours without waiting for call-up papers, including twenty-year-old Charles 'Jock' Pearson who would eventually end up serving in the *Warspite*.

> *I had always wanted to be in the Navy. My own dad was a Petty Officer stoker during the First World War and my uncle Percy was a Petty Officer stoker on the* Warspite *prior to the 1934 refit. I had tried to join when I was seventeen but my father wouldn't sign the paperwork. Perhaps he didn't want me going through what he did in the First World War. I had a job with an engineering firm in Epsom. One day, after Dunkirk and Norway and all that, I decided it was time I joined the Navy. I slung my job in and they said 'You can't you're in a Reserved Occupation'. I ignored them and went up to Croydon, the nearest place you could join up. A week later I got my papers and joining instructions. So I got on the train down to Portsmouth, off at the Harbour Station and on the ferry over to Gosport. After a short bus ride I arrived at the basic training place at Collingwood. A load of Chief Petty Officers were there to greet everybody. This old Chief comes up to me and says: 'Wait here.' He gets a crowd of us together and takes us over to the mess hall and says: 'Sit down there'.*

> *Next he says to us: 'Would you like something to eat?' 'Sure,' I says. So this Chief Petty Officer brings dinner over to me. So we have dinner and then he takes us down to our hut. Inside are the usual bunks. He says: 'Alright lads, I'll see you in the morning.' And we say goodnight to him and turn to each other commenting: 'What a nice old boy, really looked after us.Suddenly it is 5.00a.m. the next morning and all the bugles and trumpets are going. Then our hut door bangs open. In springs our Chief Petty Officer from the night before, all guts and garters shouting: 'Get up! Get up! Get dressed!' We are in a state of shock – Can this be the same gentle old Chief Petty Officer?*

> *Somewhat different in demeanour, he troops us out into the freezing morning and marches us off to various places. We are marched here there and everywhere and he's taking no nonsense as we get processed into His Majesty's Royal Navy.*

Screaming Death

On 28 October 1940, Italy had declared war on Greece and invaded via Albania, a campaign which brought no glory to Mussolini's army which soon found itself beset

The view from HMS *Warspite* as HMS *Illustrious* disappears behind a forest of bomb splashes.
Goodman Collection.

with problems. The widening of the war did, however, provide the British Mediterranean Fleet with a new base, at Suda Bay on the island of Crete, which became a useful staging post.

To help the Greeks out, *Warspite* and *Valiant* bombarded Valona, the main Italian supply port in Albania in mid-December. This venture into the Adriatic was made possible by the elimination of the enemy battleships during the Taranto raid. *Warspite* then went down to Malta for the first time in a year and received a rousing welcome from the people of the battered island. At this time, although Malta was under constant air attack, the enemy's impact on convoys was negligible. There was a regular run once a month, from either Gibraltar or Alexandria and, with the armoured carrier *Illustrious* on the scene carrying radar-directed Fulmar fighters, the Italians were having little luck.

'By the end of 1940, it was almost the expected thing for convoys to run without any interruption whatsoever,' said Lieutenant Commander Lamb. But the easy time was coming to an end, as the Germans were about to make their debut in the Mediterranean.

During convoy escort duty in mid-January the Mediterranean Fleet was introduced to the rather more aggressive bombing style of the Luftwaffe. Flying from airfields in Sicily on 10 January, Stukas plunged eagerly on *Warspite*, *Valiant*, *Illustrious* and their escorts. Meanwhile Italian high-level bombers also made a contribution. From his position in *Warspite*'s starboard 6-inch battery Marine Arthur Jones got a good view of attacks on *Illustrious*.

> *They gave her a real pasting. I could see it though the sighting ports on my gun. The Stukas made this terrible shriek and came in really low, unlike the Italians.*

Hit by six 1,000lb bombs, leaving her badly on fire, with heavy casualties and her aircraft lifts out of action, *Illustrious* was surely done for. But somehow she managed to make seventeen knots and head for Malta. *Warspite* and the rest of the fleet stayed close to her, trying to distract the enemy, but the Luftwaffe knew the value of bagging a brand new aircraft carrier. Still ablaze in the late afternoon, *Illustrious* was subjected to a further Stuka onslaught.

Throughout all this, the *Warspite's* luck held. She was struck only once – a glancing blow on a stern anchor by a 1,000lb bomb which ricocheted right over the ship, watched, mouths hanging open, by sailors on the

Near miss during Malta convoy. *K. Smith Collection.*

battleship's bridge. Other ships were not so lucky – the cruiser *Southampton* was lost while the *Gloucester* suffered another hit. *Illustrious* was attacked repeatedly in dock at Malta but, by the end of January, she had been repaired well enough to sail to Alexandria and from there went to America for more work. *Warspite* ended January with a collision involving the destroyer *Greyhound* which luckily caused only slight damage to the battleship. *Greyhound* survived to be sunk off Crete four months later.

The depredations of the German and Italian bombers might not have inflicted heavy ship losses as yet, but it was beginning to get on everybody's nerves. Marine Arthur Jones recalled:

> *There were plenty of near misses and somehow we were lucky, but it was very wearing. You looked at what happened to the* Illustrious *and wondered how long it might be until it happened to you. Everybody became a bit bomb happy. In fact we were getting so ragged on* Warspite *it became a punishable offence to slam a hatch because it jarred the nerves so much.*

Slaughter at Matapan

Luck is a most precious commodity in any game of chance. War is no exception.

In the Mediterranean during the Second World War Admiral Cunningham's winning streak lasted for a long time – from July 1940 to March 1941 – and, while he was aboard *Warspite*, fortune seemed to especially favour her. During a fleet action, countless air attacks, coastal bombardments and the raid on Taranto, Cunningham's flagship had escaped serious injury but the *Warspite's* luck would soon run out and she would suffer great harm. But, before disaster struck, she enjoyed a moment of glory which was Cunningham's most crushing victory at sea.

Having bitten off more than they could chew in Greece and Yugoslavia, the Italians had to be extracted from the mire by the Germans. On the brink of launching its massive assault on the Soviet Union, in early April 1941 Hitler's army found itself required to conquer the Balkans to secure its flanks. It set about the task with its usual

117

brutal efficiency, delivering another stunning Blitzkrieg blow to the Allies. To help pave the way for this lightning move towards the shores of the Mediterranean, German high command put pressure on the Italian Navy to cut supply routes between Egypt and Greece. A sortie towards Crete by the battleship *Vittorio Veneto*, together with eight cruisers and more than a dozen destroyers, was therefore planned for late March. German air cover was promised to the Italians who were worried about finding themselves at the mercy of British carrier-borne torpedo bombers.

On 27 March a Sunderland flying boat from Malta spotted three Italian cruisers and a destroyer to the south-east of Sicily, headed towards Crete. Aboard *Warspite* in Alexandria, Cunningham told his staff officers he felt certain the cruisers were part of a screening force for Italian major units. He decided the fleet should go to sea after dark and aim to place itself between Crete and the enemy. Hopefully, under cover of the night, its departure would not be noticed and by daylight the following day the Italian reconnaissance aircraft would discover the truth too late to save their fleet from being brought to action. But, even though his gut instinct told him he was on to a winner, Cunningham still had his doubts:

> ...I bet Commander Power, the Staff Officer, Operations, the sum of ten shillings that we should see nothing of the enemy.[10]

One person the British were particularly keen to deceive was the Japanese consul in Alexandria who regularly reported British fleet movements to the Germans and Italians. Cunningham treated the Japanese diplomat's rather obvious spying activities seriously enough to play a charade. The Admiral went ashore from *Warspite* with an overnight bag and his golf kit as if he had no intention of leading the fleet to sea that evening.

> This little plot worked as intended. Retrieving my suit-case, I returned to the Warspite *after dark and the fleet sailed at 7.00p.m. What the Japanese consul thought and did when he saw the empty harbour next morning was no affair of mine.*[11]

Warspite led out *Valiant* and *Barham*, together with HMS *Formidable* which had replaced *Illustrious*, and nine destroyers in escort. Unfortunately, as *Warspite* left she managed to clog up her condensers, reducing her speed to twenty knots.

Meanwhile four 6-inch gun cruisers were in the Aegean where they could give advance warning of enemy moves. Just before 7.30a.m. the following morning, 28 March, they spotted enemy cruisers. Cunningham took this to be confirmation the Italian fleet was at sea. He put his hand in his pocket for Commander Power and handed over the ten shillings. In the meantime, the enemy vessels had been recognized as heavy cruisers with 8-inch guns. Despite being out-gunned Cunningham hoped his cruisers could lure them within range of his battleships. At 8.12a.m. the Italians opened fire from a range of thirteen miles, concentrating on HMS *Gloucester* which zig-zagged vigorously to avoid being hit. The enemy warships soon caught up and, just over a quarter of an hour later, were only a mile astern of her. *Gloucester* opened up with her 6-inch guns, scoring no hits, but the Italians withdrew so the three British ships, *Gloucester*, *Ajax* and *Orion*, and one Australian, *Perth*, turned around and gave chase.

Around 11.00a.m. they spotted an Italian battleship – it was the *Vittorio Veneto*,

***Warspite*'s target at the Battle of Matapan: The Italian battleship *Vittorio Veneto*.** *M. Welsford Collection.*

armed with nine 15-inch guns, and just sixteen miles to the north. She opened fire, quickly straddling the British cruisers, which turned away making smoke. In response, HMS *Valiant* was ordered ahead at full speed to assist while *Warspite* was still grappling with her condenser problem. Cunningham also ordered the *Formidable* to launch a wave of Albacore torpedo bombers. He did this against his instincts – his preferred tactic was to hold the air attack back until his main battle fleet was close enough to take full advantage of any slowing down caused by torpedo hits. 'But in this emergency my hand was forced.'[12] True enough, the *Formidable*'s torpedo bombers saved the cruisers but 'had the unfortunate effect of causing the enemy battleship to turn away and make off while some eighty miles distant.'[13] Now the chase was really on, to run the *Vittorio Veneto* down before she could reach home waters.

Cunningham was increasingly annoyed by *Warspite*'s reduced speed. The ship's engineering officer was sick ashore and so he ordered the Fleet Engineering Officer on his staff to go and help the *Warspite*'s Deputy Marine Engineering Officer sort out the problem.

> *He went below, and in a short time I was gratified to see that the* Valiant, *which had been coming up at full speed from astern, was no longer gaining. We pressed on together.'*[14]

But Cunningham now found his chase hampered by the fact that the wind was coming from the east. It meant every time HMS *Formidable* wanted to launch aircraft the fleet had to reverse course, as she needed to be sailing into the wind. This got to be so much of a handicap that about midday *Formidable* was detached to fly off. As she dropped astern of the battle fleet a sailor serving in the carrier watched the battleships steam away.

With *Warspite* in close attendance HMS *Formidable* launches Albacore torpedo bombers.
Goodman Collection.

> *The sun was now shining and accentuated the black, white and grey camouflage of the great forms of* Warspite, Barham *and* Valiant, *steaming at speed in line ahead away from us, each with a magnificent white bow wave and a glistening wake, each with eight powerful 15-inch guns trained fore and aft. The question in all our minds was whether these guns would be in action before the end of the day, firing shells which weighed approximately a ton each. Their white ensigns contrasted with the cobalt of the sky and the ultramarine of the sea.*[15]

The Albacores returned to *Formidable* claiming a hit on the *Vittorio Veneto* and this was followed by more sightings of enemy forces – all of them moving west as quickly as possible. Cunningham ordered in a second air strike hoping to slow up the fleeing Italian battleship. The *Warspite* and *Valiant* were now being held back by the *Barham* which, with her malfunctioning boilers, was struggling to keep pace. Time was also being lost in waiting for *Formidable* to catch up. Luckily the wind dropped and changed direction, meaning she could operate aircraft without needing to turn away, so the battleships waited for her because it was better to have her with the fleet if at all possible. She had already been subjected to air attack during her detachment and would be vulnerable to more on her own.

The second strike force of Albacores returned to the carrier claiming three hits on

Pilot Petty Officer Frederick 'Ben' Rice needed a steady hand when his Swordfish landed and was picked up on the move by *Warspite* during the Battle of Matapan.
Specially commissioned painting by Dennis C. Andrews.

the Italian battleship. In fact during both attacks on the *Vittorio Veneto*, one hit had been caused by the only British aircraft to be shot down during the battle. The torpedo which caused the harm was dropped from 1,000 yards ahead, just as the Italian battleship turned slowly to starboard, presenting her stern. It hit fifteen feet below the waterline just above a propeller. Over a thousand tons of water gushed into the *Vittorio Veneto* which stopped down by the stern. After some frantic work, the Italian flagship got underway again but with her speed reduced to fifteen knots.

By now one of *Warspite*'s Swordfish, carrying Fleet Observer Lieutenant Commander Bolt, had been aloft for nearly five hours. Its pilot was 'Ben' Rice and, after scouting in vain, he reported to *Warspite* that he only had fifteen minutes of fuel left. This was not enough to reach Suda Bay where the ship's other aircraft had already gone. The Swordfish therefore had to be recovered by *Warspite* on the move – a challenging operation accomplished faultlessly. The *Warspite* lost only one mile and never slowed below 18 knots.

The British cruisers were urged to maintain close visual contact and, to clarify the picture, *Warspite*'s Swordfish was catapulted again at 5.45p.m. Before the aircraft went, Manley Power briefed Lieutenant Commander Bolt on what was needed from this mission – the location of the *Vittorio Veneto* was known, but what was her speed and the disposition of her escorts? The Swordfish arrived over the *Vittorio Veneto* at 6.20p.m. and reported the Italian battleship was forty-five miles away from *Warspite*, doing an estimated fifteen knots heading west. The enemy force was composed of half a dozen cruisers and eleven destroyers drawn tightly around the limping battleship.

The Swordfish stayed with the Italian fleet until sunset, when Petty Officer Rice watched another wave of Albacores going in for the attack provoking an immense amount of flak. The Italian ships also made smoke and tried to dazzle British pilots with searchlights. Petty Officer Rice recalled:

> We had spotted the Italian fleet from about 5,000 feet up. They didn't even bother opening fire at us. We made our report then Formidable launched the Albacores to carry out an attack. It was like watching 5 November.

With fuel getting low again, the Swordfish called it a day at 8.00p.m.

> An Albacore took up aerial tracing duties and, as there was no chance of us being picked up by Warspite, we decided to head for Crete. It was dark when we arrived and we dropped our own flares to make a path for landing. I had landed at Suda Bay three or four times previously so I knew what I was doing. We landed and went to the boom. They asked us what vessel we were and we said a floatplane. After shining a big light on us to check us out they let us in. We refuelled and then flew back to Alex.

Cunningham now had to decide if he should work his way carefully to the north-west, to catch the *Vittorio Veneto* the following day, or race after her into the night.

> Some of my staff argued that it would be unwise to charge blindly after the retreating enemy with our three heavy ships, and the Formidable also on our hands, to run the risk of ships being crippled, and to find ourselves within easy range of enemy dive bombers at daylight. I paid respectful attention to this opinion and as the discussion happened to coincide with my time for dinner, I told them I would have my evening

As the sun sets, *Formidable*, in close company with *Warspite* again launches another wave of Albacores against the *Vittorio Veneto*. K. Smith Collection

meal and would see how I felt afterwards.[16]

According to a staff officer who was present at the pre-dinner discussion with the Admiral he was rather more caustic in his assessment of the advice he was being given than he later let on. The Admiral thought his staff lacked guts. Rather than paying 'respectful attention' to their opinions he actually told them:

> *'You're a pack of yellow-livered skunks. I'll go and have my supper now and see after supper if my morale isn't higher than yours.'*[17]

Either way, when the Admiral came back from dinner he ordered an eight-strong destroyer striking force off after the enemy and decided on a 'steady pursuit' for the rest of the fleet. The *Vittorio Veneto* was now a mere thirty-three miles away and still only doing fifteen knots.

Meanwhile the Royal Navy cruisers had tried, and failed, to make contact. But at 9.11p.m. *Warspite* received a signal from them saying a ship had been spotted dead in the water. A mystery vessel was soon picked up by radar six miles away on *Warspite*'s port bow. Lieutenant Commander Lamb didn't have much to do during the pursuit but was fascinated how the *Warspite*'s Gunnery Officer had swiftly realized the benefits of new technology.

> *It was very interesting to see that he had established telephone communication between the air defence radar and the gunnery control system of the ship. This was the first occasion on which radar had been used to establish the range for the gunnery system.*

Admiral Cunningham hoped he would soon be able to bag himself an Italian battleship.

> *Our hopes ran high. This might be the* Vittorio Veneto. *The course of the battle-fleet*

122

*was altered forty degrees to port together to close. We were already at action stations
with our main armament ready. Our guns were trained on the correct bearing.*[18]

In that singularly aggressive turn of the battle fleet towards the enemy Cunningham
retrieved the reputation of the Royal Navy, so badly tarnished by Jutland. In May
1916 the Grand Fleet had been largely incapable of night fighting and, when there
looked to be an unknown risk, turned away from the enemy.

At 10.25p.m. Cunningham's Chief of Staff, Commodore Edelsten, was searching
the horizon through binoculars on the starboard bow and reported two large ships
and a smaller vessel crossing the path of the fleet from starboard to port. The British
battleships now ignored the mystery vessel and turned into line ahead. The Italian
warships straying into the killing zone were two Zara Class heavy cruisers, the *Fiume*
and *Zara* (10,000 tons displacement and carrying 8-inch guns) together with a
destroyer escort. They had been sent back to assist another Zara Class ship – the *Pola*
– which had been stopped dead in the water after being hit by a British airborne
torpedo earlier in the day. The Italian admiral aboard the *Vittorio Veneto* wrongly
believed the British to be ninety miles astern of him, therefore failed to appreciate the
risk involved in detaching the Zaras.

The Italians met their deaths not only completely unaware of how near the British
actually were, but also blind thanks to a lack of radar. They were also lacking the
skills, to fight at night. The British, on the other hand, had the skills – *Warspite* in
particular being an expert at night fighting. The range between the British battle fleet
and the Italians got shorter and shorter and, in the bridge wireless office, Signalman
Donald Auffret and the other ratings were getting tenser and tenser.

> *...we were receiving the radar contacts and I can remember it got down to two-and-
> a-half miles range, almost abeam and still Cunningham didn't open fire and everybody
> was saying 'For God's sake why doesn't he open fire?'*

The Admiral moved to the upper bridge, from where the Commanding Officer of the
Warspite skippered his ship, to get a better view of the slaughter his vessels were
about to inflict.

> *I shall never forget the next few minutes. In the dead silence, a silence that could
> almost be felt, one heard only the voices of the gun control personnel putting the guns
> on to the new target. One heard the orders repeated in the director tower behind and
> above the bridge. Looking forward, one saw the turrets swing and steady when the 15-
> inch guns pointed at the enemy cruisers. Never in the whole of my life have I
> experienced a more thrilling moment than when I heard a calm voice from the director
> tower – 'Director layer sees the target'; sure sign that the guns were ready and that his
> finger was itching on the trigger. The enemy was at a range of no more than 3,800 yards
> – point-blank.*[19]

Lieutenant Commander Lamb, looking at the Italian ships though a pair of
binoculars, caught tiny glowing dots and silhouettes of men taking the air on their
upper-decks. 'The officers were walking up and down their quarterdecks smoking
their cigars after dinner. They had no idea we were there.'

The Fleet Gunnery Officer, Commander Geoffrey Barnard, gave the order to fire.
There was a 'ting-ting-ting' of firing gongs 'then came the great orange flash and the

Caught cold: *Warspite* **opens fire at Matapan as a searchlight from the destroyer** *Greyhound* **catches the Italians.** *Specially commissioned painting by Dennis C. Andrews.*

violent shudder as the six big guns bearing were fired simultaneously.'[20] At the same time the destroyer HMS *Greyhound* highlighted an enemy cruiser with her searchlight – it was the *Fiume* (third in line) – which Admiral Cunningham saw as a 'silvery-blue shape in the darkness'. As the shells carved their path of death, silhouettes of the *Zara* and the destroyer *Alfieri* could be seen. Men were also visible running along *Fiume*'s upper deck. *Warspite*'s searchlights blazed forth, providing '...full illumination for what was a ghastly sight.'[21] Five of the *Warspite*'s six shells hit the enemy cruiser just below her upper deck – Cunningham described this unfortunate ship as being 'hopelessly shattered'.

Thirty seconds after the first broadside, the second from *Warspite* hit the *Fiume* and now she was listing heavily to starboard, a complete shambles gripped by severe fires. Up in the remote control office below the flag bridge Leading Telegraphist Albert Cock was concentrating on monitoring signals traffic around the fleet. 'To me inside the ship, it was like flashes of lightning.'

The carrier *Formidable* was third in line behind the *Warspite* and the *Valiant*, with the *Barham* astern of her. As soon as the firing started the carrier was pulled sharply out of line to avoid injury to such a valuable unit which had no business being in a gun fight. Lieutenant T. Campling, one of her Gunnery Control Officers, relates the opening salvos from *Formidable*'s perspective, and reveals the carrier chipped in with some of her 4.5-inch anti-aircraft guns:

> We saw a group of coloured flares fired from Warspite, which were in fact the night challenge signal, then, almost immediately, the battleship's searchlights were switched on to reveal to our amazement three sleek-looking light grey warships, their guns trained fore and aft. Within seconds there was an ear-splitting roar as the 15-inch guns of our battleships opened fire at almost point-blank range.
>
> The result was immediate and devastating. I vividly recall seeing a complete turret of the leading ship disappear over the side. Masses of flame soon enveloped all three ships.

124

> *Although we received the order to open fire the order was almost immediately*
> *countermanded as* Formidable *turned out of line to starboard. One salvo was in fact*
> *fired by* Formidable, *and this must have been one of the few occasions during the*
> *Second World War when an aircraft carrier used its main gunnery armament against*
> *enemy warships! As we retired from the scene severe explosions continued with white*
> *flashes and orange glow of fires lighting up the sky.*[22]

As *Formidable* pulled away, *Warspite's* starboard searchlights held her and orders to
fire the starboard 6-inch guns were issued. Luckily they were cancelled instantly.

In *Warspite's* X turret Petty Officer Charles Hunter was concentrating on ensuring
everything was working smoothly and could neither see nor hear the destruction.

> *I stood on this platform between the guns. I couldn't see outside, I had eyes only for*
> *the working chamber. My turret fired the most shells during Matapan. We fired six on*
> *the right gun and five on the left. Inside the turret during firing you just got a thud –*
> *the armour was a foot thick which acted as pretty good insulation. The turret was*
> *controlled from the bridge. We would follow a pointer – it moved, you turned your*
> *wheel and when the order came you fired.*

As a loader on a pom-pom anti-aircraft gun, Jack Worth had a grandstand view:

> *They never stood a chance. The Italians vanished, blown to bits before my eyes. You*
> *don't think about these things at the time. They become more incredible only with the*
> *passing of time when you reflect on what happened.*

Signalman Auffret looked across at the unfortunate Italians from the *Warspite's* bridge
in astonishment. 'The first in line had opened up like a sardine tin,' he said.

Directly astern of *Warspite*, the *Valiant* also utterly destroyed her target – the *Zara*.
From *Warspite*, Cunningham admired *Valiant's* gunnery prowess: 'Her rapidity of fire
astonished me. Never would I have believed it possible with these heavy guns.'
Beyond *Valiant*, the *Barham* was pounding another ship to pieces – the destroyer
Alfieri. After her second 15-inch broadside into *Fiume*, *Warspite* shifted fire to *Zara*.
Meanwhile the *Fiume* limped away into the dark and sank three quarters of an hour
later. The *Barham* joined the other two battleships in firing into *Zara* which was
rendered a blazing inferno, drifting off into the darkness to be scuttled later. In a letter
mailed to his wife after the battle, Manley Power was almost exultant. He wrote:

> *It was a wonderful sight. The destroyers ahead of us put a searchlight on them. There*
> *one of them was, a lovely graceful ship all silvery in the search light...and in thirty*
> *seconds she was a blazing wreck going off like a catherine wheel. Then we switched onto*
> *another one and shot her up the same and the other battleships did too. I think there was*
> *a third there who got clocked by the* Barham. [23]

During the action the *Fiume* was hit by two 15-inch broadsides from *Warspite* and one
from *Valiant*. *Zara* was hit by four from *Warspite*, five from *Valiant* and five from
Barham. The escort destroyers *Alfieri* and *Carducci* were also destroyed.

Just after 10.30p.m. some Italian destroyers strayed into the British searchlights,
one of them firing torpedoes, forcing the battle fleet to turn ninety degrees starboard
to comb them. The British mixed it with the enemy in a wild flurry of action, *Warspite*
firing her main and secondary guns, unfortunately straddling the destroyer HMS
Havock, but she escaped unhurt.

HMS *Formidable* in company with HMS *Warspite*, viewed from under the battleship's 15-inch guns.
Goodman Collection.

> *The rest of the night we were just paddling along waiting for daylight and listening*
> *to the destroyer's signals. They were all over the shop fighting like wasps all night.*[24]

At midnight the *Havock*, which had sunk the *Carducci* and witnessed the *Alfieri* capsizing, came across the *Pola*. The Italian cruiser's crew were in a state of complete anarchy. Many of them were drunk, waving bottles of Chianti about wildly and their officers could do nothing to control them. Over his headphones on the *Warspite*, Leading Telegraphist Albert Cock heard the Royal Navy destroyers jockeying to deliver the final blow:

> *Havock made a signal to Jervis, which was carrying the Captain in command of*
> *the destroyer squadron. It was in morse saying 'I am hanging on the stern of the Italian*
> *cruiser Pola – shall I blow his stern off with depth charges?' The reply from Jervis was*
> *rather brusque – 'get out of my way I have some fish left.'*

HMS *Jervis* took the crew of the *Pola* off and then, together with HMS *Nubian*, sank the ship with torpedoes at 4.10a.m. A signal was later sent from the *Jervis* to Cunningham in the *Warspite* with regard to the state of health of prisoners taken from the *Pola*. A list of injuries ended with the immortal words: 'One senior officer has piles.'Always quick with some cutting wit, Cunningham flashed back: 'I am not surprised.'

At dawn the next day scout planes sent up by *Formidable* could find no trace of the *Vittorio Veneto*. Deprived of the chance to finish her off, *Warspite* and the rest of the fleet sailed back through the scene of battle. According to Cunningham the scene was: 'A calm sea covered with a film of oil and strewn with boats rafts and wreckage with many floating corpses.'

British destroyers tried to pick up as many survivors as possible, rescuing 900, but, with German Ju88 torpedo bombers stalking the area, it was not a good idea to loiter too long. However, the British did send a signal to the Italians telling them where to pick up remaining survivors and a hospital ship rescued nearly 200.

Weathering air attacks on 29 March, the British fleet reached Alexandria on 30 March. A service of thanksgiving for 'The Great Victory Of Matapan' was held aboard ships of the fleet on 1 April. A specially written prayer said:

> *Almighty God hath made this day to be a Joy unto us instead of destruction,*

therefore among your commemorative feasts keep it a high day with praise and thanksgiving.[25]

The personal impact on the Italians was severe.

Manley Power wrote to his wife:

I met the Captain of the Pola *the evening we got in. He seemed a very nice chap – he had been very down in the dumps and trying to commit suicide which was unreasonably dramatic of him. But he cheered up when I was there and we discussed the battle in bad French until he went off to gaol.*

Power was amazed at British luck. 'Not one of the ships was even scratched. It really does seem extraordinary.'[26] It had indeed been a remarkable victory, achieved at minimal cost to the British; 3,000 Italian sailors had lost their lives but only two Fleet Air Arm aircrew were killed. The Italian Navy never recovered.

According to Cunningham:

...the supine and inactive attitude of the Italian fleet during our subsequent evacuations of Greece and Crete was directly attributable to the rough handling they had received at Matapan.[27]

Notes

1   Cunningham, *A Sailor's Odyssey.*
2   Ibid
3   Ibid
4   Ibid
5   Power Papers, Imperial War Museum
6   Ibid
7   Cunningham, *A Sailor's Odyssey.*
8   Power Papers, Imperial War Museum.
9   Cunningham, *A Sailor's Odyssey.*
10 Ibid
11 Ibid
12 Ibid
13 Ibid
14 Cunningham, *A Sailor's Odyssey.*
15 S.W.C. Pack, The Battle of Matapan
16 Cunningham, *A Sailor's Odyssey.*
17 S.W.C.Pack, *Cunningham The Commander.*
18 Cunningham, *A Sailor's Odyssey.*
19 Ibid
20 Ibid
21 Ibid
22 Andrew M. Ramsay, HMS *Formidable.*
23 Power Papers, Imperial War Museum.
24 Ibid
25 Taken from an Order of Service contained in the Power Papers, Imperial War Museum.
26 Power Papers, Imperial War Museum.
27 Cunningham, *A Sailor's Odyssey.*

Chapter Eight

DESPERATE HOURS

Suicide Run to Tripoli

The crushing victory over the Italians at Matapan was a rare shining moment for Britain. German military success more than made up for the lacklustre performance of the Italians. From the Arctic to the Pyrenees the Wehrmacht and Luftwaffe had, with the exception of the Battle of Britain, ultimately outclassed British forces and the Kriegsmarine was making life very difficult for the Royal Navy.

As far as the British Mediterranean Fleet was concerned the most worrying development was the arrival of the German-led Afrika Korps in Libya and the appearance of the Luftwaffe's ace flyers.

Cunningham had lost one of his carriers – HMS *Eagle* went home via the Suez Canal on 13 April – and his fleet was stretched covering supply convoys to Malta and conveying troops and supplies to Greece.

At the beginning of April 1941, Rommel's Afrika Korps steamrollered the British Army of the Nile back to the Egyptian frontier – Alexandria, the Suez Canal and Cairo itself were directly threatened. If this wasn't bad enough, the Admiralty, prompted by Prime Minister and Defence Minister Winston Churchill in one of his madder

The old battleship hulk *Centurion* was put forward as a block ship for a suicide mission against Tripoli, but when she could not reach the Mediterranean in time it was suggested to Admiral Cunningham that he should prepare to sacrifice the key striking elements of his battle fleet - *Barham*, *Warspite* and *Valiant*. *Goodman Collection.*

moments, now came up with a truly desperate idea. Admiral Cunningham viewed it as insanity of the highest order.

It was suggested HMS *Barham* should be sacrificed on a suicide mission to block the enemy's major supply terminal at Tripoli. Losing the elderly and unmodernized *Barham* as a block ship was bad enough, but the Admiralty's bright idea might also mean the suicide of *Warspite* or *Valiant*. The mission would mean sailing close to an enemy shore to carry out a bombardment and Tripoli was naturally heavily defended by both shore-based batteries of guns and airpower. Cunningham commented: '...I considered the risk to the ships to be completely unjustified.'[1] The thought that soon all available ships would be needed to sustain, or evacuate, British and Commonwealth troops in Greece was probably foremost in his mind. Cunningham refused to use *Barham* as a block ship, but bowed to pressure for the bombardment. Only if *Warspite*, *Valiant* or *Barham*, were badly damaged – as was highly likely – would he then be prepared to send the fatally wounded ship in to block Tripoli harbour.

On 18 April the fleet left Alexandria, ostensibly on a convoy escort mission. In addition to three battleships it also included *Formidable*, the cruisers *Phoebe* and *Calcutta* plus an oiler and escorting destroyers. By the early hours of 21 April the fleet was close in shore, four destroyers with minesweeping gear leading the way. They turned onto their bombardment heading around a navigation light on the periscope of the submerged submarine HMS *Truant*. Cunningham paints an evocative picture of this moment:

> The silence was only broken by the rippling sound of our bow waves, the wheeze of
> air pumps, and the muffled twitter of a boatswain's pipe on the Warspite's mess deck.[2]

As they approached, an air raid by Wellington bombers from Malta marked Tripoli with fire and aircraft from *Formidable* showered the port in illumination flares at 5.00a.m. Joining the other aircraft aloft over the port was *Warspite*'s Swordfish spotting the fleet's fall of shot.

The gunners on the battleships found it difficult to make out targets clearly for not only was light bad, but, once the firing started, the smoke, dust and debris obscured Tripoli rather well. Enemy anti-aircraft fire laced the sky but shore batteries were slow to respond, only waking up when the British battleships were coming back for their second bombardment run.

Despite firing hundreds of 15-inch and 6-inch shells, the Tripoli bombardment only sank one supply ship, damaged a couple of others and crippled a small warship. The port facilities easily survived the bombardment and within two days were running again. The British fleet managed to avoid any damage on the way back from this dubious mission. Despite Cunningham's fears, aside from a trio of marauding Ju88s set upon by *Formidable*'s Fulmars, there were no air attacks. Cunningham knew the impact of his bombardment would be limited – he had been a destroyer commander in the Dardanelles during the First World War where he had seen far more intensive shelling of shore positions fail.

The Admiral believed an intensive bombing campaign by the RAF, similar to the raids inflicted at that time on Germany's Baltic ports, would have been more successful. But very few air assets were being sent to the Mediterranean and lack of fighter aircraft overhead would soon leave the Royal Navy at the mercy of Germany's dive bombers off Greece and Crete.

Catastrophe off Crete

Now came Britain's darkest hour in the Mediterranean and the Royal Navy's most severe test. The power of aircraft had already been amply demonstrated by the British in the waters of Norway and against the Italians. The Germans, whose flying machines were more capable than the Royal Navy's Albacores and Swordfish or the Italian bombers, would be given almost a free hand against Cunningham's fleet. The Luftwaffe aviators who would inflict so much pain on the British, belonged to Fliegerkorps X and VIII, with 228 bombers, 205 dive-bombers and 233 single-engined and twin-engined fighters plus fifty recce aircraft.

It took a month for the Germans to occupy the whole of Greece and now they had the island of Crete in their sights. It would make an excellent jumping off point for air operations against Egypt as Rommel's forces smashed their way to victory on land. Having taken vital elements of the Army of the Nile across to Greece, sapping its strength as the Afrika Korps made its dynamic thrust for Suez, the Royal Navy now had to bring the bulk of those 51,000 troops back to avoid their capture. The Mediterranean Fleet also transported 16,000 British, Australian and New Zealand troops to Crete as its garrison.

The Germans planned their move on the island for 20 May via a massive airborne assault. An attempt to mount an amphibious attack would also be made, although the Germans had no specialized shipping to do this, or experience in such operations. The Royal Navy's task would be to prevent the Germans mounting their seaborne invasion. The evacuation of Crete's defenders was also a possibility.

The Germans suffered dreadful casualties in their airborne assault and made little headway initially. But still they came and, once paratroopers managed to capture the airfield at Maleme, troops poured in on Junkers transporters. The plight of Crete's defenders became increasingly desperate. The Royal Navy was successful in preventing the Germans from getting any forces through by sea but was obviously unable to break the air bridge.

The injuries suffered by the Royal Navy in defending the island and its evacuation were dreadful. Between 21 May and 1 June three cruisers, *Gloucester*, *Calcutta* and *Fiji*,

HMS *Formidable* arrives at Suda Bay. *Sutherland Collection.*

HMS *Warspite* at anchor in Suda Bay. *Sutherland Collection.*

As German bombers attack, the fleet leaves Suda Bay. *Sutherland Collection.*

and six destroyers, including *Kashmir* and *Kelly* of Mountbatten's squadron, were sunk. Two battleships, *Warspite* on 22 May and *Barham* on 27 May, a carrier, HMS *Formidable*, five cruisers and five destroyers were badly damaged. Two thousand sailors were killed.

Warspite did not have her lucky admiral aboard for her traumas off Crete.

The cruiser HMS *Gloucester*. Part of *Warspite*'s protective screen at Calabria and Matapan, she was sunk in controversial circumstances not far from the battleship during the battle for Crete in May 1941. *Goodman Collection.*

HMS *Valiant* seen from *Warspite* as they cruise off Crete in May 1941. *Sutherland Collection.*

Cunningham had temporarily moved his headquarters ashore so he could more closely co-ordinate operations with other service commanders. The battleship also nearly sent Marine Arthur Jones back to Britain.

I was on draft to come home. I had packed my kit bag and was getting ready to leave when I was told, 'Sorry, it's not going to happen'. We were going back out into it.

Warspite set sail as flagship of the 1st Battle Squadron, carrying Rear Admiral H.B. Rawlings. The day she was hit, the *Warspite* was about 100 miles to the west of Crete, together with HMS *Valiant*, a cruiser and ten destroyers.

During the evening of 21-22 May *Warspite*'s sailors watched as high above Luftwaffe Ju52 transporters stacked up and curved in to Crete. An attempt was made that night by the Germans to get troops through using a flotilla of small boats but it was easily thwarted.

During daylight hours, however, the British warships were utterly at the mercy of the Luftwaffe. At shortly after 1.30p.m. on the afternoon of 22 May swarms of enemy aircraft descended on the *Warspite* from all angles, including a trio of Me109s, plunging out of the flak from a height of 800ft. Turning hard to port, *Warspite*

Jack Worth (with hat) and the rest of his pom-pom crew on HMS *Warspite* during a lull in the action off Crete. *R.J. Worth Collection*

Seconds after being hit by a German bomb off Crete, *Warspite* disappears under a towering cloud of black smoke. This photo was taken from an escorting destroyer, with the silhouette of HMS *Valiant* visible astern of *Warspite*. *Sutherland Collection.*

managed to evade two bombs but a third hit on the starboard forecastle deck and caused immense damage.

On his pom-pom anti-aircraft gun Jack Worth was perfectly placed to see the bomb hit:

I remember looking forward from my position and seeing this Me109 diving towards us, and there was this chap on our B turret firing away at it with a machine gun. Then this blob came away from beneath the German plane and hurtled my way. It was a bomb and it got bigger and bigger and bigger. But it didn't hit my position, it took out the 4-inch gun beneath me. I looked down, and really didn't think much about it in the heat of the action, other than to mentally note that what had been there before was now gone, replaced by a gigantic hole and a mess of flames and wreckage.

The semi-armour piercing 500lb bomb had blown the 4-inch gun overboard, ripped up nearly 100ft of the forecastle deck and sliced open fifty feet of the ship's side. It caused a flash fire in the starboard 6-inch battery which was soon raging out of control, while flames and thick smoke invaded a boiler room via a ventilation shaft forcing it to be abandoned. Thirty-eight men, including an officer, were killed or would die later from wounds, and another thirty-one were wounded.

Among the wounded was Marine Arthur Jones, the only survivor from his 6-inch gun crew in the starboard battery.

To be honest I cannot remember too much about what happened. I know I was sitting in the 6-inch casemate reading How Green Was

Arthur Jones, pictured here, front row right, with other Royal Marines aboard HMS *Warspite*. *A. Jones Collection.*

my Valley *when the bomb hit. All the air was blown out of my lungs... I started running and my feet were on fire... I think I wasn't killed because I wasn't where I should have been, in the gun layer's position. My mate the gun trainer was in his position and we never found his body. It might have been washed overboard, who knows. They were all my mates. There was nine of us on my gun crew. One survived. Me.*

Anti-aircraft gunner Bill Page lost his best mate:

My very best friend and shipmate Bill 'Scouse' Patterson had his action station on the 4-inch gun that was blown over the side. Both our birthdays were on that day and, before we had proceeded to our guns, we'd exchanged tots of grog and wished each other a very happy birthday. I had not been on my gun a minute when I heard a swishing noise and the bomb from the Me109 hit my pal's gun. I am not ashamed to admit that tears rolled down my cheeks when I realized what a birthday it had been for my pal Bill.

Inside X turret, Petty Officer Charles Hunter knew something serious had happened:

When we got hit it rocked the turret. That bomb killed two friends of mine. One was a Regulating Petty Officer whose job at action stations was to go around making sure all the watertight doors were closed. When the bomb exploded he was right below it.

Signalman Donald Auffret had clocked off after the forenoon watch and went down for a break in the Communications Ratings Mess. 'I think I had a cold meal and then the bugle call for air attack was sounded.' Signalman Auffret decided he'd rather be on the upper deck where he could see things coming. With the Germans using armour-piercing bombs it was no safer below decks. That reasoning was to save his life.

I went to the upper deck and I sat underneath B turret. An officer poked his head out the turret and said: 'What are you doing there?' I said: 'I'm just taking some air sir.' He said: 'Get down to your retire station'. I was actually climbing down through the armoured hatch into the mess deck when it exploded in there. I was blown out of it like a cork from a bottle, hit my head on a bulkhead and blacked out.

A quarter of a century after Commander Walwyn rushed to the scene of damage inflicted on *Warspite* during Jutland, the current Executive Officer, Commander Charles Madden, led the battleship's damage control teams into the same starboard battery. On reaching the scene, Commander Madden's most urgent task was deploying sailors to tackle the raging fire. Hoses sprang to life and jets of water criss-crossed the battery. Screaming and moaning from their injured comrades tempted the firefighting teams to put down their hoses and administer morphine. Commander Madden ordered them to keep at it and went to the aid of the wounded and dying himself. When the flames had died down and the smoke cleared, appeals for more morphine were shouted up through the massive gash to sailors on the upper decks. Visible above the charnel house hell of the 6-inch battery was a blue sky speckled with in-coming swarms of German dive-bombers determined to show *Warspite* no mercy. As the enemy planes got larger and larger there was a surreal silence because the hit had knocked out most, if not all, anti-aircraft weapons on the battleship's starboard side. But then the surviving weapons opened up and the din of battle was restored. Some of the sailors below in the starboard battery vented their feelings of outrage by shaking their fists at the German aircraft.

The wounded were taken to messdecks and laid out to receive attention from the ship's surgeon. One of them was Arthur Jones, rescued from the 6-inch battery:

> When I came around I didn't know what was happening. My face, my hands and hair were burned. I had third degree burns. I can remember the Surgeon saying, 'I'll have him next' and I suppose they lifted me onto a table for him to see whether or not I was worth saving. They gave us morphine so that must have had something to do with me not remembering.

Commander Madden went to the starboard messdeck and was greeted with another horrifying sight – the overhead armoured deck had been peeled open by the explosion and the force of the blast had created carnage. Horribly burned sailors were strewn all over the place. Many of the Communications ratings off-watch had discarded their anti-flash protection, because it was so hot, and had therefore burned to death. Luckily water pouring through from overhead put out the fire.

Signalman Auffret was just regaining consciousness:

> The next thing I remember they were opening doors and bringing the dead and the wounded through to the temporary sick bay they had made and I think that was the first time in the war I was really frightened. I only had shorts on and I felt so vulnerable.

On the day *Warspite* was hit Cunningham had signalled his fleet: 'Stick it out. Navy must not let Army down. No enemy forces must reach Crete by sea.' This message hid the Admiral's deep anger over warships being sent out to face a withering Luftwaffe onslaught naked of air protection. Removed from events by his need to stay on land, Cunningham endured mental torture.

The official Certificate of Wounds and Hurts issued to Arthur Jones after Crete, and signed by the *Warspite*'s Executive Officer, Commander Charles Madden among others. It explains the nature of his injuries and how they were sustained. *A. Jones Collection.*

Warspite's company at a hospital in Alexandria after the battle for Crete. Petty Officer Wyles is back row left, wearing PO's hat. *Wyles Collection.*

In my office ashore close to the war room where the positions of all our ships were plotted hour by hour on the large-scale chart, I came to dread every ring on the telephone, every knock on the door, and the arrival of each fresh signal. In something less than twelve hours of fighting against the unhampered Luftwaffe we had lost so much...[3]

To Petty Officer Charles Hunter and others back aboard *Warspite* fell the task of committing the dead to the deep:

As the newest and youngest Gunnery senior rate on the Warspite, *I got the job of being in charge of honour guards and burial parties. It was not a pleasant duty but we did our best to give our shipmates a proper farewell.*

Having weathered so many heavy shell hits at Jutland in the May of 1916, it was a bitter irony that one bomb from a single enemy plane had done so much damage to the *Warspite* in May 1941. But, even though she was badly hurt, the *Warspite* managed to get back to Alexandria under her own steam by 24 May. That same day, far to the north in the Atlantic, the battlecruiser

Petty Officer George Wyles was a diver serving aboard *Warspite* at Crete.
Wyles Collection.

HMS *Hood*, which started life as a fast version of the *Warspite*, and served alongside her in the Mediterranean pre-war, was blown apart by the German battleship *Bismarck*. Three of her 1,400 crew survived. When would the bad news end? As the Royal Navy recoiled under this hammer blow, *Warspite*'s wounded were being off-loaded onto trains and taken to Cairo, a journey which did nothing for their condition. Among them was Arthur Jones:

> *There were so many wounded coming back to Alexandria they didn't have room. It was baking hot in that train, simply awful. Egypt is famous for its flies but, with my hands bandaged up because of my burns, I couldn't even knock the little beggars off when they crawled all over me. The hospital we went to was in a cavalry barracks. Naturally we were all in great pain and calling out for something. They gave us Aspro.*

Back in Alexandria there were a lot of furious men aboard the *Warspite*. Signalman Auffret was one of them:

> *There was a lot of anger aboard because, while we later learned that it wasn't through any fault of our Admirals, at the time we just couldn't understand why we didn't have fighter cover. The only aircraft in the sky were German. We blamed everybody and anybody. There was also a certain amount of resentment that Cunningham wasn't aboard.*

Adding to the men's anger was a fiery speech the Admiral gave when he visited the ship after her return.

> *He told us 'You're only slightly hurt, if I want you to go out tomorrow, you'll go out tomorrow'. There was muttering but the crew would have taken the ship out. I mean there would be no question, but the* Warspite's *crew were shaken. I think we were amazed to find out that we weren't invulnerable after all.*

Newly promoted Petty Officer Telegraphist Arthur Cock had not gone to sea with the *Warspite* because he was a member of Admiral Cunningham's staff. During the battle he monitored the signals traffic coming back to Alexandria with high anxiety, not only for his shipmates on the battleship but also because he had a brother serving in one of the cruisers.

> *When the bomb hit the* Warspite *off Crete it killed quite a few people that I knew. If I had still been on the ship I might have been in that mess at the time and died with them. My brother had just been sent to HMS* Gloucester *from a destroyer. He was only on there for two or three days before she went down. In fact I'd bumped into him at the Fleet Club in Alex just before the Crete battle. It was a chance meeting. I didn't even know he was in the Med. We had a few drinks and that was the last time I saw him. Apparently my brother, as a Leading Stoker, was in a damage control party on the upper deck and was killed there. At the time I held onto a romantic idea that he might have swum to Crete and somehow survived, but land was too far from where the* Gloucester *went down. I had already lost another brother who went down with an Armed Merchant Cruiser earlier in the war. It was very hard to take, but lots of families suffered great losses during the war, and we all somehow picked ourselves up and got on with it.*

The *Warspite*'s damage was well beyond the capacity of Alexandria's floating dry dock so other arrangements would have to be made. It was decided she should go to

View from the *Warspite* as she passed down the Suez Canal in June 1941, headed for repairs in the USA. *Sutherland Collection.*

Bremerton on the west coast of the USA for repairs. Although America was still neutral, it was assisting the British by offering docking facilities secure from enemy bombers. A month after getting back from Crete – and the night before she left for the USA – *Warspite* suffered more damage when a 1,000lb bomb exploded under her during an air raid on Alexandria. It caused damage to her plating, making a docking period even more urgent. Admiral Cunningham watched his injured flagship leave Alexandria with regret:

> I was grieved at her departure, and was not to see her again in the Mediterranean for two years, and then in very different circumstances.[4]

But, as one of *Warspite*'s sailors points out, the battleship's crew were not grieved to be going:

> Evacuating the defeated Allied armies from Crete had been nothing short of a bloody shambles. So, one dark night we steamed silently from our naval base in Alexandria, heading for a shipyard. Our exact destination, as always during wartime, was a secret. Seventy of our comrades would accompany us, but only in our thoughts. They had become statistics of war. To say that we were glad to be leaving was an understatement. Rommel stood at the gates of Egypt, the Suez Canal was in peril and the Mediterranean Sea had become a very insecure part of our planet.[5]

Times were indeed still grim in the extreme. But the Royal Navy's refusal to buckle under the appalling losses it had sustained in the summer of 1941 yielded signs that the tide could be turned. For, on 27 May, the killer of the *Hood* had been hunted down and destroyed to the south of Ireland.

Player in a New Theatre of War

The battered war veteran *Warspite* took passage through the Suez Canal into the Red Sea and made her way across the Indian Ocean to Ceylon. After another brief stop at Manila in the Phillipines, she called at Pearl Harbor in Hawaii to refuel before striking out across the Pacific to Bremerton. At Pearl Harbor the gunners of HMS *Warspite*, including Petty Officer Charles Hunter, were invited over to one of the American battleships.

We had this meal with our opposite numbers on the Yank battleship and they showed us how they operated their turrets by electricity whereas ours used hydraulics.

The fact that the American battlewagons were sitting ducks was patently obvious to Petty Officer Rice, especially with his knowledge of what the Royal Navy had achieved in a similar restricted harbour at Taranto.

When I saw all these battleships packed in there I said 'blimey you can't miss!' But the Americans were not at war so you can't blame them really, whereas the Italians had no such excuse at Taranto.

Warspite left Pearl Harbor on 4 August, and six days later arrived at the Canadian naval base of Esquimalt where 300 of her crew left, bound for home. The following day she sailed south to meet a US Navy destroyer escort which led her to Bremerton where she was to be refitted at Puget Sound Naval Yard.

Rating 'Tom' Boler was on the upper deck as the *Warspite* secured alongside:

Barriers were keeping a large crowd of Americans just off the port bow. They were shouting up for souvenirs. One bright spark had a 'brain wave' and, after dashing down below, reappeared with a large paper bag full of Egyptian cigarettes in packets of fives presented to the ship by none other than King Farouk of Egypt just before we left Alex. These cigarettes were thrown over the side, the crowd made a great scramble and I saw one Yank lose his shirt for them. Of course our lads were greatly amused.

One of the first jobs undertaken after *Warspite* went into dry dock at Bremerton was taking all the ammunition off her, a process which Petty Officer Hunter helped supervise:

We took it to this huge ammunition dump somewhere out in the woods beyond the city. In a canteen there the Americans had a whip round to get some dollars for us to spend on our runs ashore. It was a really nice gesture. I thought Bremerton was an appealing place but I didn't stay long before I was told that my gun crew, and a large proportion of the rest of the complement, were going to be sent across America to Philadelphia to crew the Royal Sovereign Class battleship HMS Resolution. *She had been in dock there under repair and was now going back to Britain. We were sad to leave the* Warspite *but we were more interested in going home than staying with her.*

Another of those who also headed back to Britain at this time was Petty Officer Rice who took up an instructor's post at Lee-on-Solent near Portsmouth.

Members of *Warspite*'s crew who remained with her throughout her time at Bremerton were either housed in an ex-ferry boat moored alongside, put into barracks or lodged with American families.

Able Seaman Banks was amazed by the American hospitality:

I think every member of the Warspite's *crew had a home-from-home. Every day, at about 16.00 hours, a long queue of cars would form up outside the dockyard gates, waiting for British sailors to come ashore to invite them to their homes. There were also hundreds of applications from American families to entertain us when our leave was announced.*

Warspite's crew were treated like film stars when they visited New Westminster and Vancouver just over the border in Canada during October 1941. One young sailor found himself and his shipmates 'drowning in a sea of adulation'. He continued:

As we passed over the mighty Fraser River all hell broke loose. Motorcycle police officers, sirens screaming, surrounded our two buses. Next thing we were passing between an avenue of wildly cheering citizens. 'Look,' exclaimed my mate. 'You'd think we sank the Bismarck single-handed!' Lovely girls overwhelmed us that night in New Westminster, where a dance was held in our honour. The girls turned up in droves. It didn't take long for those sweet young ladies to realize we were a shy bunch when it came to dancing. They literally dragged us onto the floor. It was a sailor's fantasy come true – a fleeting glance at fame and we revelled in it.[6]

In the meantime, away from the dancing and hero worship, the *Warspite* was under-going substantial work. Aside from repairs to the bomb damage, her bridge was improved, more anti-aircraft weapons were installed and she also received Type 221 radar for detecting surface targets and Type 281 anti-air radar.

Royal Marine Ken Smith, one of *Warspite*'s **'new boys' in late 1941.** K. Smith Collection.

A 3.7-inch howitzer acquired in 1939 was landed and protection for the 4-inch guns improved. The 15-inch guns were replaced as they were worn out. To ensure they wouldn't all be lost in one go, if a U-boat struck mid-Atlantic, the guns were sent across to the Norfolk Naval Base aboard separate ships. Special trains then carried them to the west coast. Also shortly to be carried west across the USA aboard a special train was a new draft of sailors and Royal Marines.

View from the train carrying *Warspite*'s **new draft of sailors and marines across North America to Bremerton.** K. Smith Collection.

Royal Marine gunner Ken Smith recalled their long journey to meet the train in America started at Chatham on a very cold day in mid-November 1941.

> *Approximately 150 Royal Marines and NCOs were assembled in full marching order, dress blue uniforms and greatcoats. The order 'HMS* Warspite *detachment fall in' came. The Chatham Division Royal Marines Band was already on parade playing incidental music while the detachment was inspected by the Adjutant. By now just about everybody in barracks was watching the proceedings. The formalities over, the Parade Sergeant Major called everybody to attention, the band struck up the Regimental March and off we went to war. We arrived at the dockyard railway sidings to find about 500 Naval ratings, our future shipmates, also waiting to board the train. We knew the* Warspite *had been in the thick of the action, so we were excited about going to her. I had always been a reader of naval matters in the papers anyway and so I was especially elated about going to such a famous ship. There was no finer ship. She was the best known battlewagon in the Navy. But where was the* Warspite? *Some said on the Clyde, others that she was already back in the Med. Some said she was still in the States. The train left the dockyard sidings and worked its way around London and headed north. The first stop was Leicester, my home town. We travelled on through the night and we reached Edinburgh around breakfast time. A couple of hours later our train was running down by the banks of the Clyde and finally to Greenock and Gourock. Looking around we saw no sign of the* Warspite, *only a troopship called the* Pasteur, *our home for the next ten days. We were ferried aboard and found ourselves surrounded by thousands of RAF erks. After securing our billets we suffered the indignity of a health check by an RAF Medical Officer, complete with stick and torch. However, looking on the bright side, the smokers were introduced to Sweet Caporol cigs, the nutty fanatics to Babe Ruth and Oh Henry choc bars. We soon upped anchor during the night and by daylight we were well out into the North Channel, the Irish Coast disappearing on the port quarter.*

Marine Smith was taking it all in his stride and enjoying the fresh sea air, until the Naval Officer in Charge (NOIC), a Commander, assembled the *Warspite* contingent and gave them some rather worrying instructions. He told them:

> *This ship has 7,000 souls aboard and only life-saving capacity for 4,000 and you, as Naval personnel, are not included in that 4,000. In the event of being torpedoed you will go over the side.*

Once the troopship was out into the open Atlantic, the weather started to turn nasty. 'The *Pasteur* was by now really digging her nose and our escort HMS *Garland*, seemed to be disappearing every few minutes,' said Marine Smith.

> *After two days we lost our air escort and the two merchantmen with us detached off Iceland. The gale was really blowing by now,* Pasteur *rolling and pitching and she had what can only be described as a fair amount of 'human debris' waiting to die.*

One of *Warspite*'s new sailors was amused by the non-naval personnel aboard the liner all feeling rather green around the gills.

> *It was a pretty rough crossing. I remember seeing some RAF blokes hanging over the side on the first day out and hearing one of them say 'thank Christ we have a navy and thank Him that I am not in it.' That summed up the feelings of them all.7*

But the rough weather eased and, on the tenth day at sea, land appeared over the horizon. 'We saw lights,' recalled Marine Smith.

> *They were the first we'd seen since the war started. A couple of hours later we eased alongside at Halifax, Nova Scotia. Reporting to the docks, we boarded a train. This would be our home for the next six days. We steamed off into the night, the loco's bell ringing and hooter blasting. A few hours later we stopped, and were sealed and examined as we crossed the border into the USA at Maine. The US was still neutral you see. Next day the train crossed back into Canada at Quebec. Moving across the St Lawrence River, we stopped outside Montreal. We were introduced to the meal of the day – venison, which went down well. The train steamed on to Sudbury, Ontario, where we had an hour to stretch our legs. Next came the long pull skirting Lake Superior. Leaving the Great Lakes we headed out into endless miles of prairies with a couple of brief stops for a leg stretch. We passed through Moose Jaw, Swift Current, and arrived at Medicine Hat which is where it all happened. This place was the 'watering hole' for the RAF training schools out in Canada. You can imagine the potential when a train load of frustrated matelots and bootnecks arrived and were treated to four hours leave. It does not take much imagination to understand what went on in the local hostelries.*

During the Medicine Hat stop some of *Warspite*'s new draft 'jumped ship', much to the amusement of junior rating Reg Foster.

> *It was amazing – one chap found himself a lumberjack jacket, and slipped away. But they caught up with him later and ended up sending him out to meet us in Australia. He was standing on the quay when we arrived there a few months later.*

Reg Foster and Ken Smith were among those dutifully reporting back to the train. But, as Ken Smith explained, there was more than one aspiring lumberjack missing.

> *Three hours ten minutes later heads were being counted and, needless to say several were not there. Getting concerned the Naval Officer in Charge decided on a search party. However, the train driver decided it was time to go, blew his hooter and off we went, leaving the man in charge behind. There was a certain amount of gusto put into the cheering and waving. However somehow our Commander was waiting for us at Calgary. We thought someone was conspiring against us. We were now at the foot of the Rockies and, after cresting by the Blackfeet Tribe reservation where we saw Indians riding their ponies, we descended down to Vancouver via the Fraser River, and arrived at New Westminster sidings. We said goodbye to our Canadian train crew and the Americans took over. Two hours later we disembarked at Seattle, took a ferry over to Bremerton Naval Barracks and crashed. It had been a very long and eventful journey.*

Reg Foster had thoroughly enjoyed his marathon ride across America: 'I thought it was fantastic and said to myself "This is a good Navy".'

When the *Warspite* sailors and marines finally got their heads down in Bremerton it was 2.00a.m. on 7 December 1941 – the notorious 'Day of Infamy' that brought America into the war. While war warnings had been sent out to US bases throughout the Pacific there was no general alert. Instead military personnel went home for the weekend as usual. Ninety Japanese torpedo bombers and dive bombers fell upon the unsuspecting American battleships at Pearl Harbor, with a covering force of ninety-three fighters suppressing anti-aircraft guns and neutralizing attempts by US fighters to intervene.

The battlewagons USS *California*, USS *Oklahoma* and USS *West Virginia* shuddered to the impact of torpedoes, swiftly followed by hits on the USS *Nevada*, USS *Pennsylvania*, USS *Maryland* and USS *Tennessee*. The USS *Arizona* blew up and capsized, entombing hundreds of her crew. To inflict this immense damage cost the Japanese thirty aircraft. It was definitely the raid on Taranto writ large. However, the Imperial Japanese Navy had failed to destroy crucial oil reserves or American carriers in port – the USS *Lexington* and USS *Enterprise* were at sea and the USS *Saratoga* was under refit in a US dockyard. Fear of a follow-up Japanese attack on the west coast of the USA caused pandemonium within hours of the last bomb falling on Pearl Harbor.

Anti-aircraft gunner Jack Worth was on a run ashore in Bremerton when news of the raid exploded:

> The Americans went completely over the top. I lit this cigarette and someone yelled at me to put it out because they thought an air raid was due at any moment. I thought that was rich. Having been through it all in the Med, I naturally took exception to being told off by a twit thousands of miles from the nearest Japanese aircraft.

But, in the aftermath of Pearl anything seemed possible. Japanese carriers could be lurking off Bremerton at that precise moment. The *Warspite*, the American battleship USS *Colorado*, which was under refit, and some destroyers provided the only defence against air-attack Puget Sound Naval Yard had.

Warspite's gun crews were sent to Action Stations but didn't have any ammunition for their weapons so a truck went off at top speed to get some from a nearby bunker. After a short while it was realized no air attacks were developing, or likely to, so *Warspite*'s gunners were stood down. Next day *Warspite*'s 600 new sailors and marines came aboard and Reg Foster was very impressed with his new ship:

> When I saw her in the dockyard I thought 'they will never sink that thing'.

> Everybody who served aboard the *Warspite* thought her the finest ship in the Navy.

However, not every newcomer was seduced by the sight of the *Warspite*. One matelot decided to slip away and visit a mate.

> I went down to Modesto, California, without asking of course, and hitch-hiked there only to find the people were not in. After a few days of roaming I was picked up by the Police and, as I had no ID, thrown in jail. In order to get out I wrote to the British Consul in San Franciso. They contacted Warspite on Boxing Day and the ship kindly

The battlecruiser HMS *Repulse* pictured shortly before leaving for the Far East, where she was sunk on 10 December 1941, off Malaya while in company with the battleship HMS *Prince of Wales*.
Goodman Collection

The new King George V Class battleship HMS *Prince of Wales*, pictured in 1941 shortly before being sunk off Malaya by the Japanese. The loss of the *Prince of Wales* and the *Repulse* was a dark moment for the *Warspite*'s crew as they neared the end of their refit at Bremerton and prepared to sail into action against the Japanese. *Goodman Collection.*

> *despatched three lucky Royal Marines, including one burly Sergeant, to escort me back. After putting me on my honour not to escape I was more or less on my own, but during several train stops, I had to help the Sergeant round up the two marines. On arrival back aboard I had to crash down in the cell flat, as there was no room in the cells thanks to all the other miscreants.*[8]

While *Warspite*'s AWOL sailors received their punishment, spurred on by their country's brutal forced entry into the war, the naval yard workers worked ever harder to get the battleship ready for sea. Puget Sound's facilities might be needed at any moment for damaged American warships.

Three days after Pearl Harbor was blitzed, the brand new British battleship HMS

HMS *Warspite* under repair at Puget Sound Navy Yard. *US Naval Historical Center.*

A US Navy destroyer is battered by heavy weather off the west coast of the USA as she escorts the *Warspite* during final gunnery trials before the British battleship headed west across the Pacific to rejoin the war. *Specially commissioned painting by Dennis C. Andrews.*

Prince of Wales, and the old battlecruiser HMS *Repulse* were sunk by Japanese aircraft off Malaya.

It was a devastating demonstration of how vulnerable capital ships could be to air attack. The crew of *Warspite* were deeply shocked by the loss of the two British warships. Ken Smith remembered:

> *The American papers had these screaming headlines about it and it was all over the radio. When you are young you are gung-ho and your attitude is 'right let's go and get them and sort them out'. But the loss of these two ships sort of brought home the fact that war is not quite that simple, that it is a serious business in which the enemy is not to be taken lightly. You have to remember this was in the days of the British Empire which really meant something. But this was the end of it really. Perceptions were changed by the sinking of those two ships. The Royal Navy which protected that empire for so long was not invulnerable.*

> *It was because of the sinking of the* Repulse *and* Prince of Wales *that we suddenly had a lot more Oerlikons put on the* Warspite. *We realized how vulnerable a battleship might be to aircraft.*

Warspite recommissioned on 28 December 1941, and prepared to leave her American friends behind. On 7 January, exactly one month after the raid on Pearl Harbor, she set sail for Vancouver. The *Warspite* remained in North American waters for nearly three weeks more, carrying out sea trials under close anti-submarine escort from Canadian and American warships. Their worst enemy turned out to be dreadful weather which made life very unpleasant.

The *Warspite* next headed south alone, staying close to the coasts of California and Mexico to minimize the submarine threat, then headed south-west across the Pacific. She indulged in the usual ceremonies of 'crossing the line' on 1 February 1942, just a week before the Japanese began their assault on the British naval bastion of Singapore.

Out in the vastness of the Pacific it was easy for someone to be lost overboard as Able Seaman Banks recalled:

> *It was one of those beautiful tropical evenings that one reads about in romantic*

Traditional 'Crossing the Line' ceremony aboard HMS *Warspite*, 1 February 1942. *K. Smith Collection.*

HMS *Warspite* cruises across the vast Pacific headed for Australia, early 1942. *K. Smith Collection*

novels – the seas calm, the stars brilliant and the air warm. Most of us were on the upper deck enjoying the evening breeze when suddenly there was a shout of 'Man Overboard!' There was an immediate dash for the lifeboat, by those who happened to be nearest, to await the order 'away lifeboat crew'. Our Captain had to make a very big decision. For we were without any kind of anti-submarine screen. There was no hesitation on the Captain's part. The ship was stopped and the lifeboat duly lowered, but after a search lasting over an hour we could find no trace of the unfortunate man. We were all aware that these were shark infested waters and therefore knew there would be little hope of picking him up.

Admiral Sir James Somerville. K. Smith Collection.

Meanwhile new boy Royal Marine Ken Smith was getting used to life at sea.

The marines did all sorts of jobs. We manned Y turret of the main 15-inch armament which was unusual as normally aboard a battleship it was X turret for the Royals. We also manned the starboard 4-inch and 6-inch guns and some of the Oerlikons. I was on S3 on the starboard 6-inch guns. That was my usual action station. I was the rammer. These were 1914 pattern guns and I used a hand rammer like a big mop in a bucket. That is how antiquated the 6-inch guns were despite the Warspite getting that modernization before the war. The Valiant and the Queen Elizabeth came later and got the automatic 5.2 inch guns. Meanwhile our 6-inch guns were useless.

Loading 15-inch shells aboard HMS Warspite in the tropics. K. Smith Collection.

On 20 February, five days after the Japanese raised their flag over Singapore on taking the surrender of 70,000 British and Australian troops, Warspite reached Sydney. Local people showed commendable hospitality during Warspite's time in port, despite being justifiably angry at Britain's incompetent squandering of Australian troops at Singapore when their country was under threat of invasion. The Captain warned his crew to be on their best behaviour during shore leave.

Ken Smith recalled:

It was a grim time – Singapore had just fallen and the Japanese were rampaging everywhere. We didn't know what was happening to us and where we would go. I don't *think they had decided. The whole idea of sending a battleship without proper air cover anywhere near the Japanese was not on. It was a bit of a humiliating time really. The Aussies did feel let down but on the whole they treated us pretty well. In those days the Australian bars opened at six in the morning and closed at six at night so you can imagine people were well entertained. The defaulters line aboard ship was certainly long. I wasn't much of a drinker so I went to the cricket and also sight-seeing.*

Among those who joined the battleship at Sydney, having come out with a new draft from the United Kingdom, was Ordnance Artificer Charlie Pearson who was assigned to A turret.

After gunnery practice off Sydney *Warspite* was destined to call at Fremantle but reports of Japanese submarine activity in the area meant she diverted to a safe anchorage near Adelaide.

The cruiser HMAS *Sydney* had been sunk the previous November and no one knew how at that time. In reality she had been in action with a German raider and both vessels had gone down, but before those facts became clear it was feared Japanese submarines had struck.

Warspite was eventually ordered to join the Eastern Fleet at Ceylon and arrived at Trincomalee in mid-March where she piped aboard one of her former captains to raise his Admiral's flag in her for one of the most frustrating, and dangerous, moments of the Second World War.

Shadow Boxing With Nagumo

Continuing heavy losses in the Mediterranean, and the need to keep the most modern and powerful fighting units in home waters to guard against the German threat, deprived the Royal Navy of forces to put together an effective fighting fleet in the Far East.

Hence the Eastern Fleet under Admiral Sir James Somerville was a vulnerable collection of vessels, with the exception of his flagship, HMS *Warspite*. The Americans – still reeling from the shock of Pearl Harbor which had for the moment removed most of their Pacific fleet from the scene – were temporarily of no assistance. The Japanese seemed to be on the brink of invading Australia and adding Burma and India to their long list of conquests. As the *Warspite* arrived in the Indian Ocean, the Imperial Japanese Navy was not far behind her, surging forward to put to the sword the last significant naval force that could stand in the way of further conquest – the Royal Navy's Eastern Fleet.

Inadequate though it was, never has the preservation of a 'fleet in being' been more vital – for to have handed the enemy complete and undisputed control of the seas could only have made Burma and India more open to the rapidly advancing Japanese armies than they already were. Destruction of the Eastern Fleet would secure the flanks of fresh Japanese conquests in south-east Asia.

And, if the whole of Burma and then India fell, and the Japanese moved even further west, they would be in a superb position to cut the convoy route up the eastern coast of Africa.

Admiral Somerville had commanded the Royal Navy's Gibraltar-based Force H

HMS *Warspite*'s Walrus amphibian aircraft alongside the battleship, with HMS *Formidable* in the background. *K. Smith Collection.*

and earned a formidable reputation fighting his way through to Malta while escorting badly needed convoys. But, when he was handed the job of heading a new Eastern Fleet, Somerville knew he was getting an inadequate force. With the *Prince of Wales* and the *Repulse* he might have felt more optimistic, but Winston Churchill's unwise sacrifice of the ships in defence of Singapore and Malaya had deprived him of that sliver of hope. The fleet he commanded was not only fatally hampered by lack of adequate carrier air groups with which to counter the Japanese superiority, the bulk of his battleships were deeply inadequate Royal Sovereign Class vessels. Somerville had no choice but to divide the Eastern Fleet into two forces, to try and give some cohesion to any moves in response to the Japanese thrust. Force A (the faster ships)

Commander Charles Madden (left), chatting with Captain F.E.P. Hutton who commanded *Warspite* during her time with the Eastern Fleet, March 1942-March 1943. *Foster Collection.*

Admiral Somerville in conversation (centre). *K. Smith Collection.*

The Royal Sovereign Class battleship HMS *Resolution*, one of four inadequate R Class capital ships tasked with taking on the Japanese in April 1942 while under the flag of Admiral Somerville. *K. Smith Collection.*

was composed of HMS *Warspite*, the carriers HMS *Indomitable* and *Formidable* plus the heavy cruisers *Dorsetshire*, *Cornwall*, light cruisers *Emerald* and *Enterprise* and six destroyers.

Force B (the slower vessels) was led by the four R Class battleships *Resolution*, *Ramillies*, *Royal Sovereign* and *Revenge*, plus the carrier *Hermes*, the light cruisers *Caledon*, *Dragon* and *Heemskerck* plus eight destroyers. The British carriers could only muster forty fleet fighters and around sixty torpedo bombers combined. In addition to flying machines that were inferior to Japanese naval aircraft, many of the British aircrews were very inexperienced and simply not up to combat standard.

One valuable addition to Somerville's team was Commander William Lamb. He had volunteered that March to become Fleet AA Officer for the Eastern Fleet, as his way of avoiding a desk job in Britain.

I had embarked on an Imperial Airways flying boat in Alexandria and flew out via the Sea of Galilee and the Gulf to Karachi and then via Indian Airlines to Bombay. It was slightly strange that I should find myself in exactly the same place as I had been in Warspite *in the Med, in the same little corner that I used when I was at sea there. However, following the battleship's big refit in the USA, it had been buffed up into a real cabin that was allocated to me.*

At the time Commander Lamb rejoined the *Warspite*, Somerville's nominal fleet was still scattered and time to concentrate was fast running out.

Commander Lamb:

There had been intelligence the Japanese were planning some sort of raid or foray

150

The Japanese carrier *Hiryu*, one of the vessels hunting for the *Warspite* and the Eastern Fleet, April 1942. *US Naval Historical Center,*

Japanese Zero fighters outclassed the aircraft of the Eastern Fleet. *US Naval Historical Center,*

Colombo Harbour before the Japanese raid.
K. Smith Collection.

View over the forward guns of HMS *Warspite* in the Indian Ocean in the, summer of 1942.
K. Smith Collection.

into the Indian Ocean and we felt we had very little time to get ourselves in a fit state to meet them. The Warspite was at Bombay, the four R Class battleships were coming around the Cape to join, and the aircraft carriers, which had been occupied ferrying aircraft into Singapore for defence, had no recent combat action to ready them to defend the fleet. About a week after I arrived in Bombay the Warspite sailed and rendezvoused with this fleet. On paper it was most impressive. But in fact, when we finally all met up at sea, Admiral Somerville had not even had an opportunity to meet his captains or more junior admirals before undertaking the fleet's first operation.

The Japanese Carrier Striking Force sent into the Indian Ocean was under the command of Vice Admiral Chuichi Nagumo. His five major vessels – *Akagi, Soryu, Hiryu, Zuikaku, Shokaku* –

The cruiser HMS *Exeter*, another Devonport-built warship, which was not as lucky as *Warspite* in avoiding the rampaging Japanese. *Exeter* was sunk in March 1942. *Photo: Strathdee Collection.*

and the aviators they carried, were the elite of the Japanese Navy, having carried out the raids on Pearl Harbor and Darwin in northern Australia. Nagumo's carriers could launch over 100 Zero fighters, plus 240 bombers and torpedo bombers.

The squadron of battleships which escorted the carrier force – *Kongo, Hiei, Kirishima* and *Haruna* – were equally as old as the British battlewagons but, crucially, had all received extensive modernization. Meanwhile Vice Admiral J. Ozawa with the light carrier *Ryujo* and five heavy cruisers was prowling in the Bay of Bengal to attack merchant shipping.

On 28 March – the first anniversary of the victory at Matapan – Admiral Somerville received further intelligence reports which confirmed powerful Japanese naval forces were heading his way and air strikes on Ceylon were highly likely. His two main bases of Colombo and Trincomalee would therefore be untenable. Somerville had at least managed to find a secret and secure base for his

HMS *Indomitable*, one of two modern carriers with the Eastern Fleet in April 1942. *K. Smith Collection.*

fleet 600 miles to the south-west of Ceylon at Addu Atoll in the Maldives. It was not the most attractive of bases, but it had the benefit of being so obscure it was unlikely the Japanese would ever find it.

While he steamed south with Force A, the other half of Somerville's force steamed north from Addu and they met up eighty miles off Ceylon on 31 March.

Caught on its own, Force A might have put up a brave fight but *Warspite* and her carriers would soon have gone to the bottom. Allowing Force B to come anywhere near the Japanese would have been sheer murder – the four R Class battleships were slow, their guns lacked range, their deck armour was too thin to resist bombs and they guzzled water and fuel at an alarming rate. Yet Somerville was still trying to wield this force in a deterrent fashion, praying that under cover of darkness he might skirt close enough to the rapidly approaching Japanese to launch a torpedo bomber attack. One of Commander Lamb's first jobs on *Warspite* was to draft AA gunnery policies,

HMS *Warspite* cruising in the Indian Ocean in 1942, while flagship of the Eastern Fleet. *C. Pearson Collection.*

bearing in mind friendly aircraft from the Eastern Fleet's own carriers would be flying in close proximity. He said: 'This had to be done on one sheet of foolscap and signalled visually to the fleet as we did not wish to break radio silence.' By 2 April, with no sign as yet of the Japanese, and with the R Class ships needing to refuel and take on water, the whole fleet withdrew to Addu. On seeing it for the first time Ordnance Artificer Pearson felt he would willingly let the enemy occupy Addu in exchange for leaving Ceylon alone. 'It was a dreadful desolate place. Nothing there,

The *Warspite*'s Walrus launches in the Indian Ocean during 1942. *C. Pearson Collection.*

Japanese aircraft failed to find HMS *Warspite* off Ceylon in April 1942, but sank HMS *Hermes*.
Taylor Library.

barren as anything. Some people called it "Scapa with palm trees".'

HMS *Dorsetshire* was sent to Colombo to resume a refit and *Cornwall* was ordered to accompany her and then escort a convoy. *Hermes* and the destroyer *Vampire* were ordered to Trincomalee to prepare for a mission to take the French island of Madagascar which it was feared might fall into Japanese hands. Somerville's decision to send these elements of his force back to vulnerable ports about to be subjected to intense Japanese air attack was later to provoke severe criticism.

On the afternoon of 4 April the Japanese carriers were spotted by an RAF Catalina flying boat. Force A set sail from Addu, intent on obtaining a position south of Ceylon to launch a night strike on the Japanese by 6 April, while Force B would follow after finishing replenishment. Somerville called *Dorsetshire* and *Cornwall* back to him from Colombo and *Hermes* was ordered to clear Trincomalee and seek protection by hiding out along the coastline of India. The Japanese launched their air attack against Colombo on the morning of 5 April. Among the casualties in harbour was the destroyer HMS *Tenedos*, the Armed Merchant Cruiser *Hector* and a

Prayers in *Warspite*'s chapel for those lost on the *Dorsetshire*, *Exeter* and *Hermes*.
K. Smith Collection.

The Admiral's barge comes back aboard the *Warspite* after a fleet conference afloat. *K. Smith Collection.*

merchant ship.

At 1.44p.m., HMS *Warspite*'s radar picked up a swarm of blips – these were Japanese planes in the final moments of sinking the cruisers *Cornwall* and *Dorsetshire*. The two British warships stood no chance as they were attacked by eighty-eight aircraft.

A scouting aircraft from the Japanese cruiser *Tone* was also picked up on radar, but luckily it never found the British fleet. British Albacores soon managed to locate the main Japanese fleet but their sighting reports were fragmented as they were set upon

HMS *Warspite* **takes on fuel at the Seychelles, 1942**. *C. Pearson Collection*

Warspite's Royal Marine buglers sound the Last Post in memory of their fallen comrades, lost in action against the Japanese off Ceylon in April 1942. K. Smith Collection.

by Japanese fighters.

At 5.00p.m. on the 5 April, a scouting RAF Catalina spotted five ships heading towards Force A so Somerville pulled back, waiting for night to launch a torpedo strike against them. Though the torpedo bombers were armed and ready to go, with their crews sitting in them, Somerville hesitated, needing more accurate reports on the location of the enemy before he sacrificed any of his young aviators. He knew well the hazards faced by torpedo bomber crews having astounded his staff while commanding Force H by flying off HMS *Ark Royal* to get a taste of the naval aviator's lot. He once remarked: 'How I hate seeing them go off and wondering how many of the brave lads will return.'[9]

In reality Nagumo's force was sailing away, so the distance between the two naval groups was opening not closing. Aboard *Warspite* Somerville's staff warned him against going to the last known position of *Cornwall* and *Dorsetshire* with his main force. Instead he

HMS *Warspite* coming up fast behind the Australian destroyer HMAS *Norman*.

K. Smith Collection.

Above and below: The view from *Warspite* as she replenishes an escort destroyer in the Indian Ocean. *K. Smith Collection.*

sent ahead *Enterprise*, *Paladin* and *Panther* which managed to pick up 1,122 survivors.

Most of the *Warspite*'s crew had no idea what was happening and only learned later about the day's events. Ken Smith remembers an agonizing day of uncertainty:

We were at action stations for most of the time. It all felt very tense and dangerous. You were closed up for hours and hours. Your nerves were jangled every time alarm bells rang to warn that action was imminent. Sometimes they did this because they genuinely thought it might be and other times they did it just to keep us on our toes.

A 6-inch gun battery is a long passageway, each of the guns in its own compartment with only a semi-divide between. You could see the other gun crews over it but that was all. Nothing else. It was pretty tedious. There was a crew of about seven on each gun and there was no sitting down – you stood for hours. When they stood down the alert status then you might be able to sit on the floor, but there would always be someone stood by the phone. You even had crews sleeping by their guns. We were not certain what was going on at all. They did tell us they were hoping to make a night attack. But whether that was propaganda to keep our spirits up or a serious intention I don't know. We were told very little about what was happening – we found out the detail later.

I believe had we gone on towards the Japanese for another five or ten minutes we would have been picked up by the Tone's scouting aircraft. Thank goodness we turned about – there was no sense risking the whole fleet in seeking a hopeless battle with the same carriers which destroyed the American fleet. There but for the grace of God went I.

Early on 6 April, Force A and Force B joined up and mounted a sweep towards the east. Two days later, with no contact having been made, the British withdrew again to Addu Atoll which the Japanese were still completely unaware of. Still seeking to destroy the Eastern Fleet, Nagumo's strike force pounced on Trincomalee on 9 April. Having only damaged the monitor HMS *Erebus* and a merchant ship, the Japanese were disappointed at their catch but delighted to find HMS *Hermes* returning to Trincomalee, swiftly sinking her and two escort warships. Throughout this *Warspite* and the rest of the fleet stayed at a discreet distance. Commander Lamb recalled:

We continued to maintain a position between the Maldives and Ceylon and we could just see on the edge of our radar screens the Japanese aircraft.

With Ozawa's roving group ravaging merchant shipping off the coast of India, Admiral Somerville convened a meeting aboard *Warspite* to announce his next course of action. It was perfectly feasible the Japanese could be preparing a pincer movement to trap and annihilate his sickly fleet.

At the conference aboard the flagship, Somerville explained how he was convinced of the undesirability of operating his battle fleet, which lacked speed, endurance and AA gun power in Ceylon waters in the face of such superior Japanese naval and air power.[10]

He therefore decided to send Force B to East Africa, to guard convoy routes to North Africa, while Force A would go to Bombay to try and deter Japan from raiding waters off India.

The only strike on Nagumo's force was conducted by some RAF Blenheim bombers which managed to slightly damage Nagumo's flagship, the carrier *Akagi*, on 9 April.

The Japanese left the Indian Ocean several days after the raid on Trincomalee. While the Indian Ocean was now there for the taking, the Imperial Japanese Navy failed to exploit it to support the Japanese Army's attempted invasion of India. However, the IJN had managed to chase away any serious naval threat to its newly conquered territories in Indonesia and Malaya. Somerville's actions in April 1942, were seen by many as cowardice and it was deeply dispiriting for a force as proud as the Royal Navy to avoid a fight. Gordon Wallace, one of the young aviators of HMS *Indomitable* who might have carried out the strike on Nagumo's force, said in his book *Carrier Observer*:

> *At the time and for many years after these events I was convinced that we had simply run away from the enemy...*

But, as Wallace acknowledged when he wrote his book half a century later, Somerville's sober reflection on the choices he faced, and the assets at his disposal, meant he had no other choice of action.

Commander Lamb was also convinced Somerville did the right thing.

> *It must have been very difficult for the C-in-C. It was more important that he kept his fleet in being, as a continuing deterrent to the Japanese coming westwards into the Indian Ocean. In the circumstances I am not only grateful for my own skin that he did take that line but feel it was a fully justified one.*

Having narrowly avoided destruction at the hands of the Japanese, the *Warspite* soon found herself operating from Kilindini, near Mombasa. The enemy threat was more imagined than real.

'Japanese submarines did operate off Madagascar,' said Commander Lamb.

> *But I believe there were more German than Japanese U-boats in the Indian Ocean. I don't remember any enemy submarines being reported off the Kenya coastline.*

Commander Lamb was soon on his travels again, this time sent as a liaison officer to the American fleet, to try and learn from its combat against the Japanese in the central Pacific.

Admiral Somerville continued to use the *Warspite* off and on as his flagship and managed to retain the good opinion of her crew. Ordnance Artificer Charlie Pearson was one of those who came into contact with the Commander-in-Chief from time to time when maintaining AA weapons about the ship.

> *I think Somerville was a gentleman. He had a good sense of humour and whenever he was ashore and sending us a signal would say: 'I see Pluto is in position,' meaning our ship's mascot, Pluto the dog.*

For their part, the Japanese still hungered after humiliating the Royal Navy by inflicting another body blow. They were so desperate to destroy the legendary *Warspite* they claimed to have sunk her during the Battle of the Coral Sea in early May.[11] Using hopelessly outdated intelligence reports they next ordered a midget submarine attack on Sydney Harbour at the end of May, hoping to catch *Warspite* there. They sank the depot ship HMAS *Kuttabul*, killing nineteen sailors and wounding another ten. Meanwhile, eluding the Japanese, the *Warspite* led an uneventful life punctuated by exercises and action alerts plus the odd episode of humour. One of her sailors remembered one such incident:

> *One morning in 1942, the* Warspite *was out in the Indian Ocean on exercises with her screen of destroyers. As flagship,* Warspite *announced the speed of the fleet by hoisting the signal flag 'speed' followed by the numeral flags for 'one' and 'six' (ie: speed*

Scetches shewing battleships, craisers and aircraft carriers

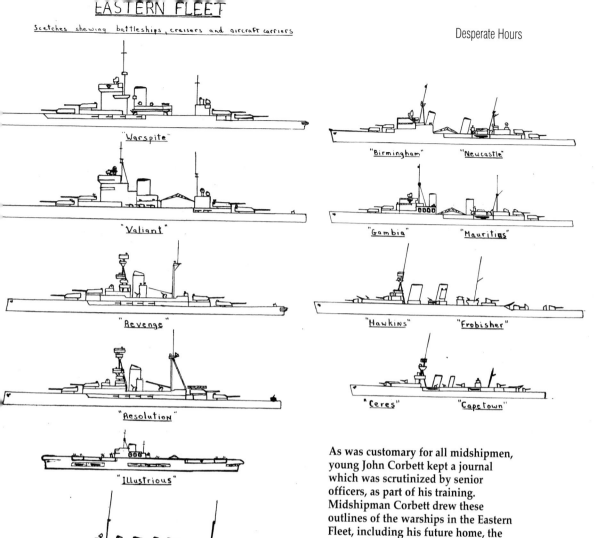

"Warspite"

"Birmingham"   "Newcastle"

"Valiant"

"Gambia"   "Mauritias"

"Revenge"

"Hawkins"   "Frobisher"

"Resolution"

"Ceres"   "Cape town"

"Illustrious"

As was customary for all midshipmen, young John Corbett kept a journal which was scrutinized by senior officers, as part of his training. Midshipman Corbett drew these outlines of the warships in the Eastern Fleet, including his future home, the battleship *Warspite*. J. Corbett.

"Devonshire"

sixteen knots). A destroyer on the far edge of the screen incorrectly acknowledged the instruction by rapidly hoisting flags 'six' and 'one' (sixty-one knots). Quick as a flash the Warspite's Yeoman was ordered to make by Aldis Lamp the signal 'circle the fleet twice and take off...' which made us laugh a little.[12]

In the tropics, conditions aboard *Warspite* were intolerable, as she had been built to fight the Kaiser's fleet in the North Sea not cruise off the coast of Africa. Ken Smith soon found his health, and that of many others aboard the battleship, was affected:

She was a gigantic sweatbox. We're talking extreme temperatures closed up at action stations in a 6-inch gun battery for hours. There was little or no ventilation – you just sweated and sweated. Hundreds of the crew went down sick – the sickbay was always full. You got dhobi itch, you got prickly heat, all sorts of lumps and bumps. It was those *conditions that did for me ultimately. If you had any sense you got yourself a bucket and filled it with water from the shower room taps. That water was used for your first wash of the day and to bathe in later. Someone might give you a tot of rum to borrow it. You also used it for your dhobi. The bucket thing was against regulations, but, in such circumstances, a lot of things went by the board.*

But sometimes the Royal Marines got to work on the upper deck and there conditions were more tolerable, although, as Ken Smith recalled, some of the hazards they faced could threaten lives.

There was this lad called Tom Brown and we were refuelling a destroyer in the Indian Ocean. He was part of a Royal Marines party being used to haul on the hawser that kept the oil pipes linked to the destroyer up out of the water. Suddenly it wrapped itself around him and he was pulled over the side, down between the two ships. Luckily the destroyer captain saw this and took action straight away, so avoiding cutting him up with the props. The destroyer picked Tom up and amazingly he only had a few bumps and bruises. He ended up coming through the war without a scratch.

By mid-summer 1942, with the US Navy finally seizing the initiative from the Japanese at Midway, things were starting to run in favour of the Allies.

The thrust towards Australia had been halted in Papua New Guinea and, while they would push briefly into India, the Japanese would ultimately find only disaster.

In North Africa, the Battle of El Alamein would turn the tide resolutely against the Germans and Italians while at Stalingrad, the Russians would, by the beginning of 1943, halt the German advance to the Caucasus forever.

In the meantime *Warspite* went down to Durban for a docking period and to partially change her crew. With events taking such a positive turn in favour of the Allies she was to be called home to prepare for a new mission which would take her back to the Mediterranean.

Notes

1   Cuningham, *A Sailor's Odyssey.*
2   Ibid.
3   Ibid.
4   Ibid.
5   A *Warspite* veteran writing in *Anchors Aweigh*, the journal of the *Warspite* Association.
6   Edited quotes taken from article by D. Cooper in *Anchors Aweigh*, the journal of the *Warspite* Association.
7   A *Warspite* veteran writing in *Anchors Aweigh*, the journal of the *Warspite* Association.
8   Ibid.
9   Ludovic Kennedy, *Pursuit: The Sinking of the Bismarck.*
10 David A. Thomas, *Japan's War at Sea.*
11 Ibid.
12 Warspite veteran Frank Veal, in *Anchors Aweigh*, the journal of the *Warspite* Association.

Chapter Nine

DELIVERING A KNOCK-OUT BLOW

Return to the Mediterranean

During her time in dock at Durban, *Warspite* welcomed back a familiar face. Bertie Packer, who had served as a young Sub Lieutenant at Jutland and as her Gunnery Officer in the 1920s, now returned as her commanding officer.

Saying goodbye to *Warspite* when she docked at Durban was Ken Smith whose health had finally collapsed after months inside the sweatbox battleship. Following emergency treatment in hospital, including surgery, he spent many months recuperating in South Africa. Joining *Warspite* at Durban was Midshipman John Corbett. 'I suppose I was lucky to get her and not an R Class battleship,' he told his Midshipman's journal.

On 16 April 1943, *Warspite* sailed from Durban for Freetown where she was to rendezvous with a troop convoy before sailing for the Clyde to rejoin the Home Fleet.

Heavy weather revealed some limitations in *Warspite*'s design. Midshipman Corbett noted in his journal:

> ...our port 6-inch gun battery was soon flooded and the shelter deck made most uncomfortable. A wind of about Force seven carried spray right up to the bridge. We actually did some ten degree rolls which greatly surprised me as I didn't think this ship could roll at all. However she certainly buried her head. The seas broke over the forecastle completely engulfing capstans, breakwater and most of A turret.

Warspite secured to her buoy at Greenock on 10 May. The battleship had not seen home waters since April 1940 and, as Midshipman Corbett noted, no one seemed to care.

Plans showing modifications to *Warspite* as carried out during her refit at Durban in early 1943.
Goodman Collection

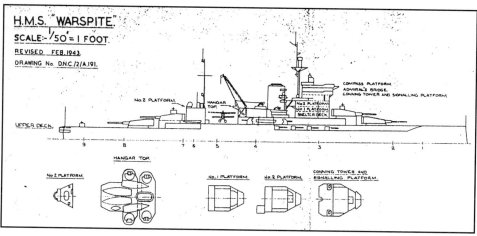

> *Such was the homecoming of the mighty* Warspite *after Narvik, Calabria, Matapan and Crete... . Two years have elapsed since Crete, the ship's company have dispersed and the ship is largely forgotten. I hope that now, with a new crew, we get a chance and succeed in once more making her world famous at the enemy's cost.*

During the voyage Midshipman Corbett had been tasked with calculating the miles steamed by *Warspite* since the beginning of the war. After arriving at Greenock he recorded the following figures in his journal:

1939 (from declaration of war in September) – 12,984 miles.

1940 – 43,978 miles.

1941 – 25,253 miles.

1942 – 61,481 miles.

1943 – 17,168 miles.

The mileage per month since Midshipman Corbett had joined the ship was:

March – 2,459 miles (twenty-three days in harbour, eight days at sea).

April – 5,119 miles (sixteen days in harbour, fourteen days at sea).

May – 3,586 miles (twenty days in harbour, ten days at sea).

Before the month was out *Warspite* visited Princes Dock in Glasgow where Bertie Packer commanded the landing party which saw off arsonists during the 1926 General Strike. This time she was there for another attempt to fix her recurring steering problem which had surfaced again on the way back from Africa.

June 1943 dawned and the *Warspite* sailed north to the anchorage of Scapa Flow where she had not been since returning from her victory at Narvik. *Warspite* was now to be prepared for a role which would occupy her for the rest of her fighting life – shore bombardment missions in support of land forces driving forward from a beachhead.

Having inflicted a devastating defeat on Axis forces in North Africa – taking the surrender of a quarter of a million German and Italian troops in Tunisia – the Allies were preparing to invade Sicily as a prelude to an amphibious assault on the Italian mainland.

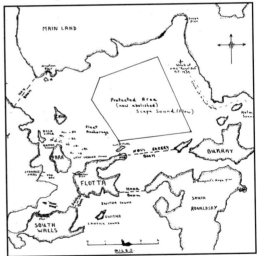

Midshipman John Corbett's map of Scapa Flow. Taken from the Midshipman's journal he kept while aboard **HMS** *Warspite*. *John Corbett.*

Admiral Cunningham, who had been replaced as Commander-in-Chief of the Mediterranean Fleet in April 1942, and sent to America as Britain's most senior naval representative on the Combined Chiefs of Staff, was now back in the Mediterranean as the Supreme Commander of Allied naval forces.

On 9 June Force H sailed out of Scapa Flow, led by HMS *Nelson* and bound for Gibraltar. With the *Nelson* was *Warspite* plus *Rodney*, *Valiant* the carrier *Indomitable* and a large destroyer escort. On the way down to Gibraltar, Force H hit more heavy weather. Midshipman Corbett wrote in his journal:

Warspite is taking the heavy weather as usual, seas breaking over the forecastle and quarterdeck carrying away ammunition lockers, carley rafts and guard rails. It has been necessary to train A turret on the port beam and close the starboard hatches.

On 28 June 1943, leave was cancelled and *Warspite*, in company with *Valiant* and *Formidable*, plus escorts, left Gibraltar bound for Algiers at sixteen knots. Arriving on 30 June, she took on some mail and passengers then departed that afternoon for Alexandria. As Cape Bon was rounded Midshipman Corbett saw the wreck of HMS *Havock* visible above the shallow waters. The destroyer, which had played such an important part in the First Battle of Narvik and at Matapan, was disabled by a 15-inch shell from the Italian battleship *Littorio* at the Second Battle of Sirte in March 1942. Making for Gibraltar dockyard, she ran aground and was later hit by torpedoes from an Italian submarine. As *Warspite* sailed past in the summer of 1943, *Havock*'s wreck was a reminder of hard times left behind.

Force H was to be divided into three Divisions of battleships with attendant carriers, cruisers and destroyers.

They were:

Division 1 – HMS *Nelson*, HMS *Rodney* and HMS *Indomitable*.

Division 2 – HMS *Warspite*, HMS *Valiant* and HMS *Formidable*.

Division 3 – HMS *King George V* and HMS *Howe* (also known as Force Z).

During the forthcoming invasion of Sicily Division 2 would leave from Alexandria and Division 1 was to sail from Gibraltar. Division 3 was to be held in reserve at Algiers as a mobile reserve, ready at a moment's notice to sail wherever the Italian fleet threatened to make an appearance.

The Mediterranean was too quiet for Midshipman Corbett's liking and he entered the following comment in his journal:

It is very much of an anticlimax if not disappointing,. It would have been grand to have left astern the wreckage of a few enemy aircraft and E boats. The

The KGV battleship *King George V* which, together with sister ship HMS *Howe*, made up Division 3 (or Force Z) in the British naval armada assembled for the final assault on Italy. *Goodman Collection*

trouble is I have joined this Navy far too late in the war to do anything.'

It was the quiet before the storm.

Warspite entered Alexandria for the first time since the bloody summer of 1941 on 5 July and two days later left for her part in the Sicily invasion.

Warspite and the rest of Division 2 met up with Division 1 south of Malta in the early hours of 9 July. By daylight the following morning this awesome gathering of firepower was arrayed off the target island. Watching the guns of other ships invest Italian and German positions ashore with severe punishment was not much fun for young Midshipman Corbett, still itching for his baptism of fire. He told his journal:

Midshipman John Corbett's map of his theatre of war. Taken from the Midshipman's journal he kept while aboard HMS *Warspite*. *John Corbett*

> We did not see Sicily but saw some flashes as we patrolled up and down some fifty miles off the coast. What was even more infuriating was seeing the cruisers Penelope and Aurora being detached to bombard Catania and other missions later. I thought they would have seen enough of the war already. It's so discouraging not doing anything after losing so much sleep preparing.

Two days after the landings at Sicily started, *Warspite* made the first visit by a Royal Navy battleship to Malta in nearly three years. She received a rousing welcome, the ramparts of the fortress island crowded with cheering people. Sailing from Malta not long after, *Warspite* took up station ninety miles off Sicily to carry on waiting for the Italian fleet to respond. During this period, the British battle fleet was subjected to repeated attacks from torpedo bombers and submarines. Midshipman Corbett's

Warspite back at Malta for the first time in three years. Note the 15-inch gun out of alignment which earned the battleship a rebuke. *C. Pearson Collection*

journal entry for 16 July 1943 revealed *Warspite* may have come close to receiving a mortal blow:

> Last evening the 1st Division of Force H struck a spot of bother which I believe was aimed at us. At 17.00 we were seen by an enemy aircraft which sent out a sighting report. Soon after we altered course to the east to fill in some time and the 1st Division, coming north from Malta, was attacked soon after midnight by torpedo bombers which I think meant to have us. Indomitable was hit by a torpedo in the boiler room and her speed reduced to eleven knots. As a result Formidable *joined the 1st Division and* Indomitable *returned with us to Malta.*

Once his ship was back at Malta, Captain Packer seized an opportunity to make representations to Admiral Cunningham at his headquarters on the island. He asked the Admiral to allow his old flagship to carry out a bombardment and was granted permission immediately. Both *Warspite* and *Valiant* were ordered to leave their anchorage and steam to Sicily to carry out a bombardment of enemy positions in Catania which was proving a tough nut to crack. Unfortunately, when it was time to sail *Valiant* had to be left behind as she got tangled up in anti-submarine nets.

Meanwhile *Warspite* had to be in position to start firing by 6.30p.m. and conclude by around 7.00p.m. She would need to do some hard steaming to make that deadline. Somehow her engineers managed to squeeze twenty-two-and-a-half knots out of the *Warspite*, which was pretty remarkable for a thirty-year-old ship. However, just when she was making good progress, her old steering problem struck again. Careering off on a mad circle, she nearly collided with one of her destroyer escorts.

Midshipman Corbett got a good view of it through his X turret periscope:

> We swung to port but the swing was arrested and then, going out of control again, we swung violently to starboard at full speed. The water washed the port side of the quarterdeck and the starboard bilge hull was almost out of the water though the sea was flat calm. We went through 180 degrees in almost our own length. We stopped as the circle was completed and then were under control again. We must have lost twenty minutes all told but, as such action is Warspite's *traditional preliminary to battle, no one was really upset.*

The *Warspite's* initial range was 15,000 yards but by 7.00p.m. this was down to 7,000 yards and each turret had fired fourteen rounds. Midshipman Corbett watched the fall of shell:

> It was very hazy and through my periscope I could see little but huge bursts and palls of smoke. A few very small shore batteries made very little effective reply. In X turret we had gun failure. But missed no salvos as the other gun fired each salvo till the jam was cleared and the right hand gun caught up. While this was going on a submarine was seen and some Focke Wulf 190s passed down the starboard side. We missed them astern by miles. The port side, not to be outdone, fired a few shots at some of our own Spitfires, there being no better target available.

At 7.02p.m. the last shell was fired and *Warspite* withdrew at top speed. Despite several air alerts, she made it back safely to Malta by morning. Proud as ever of his

The *Warspite*'s 15-inch guns firing on Catania, July 1943. *C. Pearson Collection*

old flagship, Admiral Cunningham couldn't resist sending a humorous compliment to Captain Packer. 'Operation well carried out. There is no doubt that when the old lady lifts her skirts she can run.'[1] From that moment on, the *Warspite* was known throughout the fleet as 'The Old Lady'.

Warspite's fire mission left a significant part of Catania in ruins, causing what would today be termed 'collateral damage'. This possibility evoked little sympathy in the *Warspite*'s crew who remembered the dreadful price paid by the blitzed British naval cities of Portsmouth and Plymouth.

On 19 July the enemy tried to inflict some payback via a big raid on Malta. Midshipman Corbett noted in his journal:

> *On Monday night Malta had its biggest raid for some months. I've never in my life seen such a barrage put up. It was not so much the quantity but the way the barrage just went on for so long. The amount of Bofors ammunition expended must have been colossal. I heard a buzz that* Nelson *had three near misses but do not know for sure. We had a grandstand view without any danger.*

A week later he noted:

The *Warspite*'s secondary armament firing during the bombardment of Sicily. *C. Pearson Collection.*

The view from *Warspite* of another British warship firing an anti-aircraft barrage at night to deter torpedo bombers. *C. Pearson Collection.*

After Taranto the Italian fleet avoided using its main naval port, opting for other bases including Spezia (seen here in an RAF reconniassance photograph with major units of the Italian fleet moored alongside). With a mighty Allied naval force gathered for the invasion of Sicily in the summer of 1943, the Italians preferred to stay in harbour. *Taylor Library.*

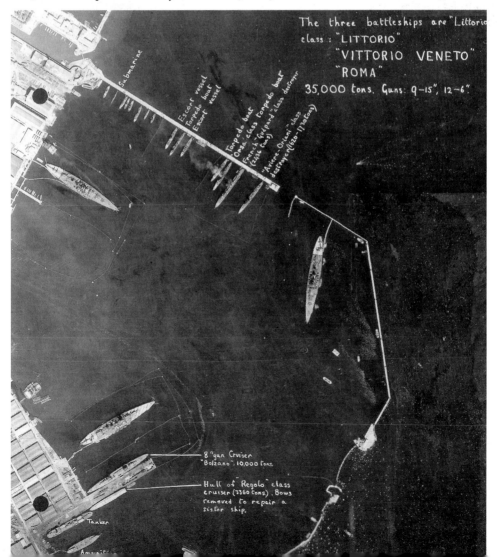

Warspite's sailors and marines being briefed on the next phase of the campaign against Italy. Crews of smaller ships were surprised by the battleship's informal dress code. *C. Pearson Collection*

Last Sunday evening excitement was caused during a raid on Valetta when a bomb landed some two cables off on our starboard beam. I thought it sounded much more like a crashing aircraft as it didn't have the whistle of a bomb and made a crash rather than an explosion. Sparks flew in a manner suggesting a petrol tank exploding....As no wreckage was seen, and a diver could find no trace of it the next day, we must, however, accept it as a bomb. During the attack a Junkers 88 was caught in a searchlight beam. Our starboard 4-inch fired two rounds as he crossed our stern and made good his escape.

Even the Italian Navy fleetingly threatened to contest the seas. Midshipman Corbett wrote in his journal:

On Monday evening we were suddenly ordered to be at half an hour's notice for steam. Next morning it was announced that two Italian battleships had risked coming out but immediately turned around and went back in to port.

The high temperatures of summer 1943 did not make the waiting easy, with *Warspite* as unsuitable for the hot climate as ever. But at least the regime aboard the *Warspite* allowed people to take suitable measures, as Petty Officer Charlie Pearson remembered:

Nobody wore what you'd call regulation uniform. We just wore shorts. It could be quite amusing when

A series of cartoons depicting a sailor's life ashore in Malta.
C. Pearson Collection.

Noel Coward entertains *Warspite*'s crew during his visit to the battleship at Malta. *C. Pearson Collection.*

people on smaller ships came alongside the Spite *and saw us dressed like that. Being the crew of a battleship, they thought we would be real Pusser's Navy's – spit and polish sticklers for regulation uniforms at all times. They would ask 'what the hell's going on?' And we'd smile back at them and say 'normal rig mate, what's the matter with you?' The* Warspite *was such an easy-going ship sometimes.*

Towards the end of July Mussolini was deposed and imprisoned, but soon set free by the Germans who returned him to power while they took full control of the conduct of the war. But this could not save Sicily and, by mid-August, Allied forces had taken the island, the Germans managing to withdraw 100,000 troops across the Straits of Messina to the mainland. While these dramatic events were happening the fleet used Malta with impunity and waited for orders to intervene which never came.

Any disappointment and frustration young Midshipman Corbett might have felt over the German escape trick was washed away with the excitement of going up for a forty minute flight in a bomber.

We had a 'dog fight' with another Wellington and dive bombed a small island, both incidents being against all the rules. We went out to sea and returned to look at the Warspite. *She looked fine from the air. There was no mistaking any of the ships and even the smallest boats were easily seen. It was just like a relief map.*

In mid-August *Warspite* received an unexpected celebrity visitor. Captain Packer bumped into Noel Coward who was putting on a show ashore for wounded troops evacuated from Sicily. As none of his crew

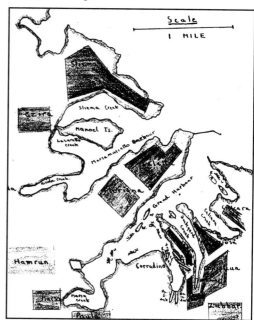

Midshipman John Corbett's map of Malta's harbours. Taken from the Midshipman's journal he kept while aboard HMS *Warspite*. *John Corbett.*

Admiral Cunningham comes aboard HMS *Warspite* in Malta. *C. Pearson Collection*

had seen Coward's film *In Which We Serve,* Captain Packer sent a midshipman ashore with a note to ask the entertainer if a copy was locally available. Luckily Coward had one with him and this was sent across to the battleship. Shortly afterwards Coward visited *Warspite* as his plane had been delayed and while aboard gave an impromptu concert.

The following morning the ship was visited by Admiral Cunningham. Midshipman Corbett noted in his journal:

> *Admiral Cunningham seems very attached to* Warspite *and takes a great interest in her. When he came aboard no one was excused divisions and the men were in Number 5s and the officers in Number 10s. Admiral Cunningham said he was glad to be back on his old flagship and that it was just over two years since he had last spoken to her ship's company. He recalled circumstances were very different. He remembered waking up one morning, in May 1941, at the time of Crete, and having in his fleet only one battleship, one cruiser and three destroyers that were not damaged.*

Admiral Cunningham addresses *Warspite*'s sailors. *C. Pearson Collection*

The Admiral told the crew he expected Italy would be out of the war by Christmas and, after Germany's defeat, there would be Japan to finish off. Shortly afterwards it was announced that, between May and July, ninety enemy submarines had been destroyed. This was the turn of the tide in the Battle of the Atlantic, with victory for the Royal Navy and its allies assured.

On 22 August the journal of Midshipman Corbett reported:

> *A court martial was held on board the* Valiant *on Thursday. A rating was charged with cowardice in the face of the enemy. It appears he was a survivor from Mountbatten's destroyer* Kelly *which was sunk off Crete in May 1941. His experiences then, when he was washed off his anti-aircraft gun position as the ship rolled over and sank, affected him. He refused to close up for action at his anti-aircraft gun on the cruiser HMS* Uganda *during a recent air attack. He eventually lost all badges, was dismissed and given a year in prison. It shows the hardness of war. Cowardice in British ships is never likely to be a serious problem and the safest place is in fact on the upper deck at a gun. The case deserves sympathy rather than punishment. However, there can be no exceptions to the rules or people might start trying to abuse them to get a soft job ashore or even out of the Navy, leaving the rest of us to fight on. So we have to be hard on the few unfortunates. It is all very different from a sailor on this ship who was recently given cells for thieving from a shipmate, a despicable crime. He escaped and jumped ship. Swimming ashore, he claimed to be a Merchant Navy seaman who had missed his ship. The authorities were naturally suspicious and caught him out during questioning. He was brought back aboard and has now been given a well deserved ninety days for desertion.*

Just under two weeks later the Allies mounted their invasion of the Italian mainland. On 2 September *Warspite* and *Valiant* sailed through the Straits of Messina to carry out a bombardment of enemy fortifications south of Reggio as part of softening up for the assault. An encounter with some fishing boats provided amusement for Ordnance Artificers working on the upper deck, including Petty Officer Charlie Pearson.

> *We passed all these Italian fishermen who couldn't have been frightened at all because they waved and smiled up at the* Warspite *as she passed. We laughed because we thought: 'It's no good you smiling and waving because we're going to blow up your country'.*

Later, together with some of his officers Captain Packer flew from Malta to Reggio to see the damage the *Warspite*'s guns had inflicted. They found a moonscape of massive shell craters.

A second landing on the mainland was to be carried out at Salerno in the Bay of Naples and, on 7 September, *Warspite* and Force H moved into position to carry out bombardment of German positions above the invasion beaches. Over the next two days and nights German aircraft made a determined effort to torpedo ships of the bombardment force and *Warspite* came close to being hit. Captain Packer wrote: 'The moonlight is a gift for determined aircraft. They attack up moon. They can see us and we can't see them.'[2]

Through a barrage of pom-poms, Oerlikons, 4-inch and 6-inch guns Captain

Packer somehow heard a low-flying aircraft which he sensed was a maximum threat.

Suddenly there was a great shape down-moon about 100ft up off the sea. Things happen terribly quickly – fractions of seconds are minutes. I saw this Ju88 drop his torpedo and I saw it splash and down the voice-pipe to the quartermaster I roared 'Port 35!'[3]

Able Seaman Peter Finnigan was also on the bridge and leapt out of his skin:

Almost to my disbelief I saw a torpedo heading straight for us. I roared: 'Torpedo off the port bow!'

Captain Packer didn't rate the *Warspite*'s chances of escaping unhurt:

I didn't think we had a hope of it missing us and it seemed about a thousand years before I saw the electric repeat from the rudderhead showing that the rudder was 35 degrees to port.[4]

Charlie Pearson was concentrating on his work and didn't notice the danger his ship was in.

I was maintaining one of the AA guns up for'ard. All of a sudden all our pom-poms and 4-inch guns start going and ack-ack guns on other ships start to send up the old blind barrage too. It was quite a well lit moonlit night and I didn't take any notice what was going on really until I saw a German plane flash by out of nowhere.

I looked over the side and saw this torpedo going past the ship as she turned very hard a port. I remember saying calmly, much as you would refer to a passing rare breed of bird: 'There goes a torpedo'.

Of the same incident, Midshipman Corbett later dryly observed in his journal:

The distance by which the torpedo missed us astern seems to be lessening each time people tell the story.

The following morning events took a really dramatic turn and Midshipman Corbett told his journal:

I was on the bridge at the time the great news came, Italy had surrendered unconditionally. We just stood amazed and then everyone from the Captain to the bridge messenger burst out laughing.

Able Seaman Finnigan was among those celebrating below decks:

Petty Officer Charles Pearson.

C. Pearson Collection

At the announcement of the surrender there was a great excitement on the messdeck. The questions were: 'How would the Italian fleet react to the surrender? Would they scuttle? Would they come over to us?' The crew ran a sweepstake on it.

The news was not unexpected for some members of the crew, including Petty Officer Pearson:

In our mess we had all the Petty Officer Telegraphists and earlier they'd told us about this signal regarding an Italian aircraft coming from Italy to North Africa which was not to be fired upon. We got an inkling something was in the offing.

In fact the surrender of Italy had been agreed with the rebel Italian government on the day Allied forces landed at Reggio. As part of the Armistice the Italian fleet was

From under *Warspite*'s 15-inch guns, the surrendering Italian fleet is seen on the horizon.

to sail from its bases at Spezia and Genoa to surrender on the high seas before being escorted to internment at Malta. The furious Germans wasted no time in launching attacks on their former comrades in arms, hitting and sinking the battleship *Roma* with a glider bomb and causing severe damage to the *Italia*, as the *Littorio* was known after the fall of Mussolini. Aboard one of the surrendering Italian destroyers were six American airmen picked up after their bomber crashed off Sardinia. The US airmen were delighted to be going to Malta rather than into a prison cage.

At 8.00a.m. on 10 September the Italians arrived at their rendezvous and were soon steaming in line astern behind *Valiant* with *Warspite* leading. Midshipman Corbett wrote in his journal:

> I think it was the biggest day for the British Navy since the surrender of the German Fleet in 1918. The Italians appeared under a great cloud of smoke, then formed up a long way astern and we set off for Malta. Shortly afterwards we passed a big convoy escorted by the cruiser HMS Delhi. It must have given them the shock of their lives to see the Italian fleet trailing along astern of the

Vittorio Veneto **passes *Warspite* as the Italian fleet sails into captivity at Malta.** *C. Pearson Collection*

The *Italia* (formerly the *Littorio*) passes under *Warspite*'s gun as the Italian fleet enters Malta.
Jack Hockley Collection

Warspite and the Valiant.

During the afternoon we took stock of what we had 'in the bag'. It appeared the Roma was the battleship which the Germans had sunk. A brand new 35,000 ton battleship, she had been hit amidships by a bomb and sank in twenty minutes. The Commander-in-Chief of the Italian Fleet went down with her. The Germans did in twenty minutes what we couldn't do in three years.

Some members of *Warspite*'s crew had been with the Grand Fleet in 1918 when it went out to take the surrender of the German High Sea Fleet. Now, as then, they felt a sense of pity rather than triumph. Pluto – the ship's mongrel dog mascot – got excited and came up to the bridge and barked at the Italian warships.

General Eisenhower's aide-de-camp, Commander Harry Butcher, was aboard the *Warspite* and later told a newspaper journalist:

They all flew a black pennant indicating their acceptance of the Armistice. This was flown from the foremast with the Italian ensign on the main mast.

An Italian battleship sails past the *Warspite* and into internment at Malta. *C. Pearson Collection*

The British ships steamed parallel to the Italians and when we first met every
gun was trained on the Italians and every man was at battle stations – the
British were taking no chances at the moment of their first meeting.[5]

There were no messages of greeting between the two fleets – merely instructions and
discussion about the mechanics of sailing to captivity.

It was in every way a calm meeting. There was no cheering, no shouting,
and the British in the true fashion of sportsmanship made no celebrations over
the fallen foe.[6]

As the formation passed Bizerta the destroyer HMS *Hambledon* came out to meet it,
carrying Admiral Cunningham and General Eisenhower. Eight years later
Cunningham wrote of this moment:

To me it was a most moving and thrilling sight. To see my wildest
hopes of years back brought to fruition, and my former flagship the
Warspite, which had struck the first blow against the Italians three
years before, leading her erstwhile opponents into captivity, filled me
with the deepest emotion and lives with me still. I can never forget it. I

Valiant (left) is directly astern in this shot taken from *Warspite*, with vanquished enemy vessels
trailing behind. *Jack Hockley Collection.*

made a signal congratulating the Warspite on her proud and rightful
position at the head of the line.[7]

On the same day Admiral Cunningham flew to Malta to give the Italians instructions
regarding the disarmament of their surrendered fleet. Afterwards he signalled the
Admiralty:

Be pleased to inform their Lordships that the Italian Battle Fleet now lies at
anchor under the guns of the fortress of Malta.

The following day *Warspite* went out to escort in more surrendering Italian vessels,
including the battleship *Guilio Cesare* which she had chased off with one hit at

Calabria in 1940. In total the British fleet took the surrender of five battleships, nine cruisers, fourteen destroyers, nineteen torpedo boat destroyers and thirty-five submarines.

Victim of the Luftwaffe... Again

Although Italy had capitulated, the German forces in the country decided to fight on with all their might. At Salerno the situation was getting critical, with the Allied beachhead squashed by a determined enemy onslaught. *Warspite* and *Valiant* were ordered home on 14 September but found themselves diverted to help solve the crisis at Salerno with their firepower.

Making top speed, *Warspite* and *Valiant* were off the beaches by 15 September and facing intense air attacks. For a night and a day, *Warspite*'s anti-aircraft guns were in constant action. Her particular targets with the big guns were German artillery, tanks and troop formations in hills beyond the beachhead.

Loaned to the Allied forces ashore to lay the 15-inch guns on target was a Captain of the Royal Marines, along with a specially trained team of three ratings from the ship. The Germans made several attempts to jam his radio reports to the battleship but he switched frequencies swiftly enough to outwit them. *Warspite*'s gunnery from half-a-mile offshore was devastating. W.E. Heard, a soldier with the 7th Battalion Oxfordshire and Buckinghamshire Light Infantry was among those grateful for the *Warspite*'s intervention.

> *From our positions we could see the battleship patrolling just off the beaches. Many years later as a schoolmaster at the local high school one of my colleagues, who was on the* Warspite *at the time, told me she was firing over open sights.*

Coldstream Guardsmen Dougie Weyhaup and Philip Gourd were almost as terrified of the *Warspite*'s gunnery as the Germans. Dougie was the Sergeant in a special intelligence section and Philip one of its three privates. Sergeant Weyhaup said:

> The Warspite *had good observers because every time we raised our heads she fired, but in reality she was after some German half-tracks trying to hide just beyond us.*

Private Gould tried to burrow into the earth every time her shells came over: 'They made a noise which I can only liken to a tube train coming down a tunnel.'

Of these bombardments Midshipman Corbett wrote in his journal:

> *During the last shoot of the day a formation of five Focke Wulf 190s worked around up into the sun on our port bow. A few moments after the last shot they dived on us. All the ships around joined in the barrage and three planes crashed on our starboard side. No hits were registered by us but it is impossible to say who destroyed the planes as so many were firing.*

The *Warspite* pulled back and, all through the night, German bombers hunted up and down off the beaches trying to find and attack her. Petty Officer Pearson had spent all day closed up in A turret and now came out of Action Stations to get some fresh air in his lungs.

> *I looked towards the shore where I could see fires and explosions as we were*

Warspite's bridge is crowded as the battleship prepares to fire a salvo at Salerno. *Jack Hockley Collection.*

only a couple of miles out. Although I didn't know it at the time, my own brother was in one of the regiments fighting ashore.

The *Warspite* may have evaded the enemy close inshore but she was still being shadowed and that night beat off an attack by six aircraft. Midshipman Corbett noted:

About 04.30am they disappeared and a few minutes later a shadower came in and dropped a bomb at random before also disappearing. On Thursday 16th we returned to the bay to carry out the good work. The range was 24,000 yards and it took us a long time to find the target. We then fired six salvos which, according to our Royal Marine spotting officer, were excellent.

Warspite's forward observer later told a Reuters reporter:

Below me on a plain I could see a tank battle going on. When our 15-inch shells rushed overhead it seemed like a sudden clap of thunder. Then I watched houses blown high into the sky and ammunition dumps going up with fearsome explosions, black smoke and debris flying into the air.

I couldn't see the Germans themselves as they were in concentrations in a deep ravine, but the ship's gunnery was extremely accurate and our shells were dropping clean on the target. The effect on the Germans' morale must have been enormous. Even where I was, which was some distance from where the shells were bursting, the earth shook and rumbled as the shells found their mark.[8]

In reply the enemy decided to take *Warspite* out with a deadly new team – aircraft carrying radio-controlled glider bombs.

Junior rating Charlie McCarthy was at the time temporarily acting as the Gunnery Officer's steward.

My action station was one of three on the starboard range finder alongside two Royal Marines, Ron Cave and Blossom Dorman. When the Warspite *finished bombardment, I got a request to attend to the Gunnery Officer as he wanted a shave. 'Could I leave my position, as things were quiet, and get some hot water to his cabin'. As he shaved, the Gunnery Officer said our bombardment had been a success. The Americans hadn't believed* Warspite *could knock out given targets from a ten mile range. But we apparently did and, as ammo was still available to use, we were waiting for fresh targets.*

179

At around 2.00p.m. *Warspite* was pulling back from her bombardment position when a dozen Focke Wulf 190 fighters plunged onto her, provoking an intense response from her AA guns. While the *Warspite*'s attention was fully focused in beating off this swarm, three glider bombs, each packed with almost 3,000lbs of explosive, were launched from 20,000ft.

Newly promoted Petty Officer H. Banks was looking at the approaching threat through high-powered lenses in the High Angle anti-aircraft weapon director position.

> *I had been tracking it for a few moments. It looked like a Heinkel bomber. It was too high for our High Angle guns and we decided to leave it to our fighter cover, unaware they had been diverted to carry out strafing in support of the troops ashore. It seemed like the plane might ignore us anyway but then suddenly I noticed what looked like a smaller plane flying directly beneath the bomber. When they were both directly overhead the smaller one tipped up, flames shot out its tail and it plummeted straight down.*

In another AA director position Midshipman Corbett also watched death approach from on high:

> *...three white streaks overhead at a great height. They were too high for the guns and even as I watched the centre one flashed and it looked as if a plane was crashing.*
>
> *The starboard 4-inch opened up with a barrage, believing it was a diving aircraft... There was a tremendous crash followed by a colossal 'woof' of air, the ship shuddered and lurched in every direction at once for a couple of seconds and then gave a final convulsive heave, then silence and stillness reigned.*
>
> *I found myself crouching down with everyone else. Standing up I felt mentally and physically sick – to think that one bomb had, in a few brief seconds, crippled us. A few moments before,* Warspite *was the most deadly warship in the world. At first we did not realize the extent of the damage as we were stopped for bombardment and so did not notice the loss of steam.*

Junior rating Charlie McCarthy was back at his action station:

> *Looking back and upwards to the funnel area, there was thick, dense smoke rising. Blossom Dorman looked at me and said: 'Quick Charlie, put your earplugs back in there's going to be a great big bang!'.*

Captain Packer later noted in his private war diary: 'For a moment I thought we were probably sunk and was quite prepared for the ship to break in two.'[9]

As usual Petty Officer Charlie Pearson was more relaxed about events, until it appeared the *Warspite* might keel over:

> *The 4-inch guns were still firing, the Oerlikons were as well. The loss of power would have been noticeable if the 15-inchers were firing but they weren't. Then she started to list to port, you could feel it. That was when things started to happen.*

One glider bomb had obviously hit the ship amidships by the funnel. A second missed amidships, but exploded in the water on the starboard side ripping open one of the battleship's torpedo bulges. The third glider bomb missed aft. A fire in the

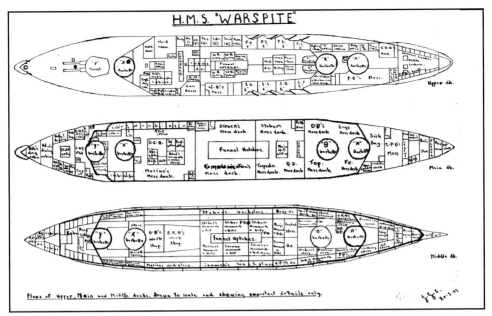

Plan drawings of the *Warspite* by Midshipman John Corbett, taken from his wartime journal. *J. Corbett.*

hangar was quickly put out and Captain Packer was determined to carry on firing, saying to his Gunnery Officer: 'If we can steam and shoot we'll carry out our final bombardment.'[10]

The ship made her way up the swept channel at six knots but then things began to go badly wrong.

> Then the ship would not steer. We were in the swept channel and we steered in a circle. I stopped engines. We were heading straight into the mines. A mine sweeper sent us violent signals to get out of it. I couldn't for the helm was hard over, and finally the starboard engine room died out too. So there we were, once again, going round in circles...[11]

While others later asserted the bomb went right down through the ship and out through her bottom without exploding, Midshipmans Corbett's journal, written a few days after the event, recorded it somewhat differently:

> It cut through the boat deck, caused a small fire in the port hangar, left a neat round hole about two foot diameter in the hangar deck, went through the ward room galley and deck, through the stokers' messdeck and finally pierced the armoured middle deck and entered Number 2 boiler room.
>
> It is believed to have exploded in the boiler room itself and blew open the Warspite's double bottom. All steam in the port unit failed instantly. The centre line bulkhead nudged dangerously into Number 3 boiler room which rapidly flooded. However the crew closed down before evacuating. Meanwhile Numbers 2 and 6 boiler rooms were unable to pump out for lack of steam so they had to be closed up and evacuated. It was hoped to use Number 1 boiler on reserve feed water but the tank was open to the sea and a neighbouring oil tank. A mixture of oil and water soon caused the Number 1 boiler room to be evacuated. Number 5 boiler room was also flooded. The only machinery we could run was two diesel dynamos, even they had to have fuel carried to them

181

in buckets. They undoubtedly saved the ship. We hauled over and took a five degree list to starboard and settled down about four feet into the water. At first we didn't realize our position was, to say the least, desperate. We were three hundred miles from a base, unable to move, heavily flooded and in great danger from further attacks with glider bombs.

Midshipman Corbett estimated the bomb had been packed with 2,600 pounds of explosives, and he measured the hole ripped in the *Warspite*'s bottom as twenty feet by four feet. Fortunately steering was soon restored and the cruiser HMS *Delhi* was called in close to provide AA cover.

The Germans were, however, doing their best to find the *Warspite* and finish her off. Midshipman Corbett: '*Delhi* overheard the German transmissions giving orders for their pilots to get us.'

A Constructor Captain – an officer with a special knowledge of naval architecture – was put aboard the *Warspite* to carry out an inspection of the damage which did not yield good news. Midshipman Corbett told his journal:

He announced we were floating on the main deck which in the quarterdeck messdeck was showing signs of collapse upwards.

It was shored down and counterflooding soon had the list corrected.

An American tug took her in tow and slowly the *Warspite* edged out into the Bay of Naples. Two more US tugs were called in and, at a speed of four knots, the *Warspite* set off for the Straits of Messina, a screen of destroyers gathered protectively around her.

Inside the *Warspite* there was an eerie silence. Warships never sleep, their vital systems providing a background noise to which crews become accustomed. Now, with all her machinery deprived of power she was completely silent and it was most unnerving. When night came, battery-powered lights flickered. With no possibility of preparing a hot meal, lemonade, bully beef and ships biscuit were passed around to her sailors.

Completely blacked out, *Warspite* crept by *Valiant* blazing away with her full anti-aircraft barrage. From time to time one of the escorting destroyers would let rip with a barrage too, making *Warspite*'s crew jump.

Exhausted by their efforts to keep her afloat, the *Warspite*'s sailors didn't know if

A British warship blazing away with all her anti-aircraft guns off Salerno, as seen from HMS **Warspite.** Jack Hockley Collection

their ship would make it through the night. They seemed to be losing the battle against flooding, even though 200 of them were on baling-out duty at all times. At any moment the crippled battleship could be found by a U-boat or a Junkers torpedo bomber.

Petty Officer Banks was puzzled: 'Why the German air force didn't attack us I'll never know, for we were absolutely helpless.'

Captain Packer's diary noted his crew were really feeling the strain but still determined to get the battleship back to Malta.

> With the dawn the situation had worsened and there was much fatigue for no one had had much stand-off during the past few days, and since the hit everyone was on their feet, either at the guns, hauling in wires, bailing, pumping or shoring up. Men were beginning to sit down and rest and drop off to sleep as they sat.[12]

More tugs arrived but their hawsers frequently parted and, pushed by the strong south flowing current, *Warspite* passed through the Straits of Messina sideways on.

Midshipman Corbett recorded the scene:

> Ahead of us we could see the glow of Mount Etna. It was an amazing spectacle. As we entered the straits a terrific wind sprang up from astern and an exceptionally strong current caught us. We swung to port and nothing would move us back again in spite of all efforts.

Captain Packer wrote in his war diary:

> When we struck the tide-rips and whirl pools the ship became unmanageable. From midnight until 5.00a.m. we were completely out of control and going through the straits broadside on with all tows parted except one. However just as the tide turned off Reggio to take us back up the straits again, I got a tug alongside each side aft and straightened her up sufficiently for the tugs forward to go ahead and get some way on the ship.[13]

Despite being a superb sitting target throughout 17 and 18 September, as she slowly crawled towards Malta, no enemy aircraft or submarines came across the *Warspite*.

She reached safe harbour on 19 September and was cheered in. Captain Packer's diary noted:

> All the ships' companies turned out to see us go past and I got many signals. There is no doubt there was great anxiety that we should not get back. Well, we have. So, for the second time in 27 years, I have limped into port in *Warspite* heavily damaged.[14]

Three men trapped in Number 4 boiler room throughout the trip back to Malta were grateful to be released.

It was soon plain Malta's dockyard facilities could do very little for her. In the meantime the Salerno beachhead was stabilized and the Germans, badly knocked about by the guns of bombarding battleships, were pushed back. In his journal Midshipman Corbett noted that *Warspite's* fatalities were low – two men were killed when the bomb hit, four died later from burns caused by not wearing their flash gear. Other ships hit by German glider bombs had suffered much worse, including the US Navy cruiser *Savannah*, with 200 dead, and the Royal Navy cruiser *Uganda*, on which eighteen men were killed.

Aboard HMS *Warspite* major efforts were made to discover how the bomb could have homed in so well after being dropped from such a height. Midshipman Corbett revealed in his journal:

> *We have gathered together various pieces of the bomb in the hope of discovering its secret. Some are covered with writing and look very promising.*

One thought was that the bombs rode in on a warship's radar. In reality the glider bombs were radio controlled by an aimer sat in the mother aircraft using powerful glasses to keep track of them on their way to the target. It struck Midshipman Corbett that *Warspite* might be so crippled she would never sail to war again and he might end up going to another ship. He wrote in his diary:

> *I don't want to leave the ship if it means going to* Nelson *or some old, slow ship. Besides,* Warspite *has found a place in my heart. It would have been dreadful if we had lost her.*

By late September it looked as if Midshipman Corbett's worst fear might be unfounded. He told his journal:

> *Numerous experts have been rushed out from England by air and have been inspecting the damage. There seems no doubt they consider the ship worth repairing.*

A large part of the *Warspite* was uninhabitable and a vast amount of the crew's clothing, bedding and private possessions had been ruined. The ship's bathrooms and toilets were out of action and so a makeshift area, screened carefully from the Maltese, was rigged up on the forecastle. Great efforts were still being made to pump out boiler rooms flooded with water and oil. But, a few days later, Midshipman Corbett reported: 'Our efforts to pump out Number 5 boiler room have failed. The submersible pumps failed at the vital moment...'.

The journey to Gibraltar where the dockyard was standing by to carry out major repairs would be a slow one. Midshipman Corbett would not be with her, for he had received confirmation of orders to join HMS *Nelson*. After his transfer he told his journal:

> *I was very sorry to leave the* Warspite*. There was something about her which gave her an air of supremacy. I don't know what it was. Perhaps it was the spirit I noticed when I joined her and, at first, disliked. It was as if her crew were saying: 'We are the* Warspite*, nothing can touch us.' That attitude stood her in good stead when we were hit. The men were so much above it all, as if it just couldn't happen to the*

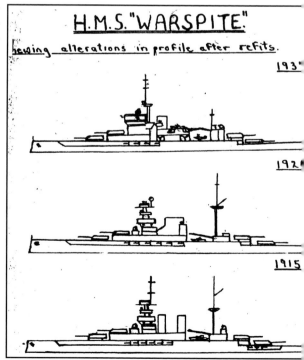

H.M.S. "WARSPITE"

showing alterations in profile after refits.

1937

1926

1915

184 **The changing silhouette of HMS *Warspite* 1915-1937 from the journal of Midshipman John Corbett.** *J. Corbett.*

Warspite. There was no question of 'will we get back', but 'at what time do we get back in'. The crew never realized just how badly we were damaged and perhaps it will be a good thing if they do not know. I hope now that they take the chance to repair her and do other essential refitting.

Midshipman Corbett hoped *Warspite* would have her 6-inch guns removed and replaced by more modern weapons. He felt she needed her anti-aircraft guns improved and more modern fire control equipment. Her hydraulics should also be renewed so *Warspite* could then go to the Far East and finally give the Japanese a good hiding.

If this is done I do not doubt the Japanese will regret their lie about sinking her at the Battle of the Coral Sea and regret they were late arriving at Sydney Harbour.

The *Warspite* started her dangerous journey under tow to Gibraltar on 1 November.

Captain Packer had left to join Admiral Cunningham's staff, so she was now commanded

Warspite under tow from Malta to Gibraltar, November 1943. *C. Pearson Collection*

temporarily by her Executive Officer, Commander the Hon. D. Edwardes.

Four tugs undertook the tow to Gibraltar and there was a quartet of destroyers on escort duty. With the Allies having virtually uncontested air supremacy over the Mediterranean, fighter cover was always close at hand to destroy any torpedo bombers cheeky enough to make a run at her.

Imagine her fate if the same journey of over 1,000 miles under tow had been attempted in 1941. Initially *Warspite* could raise steam on one boiler and proceeded at seven knots, but her engines soon failed and she had to rely on the tugs. But before the battleship could enter harbour at Gibraltar she had to sort out a tricky problem with her 15-inch guns which was down to Petty Officer Pearson's department to handle.

Some of the 15-inch guns still had their shells up the spout from Salerno. To get them out we started up some diesels to give us enough auxiliary power to operate the turrets and guns. The turrets were turned safely out to sea, the guns elevated and we put quarter charges up. As my turret wasn't involved I was on the upper deck watching. The guns were fired and, because they didn't have much charge behind them, the shells tumbled over and over. The ricochet when they hit the water was quite spectacular.

More than a week after leaving Malta for the last time the *Warspite* finally reached Gibraltar and was put into dry dock four days later. Petty Officer Banks managed to get down into the dry dock and take a look at the damage the battleship had sustained.

How the Warspite *stayed afloat I will never know. For, without exaggerating one bit, you could have driven a double-decker bus through the hole in the ship's bottom.*

On 10 October, Petty Officer Banks got his orders to head home after being recommended for promotion to officer. 'I said farewell to the beautiful ship that had been my home for four-and-a-quarter years.'

On 10 December, having been kept fully briefed on his former flagship's dangerous moments, Admiral Cunningham took time out from his busy schedule as the new First Sea Lord to visit *Warspite* at Gibraltar, touring the ship to see how her repairs were progressing. Eighteen days after Cunningham's visit the *Warspite* was released from dry dock and started some limited work-up with a virtually new crew. However, her departure was suddenly postponed and she didn't head back until March 1944. A brief call to the Clyde was followed by a trip around the top of Scotland to Rosyth for yet more

Admiral Cunningham during his visit to Gibraltar Dockyard to see how repairs to *Warspite* are progressing.
C. Pearson Collection.

substantial repairs, as two of her turrets were still out of action. Arriving on 16 March, the battleship received Captain M.H.A. Kelsey as her new Commanding Officer.

One of her new Midshipmen was Andy Hamnett who joined the *Warspite* at Rosyth in April.

> *As a midshipman, I was the lowest form of life in the Navy. I knew absolutely nothing and was really very frightened of life in this enormous metal box called* Warspite. *One of my main concerns was to find my way to and from the heads safely.*

Throughout April and May, as Midshipman Hamnett became slightly less worried about life on a battlewagon, *Warspite* rehearsed for her role in the biggest amphibious assault of all time – the invasion of Normandy. She would be without her impotent 6-inch guns which had been removed and plated in.

Notes

1   Cunningham, *A Sailor's Odyssey.*
2   Joy Packer, *Deep as the Sea.*
3   Ibid.
4   Ibid.
5   *The Malta Times, 19 September 1943.*
6   Ibid.
7   Cunningham, *A Sailor's Odyssey.*
8   Reuters report carried by the *Malta Times, 22 September 1943.*
9   Joy Packer, *Deep as the Sea.*
10 Ibid.
11 Ibid.
12 Ibid.
13 Ibid.
14 Ibid.

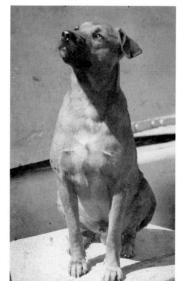

Able dog *Pluto*, who was run over while *Warspite* was at Gibraltar for repairs.
C. Pearson Collection

Chapter Ten

SWANSONG

Hammering the Atlantic Wall

Age and injuries of war were catching up with the *Warspite*. She set sail to take part in the D-Day invasion with her X turret permanently out of action and with a huge concrete caisson moulded over the large hole in her hull made by the glider bomb explosion. Though the crews of the Royal Navy's battleships did not realize it quite yet, the era of the battleship was drawing rapidly to a close. The British fleet had fought its last battleship versus battleship action during the Battle of North Cape on Boxing Day 1943, when HMS *Duke of York* played the leading role in sinking the *Scharnhorst*. The honour of fighting the last fleet action involving combat between battleships would fall to the Japanese and American navies. At the battle of Surigao Strait in late 1944, elderly US Navy dreadnoughts salvaged from the bottom of Pearl Harbor utterly destroyed a Japanese force including the battleships *Yamashiro* and *Fuso*. But Surigao lay several months in the future as *Warspite* embarked on her journey to D-Day. Midshipman Hamnett was still a worried young man:

> We sailed for Greenock via Scapa Flow and the Minches where we undertook gunnery practice and all sorts of other things which I did not understand. My action station was with the Commander in the After Conning Tower, which was the emergency position of command in case the bridge was knocked out.

The *Warspite* left Greenock on 2 June. Together with the battleship *Ramillies*, the 15-inch gun monitor *Roberts*, cruisers *Mauritius*, *Arethusa*, *Danae*, *Dragon* and *Frobisher* plus destroyers, she was to make up the Eastern Task Force. HMS *Warspite* was by 5 June off the south-west peninsula, almost within sight of Plymouth. By that evening the *Warspite* was just one of several thousand vessels waiting for the green light off the Isle of Wight, in dreadful weather which threatened to force cancellation of the whole enterprise. Petty Officer Charlie Pearson didn't envy the invasion troops:

> Standing on the upper deck you could see the landing ships passing by and you felt sorry for the troops inside them who were sick as dogs.

The Eastern Task Force sailed across the Channel behind a large force of sweepers clearing a path through minefields so they could get in as close as possible to carry out their fire missions. The troops were being landed early the following morning over a fifty mile front, on five beaches which were coded as follows: SWORD and GOLD, British,

Warspite's mighty 15-inch guns roar.
Sutherland Collection.

Sailors standing on one of *Warspite*'s 15-inch turrets gaze at the D-Day invasion fleet astern.
Topham Picturepoint

JUNO, British and Canadian, OMAHA and UTAH, American. The Eastern Task Force was to provide support for the British 3rd Division landing across SWORD beach, with the *Warspite*'s special mission knocking out gun batteries near Le Havre.

> *At 11.00p.m. they entered the eastern-most channel, between the lines of lighted buoys which the minesweeper flotillas had laid like street-lamps across to France.*[1]

To *Warspite* went the honour of being the first ship to open fire on D-Day, her shells

The *Warspite* Ordnance branch poses for a 'team photo' in 1944. Petty Officer Charles Pearson is back row, second from left. *C. Pearson Collection*

The crew of one of *Warspite*'s 4-inch guns take a cigarette break during the bombardment of the D-Day beachhead. Ray Pattenden is far left, back row. R. *Pattenden Collection.*

pummelling a German shore battery which showed signs of life. At 5.30a.m. the whole bombardment fleet fired - an awesome ribbon of flame providing the German occupiers with the rudest of awakenings. Lunging out of a smokescreen laid by Allied vessels to protect their seaward flank came three German torpedo boats from Le Havre. The young commanding officer of one was stunned:

> *The sight which he saw when he came through the smoke amazed him, prepared though he was for something extraordinary. Straight ahead of him, in the early light of dawn he saw six battleships or heavy cruisers, and so many minor warships he had not time to count them; and yet, to his further surprise not one of them opened fire.*[2]

The Germans launched seventeen torpedoes and it wasn't long before the British warships reacted on seeing the splashes. The torpedo boats turned around and made a speedy retreat back through the smokescreen, passing three of their own armed trawlers coming out to have a go. Using radar, the shells of *Warspite* and other Allied warships followed the torpedo boats back through the smoke. One of *Warspite*'s scored a hit and instantly sank a trawler.

In the meantime the German torpedoes had claimed a Norwegian destroyer, but otherwise found no victims, one of the tinfish passing harmlessly between *Warspite* and *Ramillies*. The old battlewagons had survived the only naval surface action of D-Day.

Able Seaman Ray Pattenden, who was on one of *Warspite*'s 4-inch guns, gave this verdict:

> *We did a lot of firing but I don't know what at, or if we hit anything, because we were under the gunnery director. We just followed the instruments.*

Throughout the day *Warspite* conducted fire missions – often without the benefit of an observation aircraft or a forward observer. She pounded enemy infantry and vehicle concentrations, a command headquarters and gun emplacements.

Not long after the *Warspite*'s guns had announced the seaborne part of the invasion of Europe, overhead flew the second wave of gliders carrying soldiers of the British

6th Airborne Division. Captain Kelsey drew the crew's attention to the spectacle. Over the tannoy he said: 'All personnel not on full Action Stations can come up on deck to witness a sight you will never see again in your lifetime.'

Petty Officer Pearson was one of those able to take advantage of the Captain's invitation.

At that moment there was a lull in the shelling and we came out the turret to see what was happening. Around us other ships were still firing – the Ramillies *firing her own 15-inch guns, the rocket ships letting rip. Then we saw the gliders coming over in a V for Victory formation. It was awesome. Sadly we saw some of them shot down and fall into the sea. A little while later the bodies of the dead paratroopers and wreckage of the planes floated by. It was a bit upsetting.*

German counter-fire from shore batteries sometimes came close enough to scythe her upper works with shrapnel, but no real damage was caused to *Warspite*.

Albert Cock who had been a telegraphist on the *Warspite* in the Mediterranean was now a Chief Petty Officer serving in one of the minesweepers nearby. He said:

We were fired upon by shore batteries and also bombed by German and American aircraft. We were cutting the mines free and destroying them by gunfire. We hit one mine which caused us serious damage but didn't sink us. I knew the Warspite *was there but we never made visual contact with her although we could hear the big guns banging away all day.*

Other ex-members of *Warspite*'s crew were heavily embroiled in the fighting ashore. They were Royal Marines who had served on her in the Far East before gaining entry to the commando forces and taking part in the D-Day assault. At least three of them died either during the landings or the subsequent fighting on the Normandy beachhead.

Late on the evening of D-Day *Warspite* pulled back from SWORD sector and dropped anchor a few miles off shore. The following day she fired for effect at grid references where it was thought likely enemy troops, vehicles and guns might be. Enemy strongpoints ashore also received attention.

The *Daily Mail*'s Naval Correspondent, W.F. Hatin, filed a very excited report on her invasion bombardments. He told how the pilot of a Spitfire spotting the fall of *Warspite*'s shot looked on in amazement as German troops and vehicles were blasted to bits. The Spitfire had spotted an enemy convoy moving along a road through woods some twelve miles inland. Using the pilot's report, the battleship's Gunnery Officer rapidly plotted a fire solution. 'I gave Jerry a speed of fifteen knots,' the Gunnery Officer told the *Daily Mail* man, '...and let him have it.'

Having fired more than 300 shells in just two days, *Warspite*'s magazines were low so she retired across the Channel to Portsmouth to load up with more ammo. When she returned on 9 June, she was ordered to support the American beaches where the troops were hard pressed and the US Navy's bombardment vessels, including the battleship USS *Arkansas*, were running short of shells.

Between 4.12p.m. and 6.15p.m, ninety-six rounds of 15-inch were fired, again without the aid of aircraft spotters or forward observers. *Warspite* devastated a crucial enemy artillery position and was highly praised in a signal from American

With tug in attendance, *Warspite*'s 15-inch guns pound German positions in Normandy, June 1944. *Specially commisioned painting by Dennis C. Andrews.*

commanders.

Two days later she was off GOLD beach and helped save the 50th Division from a formidable counterattack by destroying German troops and tanks assembling in a wood. The order given by Captain Kelsey for this impressive firepower display was: 'Fifty rounds 15-inch rapid fire.'

Midshipman Andy Hamnett's baptism of fire had been the incredible blast of the *Warspite*'s own guns on D-Day and since then he had learned to ignore danger.

> *Once we reached Normandy, I can remember sleeping on the deck and eating enormous quantities of pasties, or oggies as they were called. As my action station was near a 15-inch gun turret the noise was enormous.*
>
> *My principal task was running messages for the Commander, whose name I forget. Another task was to drive one of the ship's motor boats around the fleet, taking bread from our bakery to the smaller vessels and also landing war correspondents from our ship to Port-en-Bessin. I cannot remember being particularly frightened, but no doubt I took my example from the older men around me.*

As *Warspite* lay off Port-en-Bessin she was visited by Canadian radio correspondent Andrew Cowan who may well have been brought out to her by Midshipman Hamnett's boat.

Like many others who came to see the legendary vessel in action off Normandy, Cowan placed her awesome display of firepower in a lyrical frame.

> *This afternoon HMS* Warspite *stretched the long arm of her 15-inch guns fifteen miles to help the Army by bombarding enemy positions south of the little town of Tilly. She lay about a mile-and-a-half off the beach at the little fishing village of Port-en-Bessin. Through binoculars I could see the miles of yellow sands at the foot of the high cliffs, sands just made for lazy summer holidays. They were deserted except for a few landing*

craft stranded above the high water mark. The little town of Port-en-Bessin crowded into a notch in the cliffs was deserted too, so was its tiny harbour surrounded by a granite sea wall where the fishermen used to bring their boats at high tide. A French flag flew proudly over the little village. On the rim of the cliffs, looking down into the sea were the battered remains of German coastal batteries. The sea was calm and the weather typical of the Channel – cloudy and bright by turns with an occasional rain shower.

Through the ship's loud hailer the word was given that the 15 -inch guns were about to open fire. Captain Pugh, the ship's bombardment liaison officer, a Royal Artillery officer, got the targets' bearings at his action station on the bridge of the Warspite. *They came from the headquarters ship which had got them from the FOB, or Forward Observer of Bombardment, on shore.*

The ship's bombardment liaison officer telephoned the bearings and the range to the transmitting station on the ship where they were converted into terms of elevation of the ship's guns and, at a signal from the Gunnery Officer, HMS Warspite *opened fire.*

The target is on the right flank of the Canadians who are fighting around Caen. In this wood, just ahead of the British position which on the map looked to be about half - a-mile square in area was a concentration of enemy forces and into this wood the Warspite *poured fifteen three gun salvos of unobserved fire. That means the wood was saturated with a continuous bombardment without waiting for observers to check the fall of shot. When the guns fired at once the great 35,000 ton battleship gave a tremendous shudder. Everything onboard that can fall or break loose has to be fastened or battened down when the ship goes into action. Cabin doors in the bridge have to be removed or the blast that rushes from end to end of the ship when she fires would splinter the panelling.*

Looking down from the bridge at a certain angle it was just possible to see for a split second the shell as it hurtled skyward through the great puff of brown smoke. The Warspite's *second target for the afternoon was in the same neighbourhood as the first. The* Warspite's *fire was directed onto the target by an observer in a Tailor craft – one of those small planes that have a speed of about seventy-five miles an hour and can take off from a tennis court. Onto the target went nine salvos – and after each salvo the observer reported back by radio to the bombardment liaison officer onboard the ship. Six of the salvos – twelve tons of high explosives – hit the target.*[3]

The *Warspite's* main weapons were getting worn out so she was ordered to Rosyth to get replacements on 12 June. She became the first British battleship since the

HMS *Warspite* **unleashes another bombardment of German forces in support of the D-Day landings.** *C. Pearson Collection*

beginning of the war to pass through the Straits of Dover and, despite the Allies exerting almost complete control of sea and air she would still have been wiser going the long way around. Not only did a series of German coastal batteries fire at her but she set off a magnetic mine thirty miles east of Harwich early on 13 June. It caused no casualties but inflicted considerable damage. The explosion damaged her steering so that her helm jammed hard over and she made a wild turn to starboard. *Warspite* stopped dead in the water. Several hundred tons of water had poured into her and she had a list of more than four degrees to port.

Midshipman Hamnett was down below in the gunnery directing rooms when the mine went off.

> *The hatch jammed on us. We knew* Warspite *had a large concrete slab in her side, as a result of the flying bomb hit at Salerno, so everyone was a little concerned in case it might fall out.*

Petty Officer Pearson was inside one of the turrets:

> *We were just about to close down and come out of action stations when there was a hell of a thud. We said: 'Don't move, we might be needed.' We thought it might be a German surface raider having a go at us.*

Able Seaman Pattenden was off watch:

> *I was down the messdeck at the time and there was a boom and a bang, just a thump really. I was by my locker and the ship just gave a kind of shudder. We went on the upper deck and it was a bit frightening because the valves on the funnel had gone and she was making this blood curdling racket, screaming blue murder as if she was outraged at what had happened.*

The *Warspite*'s list was soon corrected by counter flooding and sixty minutes later her engines were restarted. With only her starboard propellers working, she limped northwards at seven knots. She arrived at Rosyth on 14 June and, as she crawled up the Forth, the crews of the battleships *Howe* and *Anson* cheered her in. Some of the *Warspite*'s crew got leave, including a boy sailor from the East End of London who revealed a new trick he had learned since going to sea:

> *There were a lot of things I learned aboard ship which obviously you cannot get from basic training ashore, such as making a 'Monkey's Fist'. My Sea Daddy aboard* Warspite – *the older sailor tasked with showing me the tricks of the trade – gave me a tip on how to prevent my £1 notes from disintegrating should I find myself in the drink at anytime. He said I should put my money in a* Durex, *making a 'Monkey's Fist', and put it into my money belt. This I did and thought no more of it until I went on leave. Following the custom of the East End, my family went to the local pub to welcome their sailor son home. When it was my turn to buy a round I unwittingly took the* Durex *out of my belt to get my money. Mother looked mortified, Dad chortled into his beer and the barmaid, who thought I was making her an offer, blushed.*[4]

While some of the younger members of her crew were shocking their mothers, Rosyth Dockyard worked around the clock on the old battleship. The main problem was the *Warspite*'s badly twisted shafts which, because of lack of time, couldn't be removed for straightening and so had to be worked on still mounted in the ship. To the Admiralty her main purpose now was to be a floating artillery battery – as long as she could still move at a reasonable speed and her main guns functioned, it didn't matter if the repairs were not complete. The dockyard workers persevered, got three of her shafts working again and her 15-inch guns were replaced. After some bombardment practice and a short stop at Plymouth, *Warspite* was ready by late August to take up station off the French coast again.

Petty Officer Pearson recalled that she was called to save a situation her crew had been following avidly:

> We read in the newspapers while we were lying at Spithead about this German general at Brest who said his boys would fight to the last man. The Americans were worried about the casualty rate so they had a word with the Admiralty. We were ordered to go down there and do a job of work.

American troops were trying to take the port so it could be opened up to allow in supplies to feed the big breakout from the Normandy beachhead. Forty thousand German troops were cut off, but in a perfect defensive position, entrenched in eighteenth century fortifications bolstered by new defences. The Americans needed some heavy-duty firepower to crack the enemy but, even though she fired 213 shells, *Warspite* did only limited damage before the big American attack went in and finally ousted the Germans.

One individual who found his nerves completely shot away by *Warspite's* intensive programme of gunnery was the ship's cat who had to be retired. A humorous notice was posted in the *Warspite* to mark the event:

> An Official Service Certificate, including an Honourable Discharge, has been issued on behalf of the Ship's Cat which has left HMS *Warspite* owing to shell-shock and has taken up residence with the wife of a crew member A/B George Allen of Barking, Essex.

HMS *Warspite*'s Y turret gets its new guns at Rosyth Dockyard, summer 1944. *Sutherland Collection.*

According to the true copy of the Certificate, signed by Captain Kelsey DSO, the cat is described as 'Ginger Brest' the surname having reference to service with the ship at Brest. Port Division is given as Chatham and Official number as LX.1944. Born in the ship, its denomination is described as 'Free Thinker' and has previously received special mention at D-Day: 'By his actions, proved himself an example to others'. On August 25, during the bombardment of the forts at Brest, he also acquitted himself in a very seamanlike manner.

Last Curtain Call for a Fighting Life

A week before the first anniversary of her glider bomb hit off Salerno, *Warspite* was once again bombarding German troop positions, but the possibility of a similar devastating air strike was very remote.

The Luftwaffe had been wiped from the skies and the enemy's army had been pushed back almost to the German frontier.

However, the problem of Hitler's troops hanging on stubbornly to strategically important Channel ports persisted and it was threatening to bring the Allied advance to a halt. Those ports the Allies had captured were not capable of taking vast amounts of supplies needed to keep the momentum going. In fact the majority of the Allied supplies were still coming over the invasion beaches. *Warspite* did her bit to break the German grip on Le Havre on 10 September as preparation for a British attack which finally took the port.

A week later an ill-conceived Anglo-American airborne operation to cross the Rhine took place, and faltered, at Arnhem in Holland. Many thought the effort would have been better expended in driving German forces out of the island of Walcheren which dominated approaches to the major port of Antwerp. It had the potential to feed the Allied advance the huge quantities needed to storm into Germany on a broad front. Although it had been captured on 3 September it was impossible to bring supply ships up the River Schelde to it because of powerful German gun emplacements on Walcheren. Finally, in October 1944, the order was given for an all-out attack on the island. It would be spear-headed by a British commando brigade and gunfire support provided by HMS *Warspite* and the 15-inch gun monitors *Erebus* and *Roberts*. The final major amphibious assault of the Allied campaign to liberate north-west Europe, it would be the last time *Warspite*'s guns fired.

On 30 October 1944, *Warspite* dropped anchor at Deal on the Kent coast to wait with the other Walcheren invasion ships for final confirmation *Operation Infatuate* was to go ahead. By the next morning the old battleship was ten miles off West Kapelle Lighthouse and, despite filthy weather which precluded the use of spotter aircraft, she hit her targets and on time. *Warspite* fired 353 shells in twenty-one salvos of 15-inch, concluding her mission, her part in the Second World War and her fighting life shortly before 5.25p.m.

It may have been the *Warspite*'s last starring role but, for her crew, it featured nothing worth remembering. To Petty Officer Pearson it was merely 'foggy, dull and we didn't see much... . We did our job and left.'

After a call to Rosyth the *Warspite* headed back to boring inactivity at Spithead.

The 15-inch gun monitor HMS *Roberts* which took part in the bombardment of Walcheren alongside *Warspite* in November 1944. *Goodman Collection.*

Warspite fires her guns for the last time during the bombardment of Walcheren.

Specially commissioned painting by Dennis C. Andrews.

Notes

1   David Howarth, *Dawn of D-Day*.
2   Ibid.
3   Sound Archive, Imperial War Museum.
4   A *Warspite* veteran writing in *Anchors Aweigh*, the journal of the *Warspite* Association.

Chapter Eleven

STUBBORN TO THE END

Left Behind, Sent to the Breakers

At the beginning of February 1945 the Admiralty confirmed the *Warspite* would pay off into reserve. There was no point in considering her for further service - the war had literally moved beyond her horizons.

The Allied troops in Europe were about to push deep into Germany and, while battleships were still needed in the Far East for the final assault on the Japanese home islands, there were younger vessels which could now be released from home waters. *Warspite* was too old and worn out and it was not worth giving her the major rebuild she needed to be brought back to full fighting efficiency.

By the end of February 1945 she was still moored at Spithead, with the occasional trip into Portsmouth which is where Petty Officer Pearson made his exit.

I left in April 1945 lugging my kitbag, my toolbox and my hammock. Despite all that stuff, I somehow managed a turn at the bottom of the brow to give her a last look. I was a bit choked but glad to leave as well - if they no longer needed the Warspite *then the war must be coming to an end. I was demobbed the following year.*

Fifteen months later, after more time at Spithead, she was brought back into Portsmouth Harbour to be stripped of her guns and anything else worth saving for use elsewhere. Despite calls to have her preserved as a museum ship the Royal Navy showed its usual lack of sentimentality and confirmed she would be sold for scrap. Her battle ensign had been presented to St Giles Cathedral in Edinburgh by Admiral Cunningham during his investiture as a Knight of the Thistle by King George VI in September 1945.

On 12 March 1947 the *Warspite* was towed again to Spithead and the following month the tugs *Mytinda III* and *Bustler* arrived. Their job was to tow her to the Gareloch, in the mouth of the Clyde, where Metal Industries would cut her up.

However, a storm hit the Channel on 20 April when she was off Land's End. With the full fury of the Atlantic rolling in, she bucked and struggled so violently the tow line to *Bustler* parted. Digging her bows stubbornly into the sea she began to take on water and became even more unruly. It was clear by the following morning she would get no further while the storm lasted and continuing would put the lives of eight caretaker personnel aboard at risk.

The famous battleship's final journey, and her bid for freedom on the way to the breaker's yard, were reported in all the leading national newspapers.

The *Daily Telegraph*'s man-on-the-spot wrote:

I flew over the Warspite *and her escort last night as they crept slowly along the Channel through heavy weather within sight of the shore twenty miles west of the Lizard. The tugs were straining at the tow ropes fore and aft, pulling almost at right angles to starboard, with the ship's bows to the coast. Their position hardly changed as we circled, and the tugs appeared to be doing little more than hold the great battleship in the heavy seas. Both tugs were pitching so steeply that at times their screws were out of the water.*

The *News Chronicle*'s reporter also conveyed the same high drama:

Experts who, from the shore, watched her lurching and pounding heavily among the distant breakers said that the bottom must by then have been torn out of her.

After a fresh line was put across by *Bustler*, the battleship was pulled into Mount's Bay, near Penzance, where she dropped anchor. On 23 April the violence of the continuing storm saw her breaking free of her anchor and she was carried across the bay to run aground in Prussia Cove. Her bows were ripped open, compartments flooded and she sank down by her bows – it was time to get the eight caretakers off. In a savagely undulating sea the Penlee lifeboat went out for them.

In those treacherous conditions the small vessel could easily have been smashed to pieces but somehow she managed to get the men off without coming to grief.

After this daring deed the *News Chronicle*'s man buttonholed Mr E.F. Madron, Cox of the Penlee Lifeboat. He said:

We managed to get the lifeboat between the rocks and the ship, but could not get a line to her. Every time the lifeboat was level with the decks one of the crew jumped to safety. That was the only way we could get them off.

Another newspaper sagely observed:

Her oldest loves, the wind and the sea, have helped the Old Lady of the Fleet to cheat the executioner. She is ashore, apparently for good... .

One of those who made his way to Prussia Cove was Gordon Ellis, who thirty-one years earlier as a young Surgeon Lieutenant had experienced a roller-coaster ride through Jutland aboard her. Having eventually reached the rank of Surgeon Captain before leaving the Royal Navy, his family home was in Cornwall, so he was close at hand. Taking his camera with him, Gordon Ellis stood on the storm-lashed shore not far from where the *Warspite* had run aground and captured her glorious end on film. 'He always loved the ship,' his daughter-in-law Judith recalled decades later. 'My father-in-law said that, as she was a West Country ship, it would be appropriate if she ended her days there as well.'

It was true. The *Warspite* had made her last voyage and typically did what she

Warspite hits the rocks after breaking free from the tugs taking her to the scrapyard. *Gordon Ellis.*

Savage Atlantic rollers pound the old battleship's hull as she finds her final resting place on the rocks of Cornwall. *Gordon Ellis.*

wanted, refusing to leave her native south-west of England. Where she was born she would die. There is no doubt all those who knew *Warspite* would have read the reports of her final stubborn gesture with a wry smile, not least Admiral Cunningham and Winston Churchill, two leading figures of the twentieth century whom she helped elevate to everlasting fame.

It took several more years for the *Warspite* to disappear from her last resting place, cut up and blown apart.

In the summer of 1950 what was left of the *Warspite* was refloated and towed over to Marazion beach by St Michael's Mount. The job of blasting and cutting her apart continued over the next seven years, the seaplane crane which recovered Petty Officer Rice's Swordfish at Narvik and Matapan was used to lift scrap sections over the side until it too was taken away. The scrap sections were loaded onto trains at a local siding and transported to Wales to be melted down. In the end they couldn't remove her oil-burning boilers which are still deeply embedded in the beach after being blown to bits.

It is said some members of her crew made a last pilgrimage to say a final farewell to the *Warspite* before she was completely gone, walking as close as they safely could to her remains on Marazion beach.

Frank Page, who had sailed back to Britain aboard HMS *Warspite* as an eight-year-old boy in 1929, found his emotions stirred up reading about *Warspite* running aground. Even after taking part in bombing raids on Germany in RAF Lancaster bombers during the Second World War, he found room for sentiment in his soul.

> *I always remembered HMS* Warspite *with affection, and was very sad when she went aground near Penzance.*

H. Banks, who last saw *Warspite* in dry dock at Gibraltar in October 1943 and had been demobbed as a Lieutenant two years later, keenly followed the story of her final days.

> *I nearly wept with joy when I learned no further effort would be made to get her off.*
> *The* Warspite's *epitaph was surely 'she died as she lived – fighting!'.*

For most though, including former Petty Officer Charlie Pearson, her end provoked no great overwhelming reaction.

> *At Salerno when she was hurt badly we all suddenly realized we might lose our home so we wanted the old girl to pull through with a passion. But when it came time to get rid of her, I can't say any of us was out there waving banners. We were glad the war was*

An aerial photograph of *Warspite* aground at Prussia Cove.
Goodman Collection.

over and wanted to get on with our lives. Had she been an American ship I have no doubt they would have preserved her as a museum and made a movie about her, the whole works. But not the British. Everybody loves our naval history except us. We truly are an unsentimental bunch. Sometimes it's a pity, for some things, like the Warspite, *are actually worth preserving.*

Flying high over the battleship's disappearing hulk during the 1950s was former *Warspite* junior officer John Corbett who had said goodbye to her at Malta in autumn 1943. He served in the Fleet Air Arm post-war and often piloted student navigators on training flights from the nearby naval air station at Culdrose.

At the controls of his Firefly he stared down at his old battleship and felt little emotion. 'We used her as a navigation point to mark the departure point of training exercises,' he recalled half a century later. 'She was a hulk, hardly recognizable. I felt no desire to go along to Marazion and actually see her.' Then, one day, the *Warspite* was no longer there and the Culdrose pilots had to use something else as a navigation point.

Surviving veterans of the *Warspite* Association make an annual journey to Cornwall to pay homage to their old ship, at a memorial to her on the shore at Marazion, which they commissioned to be built in the 1990s. After their annual service they stop off at a pub decorated with wood panelling salvaged from her and drink a toast to their old ship, to the immortal memory of the *Warspite*'s fighting life.

***Warspite* drew many visitors after going aground at Prussia Cove in 1947.** *Goodman Collection.*

The wreckers get to work.
Topham Picturepoint.

Epilogue

COLD WAR WARRIOR

As battleship *Warspite* was being broken up on the rocks in Cornwall, a new global confrontation was evolving.

In the opening phase of the Cold War, Russia was investing heavily in submarine construction, transforming its fleet from an ineffectual coastal force to a formidable, if crude, blue water navy. The West tried to match Soviet naval expansion and the eighth HMS *Warspite* was born during a construction competition similar to the one which created her immediate predecessor.

By the early 1960s, Britain's ability to sustain any kind of mass warship building programme was largely gone, along with her battleships. In 1960 the Royal Navy's last battleship, HMS *Vanguard*, had been sent to the scrapyard. Launched on 30 November 1944, the last, and largest, battleship built for the British fleet wasn't completed until the summer of 1946. She had a displacement of 44,500 tons and carried belt armour fourteen inches thick. Aside from eight 15-inch guns - one of them previously mounted in *Warspite* and two from HMS *Queen Elizabeth* - she also possessed sixteen 5.25-inch guns and mounted more than seventy 40mm Bofors anti-aircraft guns. Her top speed was an impressive thirty knots. *Vanguard* never saw

Britain's biggest and last battleship, HMS *Vanguard* going into dock at Devonport. *Goodman Collection.*

HMS *Vanguard* at sea in the late 1940s, carrying 15-inch guns taken from the *Warspite* and *Queen Elizabeth* among others. *Goodman Collection.*

The eighth *Warspite* being launched. *Goodman Collection.*

action. By the time she went to the breakers in 1960 it was becoming clear that for the UK to continue 'dining at the top table' of international affairs, and play an effective part in the Cold War, new super dreadnoughts called nuclear-powered submarines would have to be built.

Despite entering the nuclear submarine construction race late, and in very small numbers compared with the Russians and Americans, the quality of British boats was very high, including the new HMS *Warspite*.

Like the Queen Elizabeth Class battleships, submarine *Warspite* and her sisters - including a new HMS *Valiant* – were examples of cutting edge British naval architecture. The first British nuclear hunter-killer boat was HMS *Dreadnought*, completed in April 1963, around eight months before *Warspite* was laid down and the new *Valiant* launched. Launched on 25 September 1965, at Barrow-in-Furness, by Vickers, *Warspite* was commissioned into the fleet on 18 April 1967. With a displacement of 4,500 tons and length of 285 feet, the eighth *Warspite* had six 21-inch torpedo tubes and was powered by a British-made pressurized water-cooled nuclear reactor.

An illustrated booklet printed for the occasion of her commissioning included an introduction by her Commanding Officer, Commander R. R. Squires, who made a direct connection between the first *Warspite* and the nuclear attack submarine of the 1960s.

> With her high speed, long endurance and sophisticated weapons system, she is a ship thoroughly worthy of an illustrious name in this modern age.

Like the battleship of 1913, submarine *Warspite* contained many innovations including being the first British naval vessel to rely entirely on gyroscopes rather than a magnetic compass. Because of her nuclear power, submarine *Warspite* could stay submerged for months without coming up for air, a feat made possible by air conditioning, purification systems and electrolytic gills.

The *Warspite*'s first deployment took her to the Far East on a voyage which included the longest submerged run achieved by a British submarine to date, from Gibraltar to Singapore. Submarine *Warspite* returned to her home base at Faslane on the Clyde in March 1968 and that September visited Plymouth for the first time. There was great interest not only from the local press but also from the families of her crew. They were all keen to get an insight into the secret world of the Cold War British submarine force.

Warspite's Executive Officer, Lieutenant Commander Tim Hale, welcomed aboard his mother and discovered a connection with the seventh *Warspite* he had not previously suspected. Mrs Hale explained how, as a girl, she had visited battleship *Warspite* in Plymouth during the First World War. The invitation had come about because 'Uncle Monty was the Captain'.

'I must confess I hadn't been aware of it at all ,' Mr Hale recalled more than thirty years later. 'Naturally I knew about Jutland and *Warspite*'s part in it, but I had no idea there was a family connection until my mother came aboard the submarine.'

The dimensions of the eighth *Warspite* and the veteran of two world wars were of course vastly different but the two vessels had much in common.

'The sea-faring tradition of the first *Warspite* under Raleigh, and the fighting spirit of the seventh definitely carried on into the nuclear submarine,' said Mr Hale. 'In my experience the eighth *Warspite* was also a "happy ship" and lucky.'

But good luck is earned with hard work, not given away.

Nuclear submarines travel under water, at speeds of more than thirty knots and, because there is no room for error, the *Warspite* was always run at war pitch, with procedures for every eventuality imaginable rehearsed endlessly. Mr Hale recalled:

> *You are always envisaging situations that might arise where things go wrong. When they do, you will survive if the reaction in the first ninety seconds is a conditioned one, created by endless practice. There is only one way to operate an SSN – in absolute safety. If it isn't operated safely you are dead.*

A shot of submarine *Warspite*'s fin (conning tower), taken in October 1970. *Topham/UPP*

Commander Jonathan Cooke pictured in the early 1980s after *Warspite*'s record-breaking long patrol. *J. Cooke Collection.*

Fire, flooding, loss of reactor and/or hydroplanes were the chief disasters the crew of submarine *Warspite* hoped never to encounter. Added to them were the stresses and strains of jousting with the Russians.

At the end of 1969 submarine *Warspite* received a new commanding officer – Commander John Woodward. He would later find fame as Admiral Sir Sandy Woodward, commander of the British task force which liberated the Falklands after the Argentinean invasion of 1982. But back in 1969 nobody would ever have imagined the Royal Navy would go to war in the South Atlantic. The focus was much closer to home.

With the Russian presence in the Mediterranean growing in the late 1960s, it was inevitable submarine *Warspite* would sail the same waters her battleship forebear had mastered as Admiral Cunningham's flagship. By the summer of 1971, after deployments to the Mediterranean, *Warspite* was back at Chatham for a refit which included refuelling her reactor. Recommissioned more than two years later, she subsequently deployed to the Far East in September 1975, returning home the following June. The submarine suffered a serious diesel generator fire while alongside at Liverpool and was out of action for more than a year. After extensive repairs she went back to the Cold War frontline in 1978 and then entered a major refit at Chatham in 1979.

Three years later, as the Falklands War blew up, *Warspite* was finally coming to the end of that refit.

It made her a virtually new submarine and was therefore the equivalent of battleship *Warspite*'s 1934-37 rebuild. The old reactor core was replaced as were weapons systems and sensors. The refit included installation of Sub Harpoon, a lethal anti-shipping missile. *Warspite* was one of the first British boats to receive it. It was a handy weapon to use against the Argentinean navy so *Warspite*'s captain, Commander Jonathan Cooke, was told to get his boat out of refit and into action as soon as possible. 'We got the red alert to go to war,' he recalled. 'Rather than have six months post-refit work up, we compressed everything into four weeks.'

Once *Warspite* arrived in the South Atlantic she secured an uneasy peace in the wake of the British victory by patrolling waters around the Falklands and lurking off the coast of Argentina.

Warspite's deployment ended up being a remarkable record-breaking patrol of 112 days, eighty-eight of them submerged. At the time it was a fortnight longer than any other British submarine had achieved. When she returned to Faslane in mid-March 1983, *Warspite* sported model penguins on her outer casing (to signify the South Atlantic aspect of her patrol) and it was disclosed her food had almost run out. Her Commanding Officer revealed nearly twenty years later:

> *All we had left in our deep freeze was a trio of lonely herrings and a couple of lemons.*
> *We were eating tinned tomatoes and steak and kidney pudding.*

Commander Cooke was late for his wedding by four days.

> *Warspite's cooks made the wedding cake and if we had stayed at sea any longer I believe we would have been forced to eat it.*

The following year *Warspite* became a TV star when the BBC sent a camera crew aboard her as part of a series looking at the Royal Navy's nuclear submarine force. During the time she had the BBC aboard *Warspite* took part in a large NATO exercise and, after some initial difficulty avoiding the attentions of Maritime Patrol Aircraft, managed to sneak right into the middle of a 'convoy'. Television viewers saw the *Warspite* picking off the escorting warships first and then sinking the 'merchant ships' one-by-one. The submarine's score for the exercise was a dozen warships, four fleet auxiliaries and thirteen merchant ships. However, *Warspite* was also 'sunk' twice.

Commander Cooke left the *Warspite* in 1984 but she was to soldier on without him for another seven years. For during the 1980s the Cold War continued unabated. Commander Cooke was promoted to Captain and found himself over-seeing *Warspite*'s frontline operations as the Commanding Officer of Faslane's 3rd Submarine Squadron between 1986 and 1989.

Following the beginning of the Soviet Union's fragmentation in 1990, it was clear the Cold War had ended in victory for the West. Yet, more than a decade on, the war beneath the waves which the eighth *Warspite* played an important role in winning is still shrouded in secrecy.

The surviving veterans of battleship *Warspite* can talk openly of their dangerous moments, but those that served on the nuclear submarine remain tight-lipped.

Only hints of their dangerous cat-and-mouse game with the Soviets can be gleaned. There is, however, enough fascinating detail to compose an outline sketch of what *Warspite* got up to.

It is widely known British attack boats stalked likely Soviet submarine operating areas in the North Norwegian and Barents Seas and also ventured under the polar ice cap. Passive listening equipment provided the primary method of finding and

The eighth HMS *Warspite* arrives at Devonport Dockyard flying her paying off pennant, ready for a refit in 1990. *DML*

tracking the opposition rather than active pinging on sonar which might have masked an adversary's noise.

One of *Warspite*'s submariners said of his Cold War:

> There were plenty of tasks to keep you busy but a fair proportion of it was just routine business. Obviously Warspite *was involved in the trailing and tracking of Russian submarines, attack boats and ballistic missile vessels. Much of it was really*

HMS *Warspite* under-going her final refit at Devonport. It was cancelled mid-way and she remains in a moth-balled condition. *DML.*

boring. Thirty days out there in the grey Atlantic in bad weather really lacked glamour.

Shadowing a Russian missile-carrying submarine too closely was not really on as it would have been too provocative but some close attack boat-to-attack boat stuff happened. Certainly Royal Navy submarine skippers and their crews were, and still are, regarded as very good. In the Royal Navy we were all trained to a high standard. In the US Navy and Russian fleet during the Cold War there was more variety in skill because there were so many of them. The Russians would put all their key resources and best people into the latest boats while the older boats and crews were second division, as we found out when we encountered them in Warspite.

With the Cold War over, the Royal Navy faced the immediate 'peace dividend' cutbacks of 1990-91 which included *Warspite* being retired from service mid-way through a refit at Devonport Dockyard. And that is where she is today, discarded like her illustrious immediate predecessor in the wake of a war. The hulk of submarine *Warspite* is moth-balled and tied up alongside sister vessels HMS *Conqueror*, which sank the *Belgrano* during the Falklands conflict, HMS *Valiant* and HMS *Courageous*.

These relics of the Cold War have not yet been scrapped like the redundant capital ships of the Second World War because of their residual radio activity.

However their end is nigh. In 2000 the UK Government announced it was hoping to finally rid itself of *Warspite* and other decommissioned nuclear submarines by cutting them up and storing them on land – provided safe procedures could be devised.

There are no current plans to revive the name *Warspite* in Royal Navy service. New Type 45 air defence destroyers will be D Class vessels, including names such as HMS *Dauntless* and HMS *Daring*, and a trio of next generation nuclear-powered attack submarines are to be called *Astute*, *Artful* and *Ambush*. But Britain is hoping to build revolutionary trimaran surface warships which may enter service about 2012, a century on from the seventh *Warspite* taking shape on the slipway at Devonport.

Bearing in mind the cutting edge nature of *Warspites* of the past, it might be appropriate to reserve one of those vessels as a future bearer of the name.

Appendix

Other vessels of the
QUEEN ELIZABETH CLASS

HMS *Queen Elizabeth*

Built by Portsmouth Dockyard and launched in October 1913, the lead ship of the Queen Elizabeth Class first saw action in the Dardanelles during the First World War.

At the time of Jutland she was in refit at Rosyth but was Admiral Sir David Beatty's flagship at the surrender of the German High Sea Fleet in 1918.

HMS *Queen Elizabeth* was undergoing a substantial rebuild when the Second World War started, including improved main guns, new secondary armament, a reconstructed bridge structure and increased armour. She emerged from this in February 1941, coming out to the Mediterranean that May on escort duty. After seeing action during the bloody evacuation of Crete, *Queen Elizabeth* became Admiral Cunningham's flagship, as *Warspite* had gone to the USA for bomb damage repairs and a refit. In December 1941, HMS *Queen Elizabeth* and HMS *Valiant* were badly

A stern view of HMS *Queen Elizabeth* **in the summer of 1943.** *Goodman Collection.*

H.M.S. QUEEN ELIZABETH
1943.

Another view of HMS *Queen Elizabeth* in 1943. *Goodman Collection.*

damaged by Italian frogmen while at anchor in Alexandria Harbour. The frogmen came from the submarine *Scirce*, rode through the harbour on modified torpedoes and then dropped charges under the battleships. Both battleships settled on the bottom of the harbour. The fact that they would be out of action for many months was kept secret. By May 1942 *Queen Elizabeth* had been restored enough to sail for an American dockyard for substantial repairs.

Returning to Britain in June 1943 she saw service with the Home Fleet before joining the newly reformed Eastern Fleet, alongside *Valiant*, in late 1943.

After attempting to hunt down rogue Japanese warships in the spring of 1944, *Queen Elizabeth* became the flagship of Eastern Fleet Commander-in-Chief Admiral Sir James Somerville.

Following a refit at Durban in late 1944 she was flagship of the 3rd Battle Squadron in the Eastern Fleet and in the New Year took part in bombardments of Sabang. Following further fire missions against Japanese facilities in the Andaman Islands, in the spring of 1945 she attempted to intercept enemy shipping off Malaya. In July 1945, with more modern battleships coming to the Far East following the end of the war in Europe, HMS *Queen Elizabeth* headed home to be put into reserve. She was sold off for scrap in 1948.

HMS *Barham*

Completed on the Clyde by J. Brown & Co. in October 1915, HMS *Barham* was the 5th Battle Squadron flagship at the Battle of Jutland, carrying Rear Admiral Sir Hugh Evan-Thomas. During the 1920s and 1930s she served with the Mediterranean, Atlantic and Home fleets and was at Alexandria when the Second World War started. Withdrawn from the Mediterranean, she carried out convoy escort work in the Atlantic and was torpedoed by a U-boat off the west coast of Scotland in December 1939. She went to Cammell Laird at Birkenhead for six months of repair work.

In late August 1940 *Barham* was ordered on a mission to Dakar carrying Free French troops under the command of General Charles de Gaulle. During this ill-advised attempt to take the Vichy-controlled naval port, *Barham* was slightly damaged by shellfire from a shore battery.

In March 1941 she took part in the crushing victory over the Italians at Matapan but was put out of action by German dive-bombers during the evacuation of Crete two months later. She ended up in Durban for repairs lasting eight weeks. Returning

HMS *Barham* after her 1930-33 refit. *Goodman Collection.*

HMS Barham in the 1930s *Taylor Collection*

to the fray, *Barham* took part in several convoys.

On 25 November 1941, she was hit by torpedoes from U-331 while sailing with the battle fleet, including sisters *Valiant* and *Queen Elizabeth*, off Sidi Barrani. She capsized and exploded.

The Admiralty's Summary of Circumstances of Loss says:

> From captured documents it is now known that the German Naval War Staff on 7 September had ordered six boats into the Mediterranean to operate from Salamis, where the first arrived on 10 October. U-331, the second of the six, arrived at Salamis on 11 October. At 16.25 on 25 November, when the Battle Fleet was in position 32 deg 29' N, 26 deg 27' E., the *Barham* (Captain Geoffrey Cooke) was hit by three torpedoes from U-331 and blew up within five minutes.

> The rapidity with which she sank caused heavy loss of life – 56 officers and 806 ratings. The destroyers *Jervis* and *Jackal* were immediately ordered to hunt the submarine and the *Nizam* and *Hotspur* to rescue survivors while the Fleet continued on its course. About 450 were rescued by the destroyers. Among them was Vice Admiral Pridham-Wippell. Captain Cooke was among those missing.

The loss of *Barham* was kept secret until late January 1942. This was possible because the U-boat had been forced to dive deep without seeing the results of the attack. In fact, such was the secrecy over *Barham's* dreadful loss that special Christmas and New

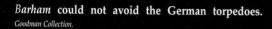

Barham could not avoid the German torpedoes.
Goodman Collection.

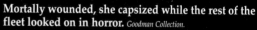

Mortally wounded, she capsized while the rest of the fleet looked on in horror. *Goodman Collection.*

The veteran battleship exploded, with HMS *Valiant* luckily out of harm's reach (on right) *Goodman Collection.*

Hundreds of *Barham's* sailors died, and the survivors clung to life under the massive cloud of black smoke as destroyers went in to try and rescue them.
Goodman Collection.

Year card greetings prepared for her crew were still printed.

HMS *Malaya*

Notable for being funded by the Federated Malay States – at a cost of £2,945,709 – *Malaya* was built on the Tyne by Armstrong Whitworth & Co. and commissioned into service at the end of January 1916.

She was badly damaged during the Battle of Jutland, sustaining two officers and sixty-one ratings killed plus thirty-three wounded.

Sometimes playing a diplomatic role between the wars, *Malaya* carried members of the Allied Naval Armistice Commission on an inspection of German ports in 1920 and in early 1921 made a visit to the Malay States before joining the Atlantic Fleet. During the final moments of the horrific Greek-Turkish War of 1922 *Malaya* sailed for Constantinople (Istanbul) to rescue British nationals and ended up taking the deposed Ottoman Sultan of Turkey to Malta.

In early 1937 *Malaya* was in collision with a Dutch merchant ship off the Portuguese coast. Returning to Britain for major repairs it was decided she should receive a moderate modernization costing nearly a million pounds. *Malaya* was serving in the Mediterranean at the outbreak of war and in October 1939 was sent to the East Indies Station to form a hunting force with the battleship HMS *Ramillies* and the carrier HMS *Glorious*.

After convoy escort work in the Atlantic, *Malaya* returned to the Mediterranean where she joined sisters *Barham* and *Warspite* under the command of Admiral Cunningham. After sailing into action alongside *Warspite* at the Battle of Calabria in July 1940, *Malaya* took part in the August 1940 bombardment of Bardia and was then engaged in convoy escort work before transferring to Force H at Gibraltar.

In March 1941 HMS *Malaya* had an unsatisfying encounter with German capital ships off West Africa. The Admiralty history of HMS *Malaya* states:

> While escorting a convoy bound from West Africa to the United Kingdom, the Malaya *sighted the German ships* Gneisenau *and* Scharnhorst *about 180 miles WNW of Cape Blanco, West Africa on 8 March 1941. The enemy vessels were shadowed for a short period but* Malaya *and the other escorts returned to the convoy when darkness fell. Earlier on the same day five vessels in the convoy had been sunk by U-*

HMS *Malaya* in 1937 after her reconstruction. *Goodman Collection.*

HMS *Malaya* at speed, January 1943. *Goodman Collection.*

boat attack.

More convoy duty followed in late March 1941 and this time *Malaya* suffered a torpedo hit which caused considerable damage. She was repaired at the Brooklyn Navy Yard, the first British naval vessel to receive repairs under the Lend-Lease Act.

In July 1941, HMS *Malaya* re-entered service, escorting a troop convoy from Halifax to the UK.

In October 1941 she became flagship of Gibraltar-based Force H and was engaged in convoy escort work until the end of 1943, when she was put into mothballs. She was recommissioned in late June 1944, after the D-Day landings, as a bombardment ship. In this role she pounded German strongpoints along the coast of northern France in September 1944, trying to persuade them to surrender.

By May 1945 *Malaya* was a torpedo school accommodation ship at Portsmouth. In 1946 she was placed in reserve with the intention of scrapping her. Two years later she was handed over to the British Iron and Steel Corporation.

HMS Valiant

Constructed at Govan in Scotland by Fairfield Shipbuilding & Engineering Co., *Valiant* was completed in February 1916. She saw action alongside *Warspite*, the *Malaya* and *Barham* at Jutland.

Between the world wars HMS *Valiant* served with the Atlantic, Home and Mediterranean Fleets and, in March 1937, began an extensive refit at Devonport which involved new engines and radical structural modernization. HMS *Valiant* emerged in December 1939 and, after convoy escort work in the Atlantic, joined the Home Fleet. She took part in the Norwegian naval actions of April 1940 and two months later was in the same waters on convoy escort work when subjected to intensive attack by Luftwaffe Stukas. *Valiant* put up a good fight during this two hour battle, surviving some near misses and managing to shoot down at least one of her attackers. Joining Force H in early July 1940, *Valiant* took part in an attack on the

Another picture of HMS *Valiant* taken in early 1943. *Goodman Collection.*

French fleet at Oran to stop it being used by the Axis powers.

Transferred to the Mediterranean Fleet, HMS *Valiant* sailed with HMS *Warspite* to shell the Albanian port of Valona in December 1940, as it was the main entry and supply point for Italian forces waging war in the Balkans. The two battleships poured nearly 100 shells into the port. *Valiant* was in action with *Warspite* and *Barham* during

HMS *Valiant* in 1943, shortly after returning to service. *Goodman Collection.*

the Battle of Matapan in March 1941 and was with them during operations off Crete that May when she was hit by two enemy bombs but suffered little damage.

Sustaining major damage during the December 1941 attack by Italian frogmen at Alexandria, after repairs she was assigned in the spring of 1942 to the Eastern Fleet where she served alongside *Warspite* again. The two ships saw service together in the Mediterranean the following year as part of Force H supporting invasions of Sicily and mainland Italy.

After another refit *Valiant* went back to the Far East at the end of 1943 and the following April began a series of offensive operations against the Japanese. While *Valiant* was in a floating dock at Trincomalee, Ceylon, in August 1944, it collapsed and sank beneath her, causing considerable harm to the battleship.

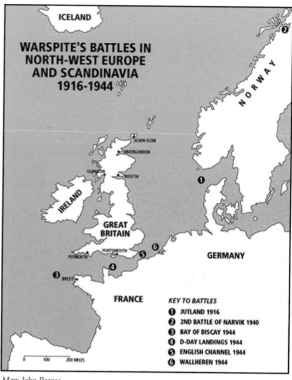

Map: John Pearce.

Bad luck struck again in October of the same year when she grounded in the entrance to the Suez Canal on the way home. Refloated after six hours, she took the Cape route to Britain and was then put into refit for the rest of the war. *Valiant* was sold off for scrap in 1948.

BIBLIOGRAPHY

Arthur, Max, *The True Glory - The Royal Navy 1914-1939,* Corona Books/Hodder & Stoughton, 1997.
   The Navy - 1939 to the Present Day, Hodder and Stoughton, 1997.
Blackman, Raymond V.B., *The World's Warships*, Macdonald & Co, 1969.
Brownstone, David and Franck, Irene, *Timelines of War - A Chronology of Warfare from 100,000 BC to the Present*, Little Brown and Company, 1996.
Buckmaster, Henrietta, *All About Sir Walter Raleigh*, W.H. Allen, 1965.
Burt R.A. and Trotter W.P., *Battleships of the Grand Fleet - A Pictorial Review of the Royal Navy's Capital Ships in World War One*, Arms and Armour Press, 1982.
Castleden, Rodney, *British History*, Parragon, 1994.
Churchill, Randolph S.,*Young Statesman, Winston S. Churchill 1901 - 1914*, Minerva, 1991.
Churchill, Winston S., *The World Crisis 1911 - 1918, Vol 1*, Odhams Press, 1938.
Conway's All the World's Fighting Ships 1922-1946, Conway Maritime Press, 1995.
Conway's All the World's Fighting Ships 1947-1982 - Part 1 The Western Powers, Conway Maritime Press, 1983.
Crane, Jonathan, *Submarine*, British Broadcasting Corporation, 1984.
Cunningham of Hyndhope, Viscount, Admiral of the Fleet, *A Sailor's Odyssey*, Hutchinson & Co, 1951.
Divine, David, *Mutiny at Invergordon*, Macdonald, 1970.
Edwards, Bernard, *SALVO! Classic Naval Gun Actions*, Brockhampton Press, 1999.
Finnigan, Peter, *An Able Seaman's War 1941 - 1945, The Story of a Love Affair (with a Ship)*, self-published.
Goodenough, Commodore William, *Rough Record*, Hutchinson, 1943.
Goodman, Syd and Ballantyne, Iain, *Plymouth Warships 1900 - 1950*, Halsgrove, 1998.
Gordon, Andrew, *The Rules of the Game - Jutland and the British Naval Command*, John Murray, 1997.
Gray, Edwyn, *Hitler's Battleships*, Leo Cooper/Pen & Sword Books, 1999.
Groos, Fregattenkapitän Otto, *Der Krieg in der Nordsee*, Official, 1920.
Hibbert, Christopher, *Nelson A Personal History*, Penguin Books, 1995.
Hill, Richard, *The Prizes of War*, Royal Naval Museum/Sutton Publishing, 1999.
Hodges, Peter, *The Big Gun, Battleship Main Armament 1860 - 1945*, Conway Maritime Press, 1981.
Hoehling, A.A., *The Great War at Sea*, Corgi, 1967.
Hough, Richard, *The Hunting of Force Z*, New English Library, 1971.
   The Great War at Sea, Oxford University Press, 1986.
   Bless Our Ship - Mountbatten and The Kelly, John Curtis/Hodder & Stoughton, 1991.
Howarth, David, *Dawn of D-Day*, Companion Book Club/Odhams, 1959.
Howarth, Stephen, *To Shining Sea - A History of the United States Navy 1775 - 1991*, Weidenfeld and Nicolson, 1991.
Ireland, Bernard and Grove, Eric, *Jane's War at Sea 1897 - 1997*, Harper Collins, 1997.
Ireland, Bernard, *Jane's Naval History of World War II*, Harper Collins, 1998.
Jordan, John, *Soviet Submarines 1945 to the present*, Arms and Armour Press, 1989.
Kennedy, Ludovic, *Pursuit: The Sinking of the Bismarck*, Fontana, 1975.
   Nelson and His Captains, Fontana, 1976.
King, Cecil, *H.M.S. (His Majesty's Ships) and Their Forebears*, The Studio Ltd, 1940.
Ladd, James D.,*The Royal Marines, 1919 to 1980, An Authorised History*, Jane's Publishing Company, 1980.
Lee, Christopher,*This Sceptred Isle, 55BC - 1901*, Penguin Books/BBC Books, 1998.
Legg, Stuart and Hart-Davis, Rupert eds., *Jutland, An Eye-witness Account of a Great Battle*, 1966.
Macintyre, Captain Donald, *Narvik*, Evans Brothers Ltd, 1959.
   Jutland, Pan Books, 1966.
The Battle For The Mediterranean, Pan, 1970.
Massie, Robert K., *Dreadnought: Britain, Germany and the Coming of the Great War*, Jonathan Cape, 1992.
Miller, David, *U-Boats-History, Development and Equipment 1914 - 1945*, Conway Maritime Press, 2000.
Morris, Jan, *Fisher's Face*, Penguin Books, 1996.
The Oxford Illustrated History of the Royal Navy, Oxford University Press, 1995.
Pack, S.W.C., *The Battle of Matapan*, Pan Books, 1968.
   Cunningham The Commander, Purnell Book Services, 1974.

Packer, Joy, *Deep as the Sea*, Corgi, 1977.

Pears, Commander Randolph, *British Battleships 1892 - 1957*, Putnam, 1957.

Penn, Geoffrey, *Fisher, Churchill and the Dardanelles*, Leo Cooper/Pen & Sword Books, 1999.

Rodger, N.A.M, *The Wooden World - An Anatomy of the Georgian Navy*, Fontana Press, 1988.

Roskill, Capt S. W., *HMS Warspite*, William Collins, 1957.

The Navy at War 1939 -1945, Wordsworth Editions, 1998.

Rowse, A.L., *Raleigh and the Throckmortons*, MacMillan and Co Ltd, 1962.

Smith, Gordon, *The War at Sea - Royal & Dominion Navy Actions in World War Two*, Ian Allan, 1989.

Strabolgi, Lord, *Narvik and After*, Hutchinson Universal, 1940.

Sturton, Ian, ed., *All The World's Battleships*, Conway Maritime Press, 1996.

Tarrant, V.E., *Battleship Warspite*, Naval Institute Press, 1990.

    Jutland, The German Perspective, Arms and Armour, 1995.

Thomas, David A., *Japan's War at Sea - Pearl Harbor to the Coral Sea*, Andre Deutsch, 1978.

    Battles and Honours of the Royal Navy, Leo Cooper/Pen & Sword Books, 1998.

    Malta Convoys, Leo Cooper/Pen & Sword Books, 1999.

Tomlinson, Michael, *The Most Dangerous Moment*, GRANADA/Mayflower, 1979.

Thompson, Julian,*The Imperial War Museum Book of The War at Sea*, Sidgwick & Jackson, 1997.

von der Porten, Edward P., *The German Navy in World War Two*, Pan Books, 1972.

von Hase, Georg, *Kiel and Jutland*, Skeffington, 1921.

von Schoultz, Gustav, *With the British Fleet*, Hutchinson, 1925.

Wallace, Gordon, *Carrier Observer*, Airlife Publishing, 1993.

Williams, Penry, *The Later Tudors, England 1547-1603*, Oxford University Press, 1998.

Williamson, Hugh Ross, *Sir Walter Raleigh*, Faber and Faber Limited.

Wilson, H.W, and Hammerton, J.A., eds., *The Great War – The Standard History of the All-Europe Conflict*, The Amalgamated Press Ltd., 1916.

Winton, John, ed., *The War at Sea 1939-1945*, Pimlico, 1994.

Woodward, Admiral Sandy with Robinson, Patrick, *One Hundred Days - The Memoirs of the Falklands Battle Group Commander*, Harper Collins, 1992.

Other Sources of Information

Imperial War Museum Collections

The Papers of:

    Bickmore, Dr G.H.

    Chessman, John.

    Ellis, Surgeon Captain G.E.D.

    Phillpotts, Captain E. M.

    Power, Admiral M.

    Vaux, Sub Lieutenant P. E.

Imperial War Museum Sound Archive

Eye Witness Recordings:

    Auffret, Donald Victor (ID No. 10681/4)

    Clements, Norman (ID No. 5821/1)

    Cowan, Andrew (ID No. 1669/H/A)

    Hazelwood, J J (ID No. 4125/B/A)

    Lamb, William John (ID No. 10723/4)

    Raikes, Dick (ID No. 17259/7)

    Ramell, Sidney Gordon (ID No. 6671/2)

    Tyler, R A (ID No. 5803/1)

    White, Arthur Royal (ID No. 12431/4)

Miscellaneous Sources

Article on 15-inch guns of Britain's last battleship, HMS *Vanguard*, *Navy News*, September 1999.

Fairthorne, Richard, *A Midshipman's Experiences at Jutland*, *Nautical Magazine*, December 1973.

HMS *Warspite* - Fleet Submarine, booklet, HMSO, 30 November 1967.

Poland, Captain Raymond, letter to his brother after Jutland, *Naval Review*, April 1985.

Service for the Blessing of Her Majesty's Ship *Warspite*, 18 April 1967.

HMS *Valiant Summary of Service 1916 - 1945*, Admiralty Historical Section, Revised S.4046, February 1962.

HMS *Malaya Summary of Service 1916 - 1948*, Admiralty Historical Section, Revised S.5610, September 1962.

HMS *Barham Summary of Service 1915 - 1941*, Naval Historical Branch, Reprint S.3500, November 1964.

HMS *Barham Summary of Circumstances of Loss, 24th November, 1941*, Naval Historical Branch, Reprint S.2164, September 1964.

Newspapers

Daily Mail, 15 June 1944.

Daily Sketch, 13 September 1944.

Daily Telegraph, 21 April 1947.

Malta Times, 15 August 1943, 19 September 1943 and 22 September 1943.

News Chronicle, 23 April 1947 and 24 April 1947.

Western Evening Herald, 25 November 1913 and 26 November 1913.

Western Morning News, 26 November 1913, 27 November 1913, 3 June 1916, 5 June 1916 and 6 June 1916.

Unpublished Documents

Banks, H. *An Outline of My Life Aboard The Grey Lady*.

Corbett, J.G. *The Journal of J.G. Corbett, Midshipman, Royal Navy*.

Goodman, S. *HMS Warspite - From 1596 to Today*, 1975.

INDEX